C000063001

HORSHAM'S
INDEPENDENT
BUS SERVICES

HORSHAM'S
INDEPENDENT
BUS SERVICES

LAURIE JAMES

TEMPUS

First published 2007

Tempus Publishing
Cirencester Road, Chalford,
Stroud, Gloucestershire, GL6 8PE
www.tempus-publishing.com

Tempus Publishing is an imprint of NPI Media Group

© Laurie James, 2007

The right of Laurie James to be identified as the Author
of this work has been asserted in accordance with the
Copyrights, Designs and Patents Act 1988.

All rights reserved. No part of this book may be reprinted
or reproduced or utilised in any form or by any electronic,
mechanical or other means, now known or hereafter invented,
including photocopying and recording, or in any information
storage or retrieval system, without the permission in writing
from the Publishers.

British Library Cataloguing in Publication Data.
A catalogue record for this book is available from the British Library.

ISBN 978 0 7524 4441 3

Typesetting and origination by NPI Media Group
Printed in Great Britain

CONTENTS

ACKNOWLEDGEMENTS

Like any book of this nature, it could not have been written without the help and advice of many people and I am extremely grateful to them all, both during the research for my original book and in more recent times. Some of those who assisted or were interviewed in the 1970s and 1980s are no longer with us.

First I must pay tribute to all those who supplied information, memories, anecdotes, documents and photographs, whose contribution may have been large or small. These include Arthur Beaver, John Belson, Tom Brady, George Burnett, Paul Churchman, Tom Cunnington, John Gaff, Martin Gilbert, Andy Hamer, Peter Holmes, Derek Jones, Fred and Mary Kilner, Barry King, Linda Kirk, Fred Knight, Alan Lambert, Barry Lejeune, Ted Longhurst, Tony McCann, Tom Merritt, Mabel Mitchell, Alan Murray, Evelyn Naldrett, Martin Noakes, Mrs B. Overington, Mrs M. Rayner, David Stewart, Celia Sendall, Bill Walker, Philip Wallis, Mary Weller, John Whatford, Allen Whitehart and Andrew Whitlam. Tickets are from the David Seddon collection, whose kind assistance is acknowledged.

Thanks must also be extended to the Omnibus Society Library & Timetable Collection, David Gray of the PSV Circle, Surrey County Council's Passenger Transport Group, the *West Sussex County Times* newspaper and those involved in checking the manuscript.

At the back of this book is a selected bibliography and those titles mentioned have all been consulted to varying degrees and certain information extracted. I am indebted to all the authors, compilers and publishers.

I am very grateful to everybody at Tempus Publishing for making this book happen and last, but in no way least, my love to my wife Michaela, whose word processing and document management advice has been invaluable, together with her superior mastery of the Excel spreadsheet for the fleet lists.

In writing about the 1920s and 1930s there is frustration caused by the lack of or conflict in documentary evidence. The licensing records of Horsham Urban District Council up to 1931 have unfortunately proved untraceable. Even in the 1980s, the memories of some of those involved fifty years previously could not reveal the level of detail that the researcher ideally seeks and contradictions were discovered. Now, we will probably never know. Therefore, as is only right, any error of interpretation or omission is mine alone and I humbly apologise if I have inadvertently conveyed an inaccuracy.

I have tried to trace the origin and give proper credit to the photographs but some were not labelled on the reverse and have been attributed to the collection of the person who supplied it. The rights of Joe Higham's photographs are held by Alan Cross and the rights of those by John Parke are held by the Omnibus Society and are reproduced with permission.

If any reader can add to or correct anything in the book, I would be delighted if they came forward via the Publisher.

Laurie James, Walton-on-Thames, 2007

The complete Mitchell fleet, *c*.1925/6. Either side of the Guy twenty-seater PX 2414 are Fords BP 5373 and 7813 and GMC fourteen-seaters PX333 and 383. Both James and Mabel Mitchell are in the picture, believed to have been taken at their yard next to Warnham Station. (Author's collection, courtesy M. Mitchell)

PREFACE

In 1983 the author's book *Independent Bus Operators into Horsham* was published by Rochester Press. Now, twenty-four years later, the book you are reading is not merely a reprint, but a fully revised and expanded version making use of additional information which has come to light. It also continues the story of the activities of independent bus operators to the present time, detailing the various names to have appeared on the scene since the deregulation of the bus industry from 1986.

The Transport Act of 1985 opened the door for any operator with the requisite licence to run their own services on a commercial basis, or to bid for contracts from the local authorities to provide subsidised services. The battles for Road Service Licences in the traffic courts, which were usually unavoidable for the enterprising service provider for nearly fifty years from 1931, are now a thing of the past.

It is necessary to set some boundaries for the coverage of this book and the definition used during the different eras of an independent operator. Generally, students of the industry define an independent as a business that is not a part of the major groups or 'combines', nor municipally-owned and – in the area being studied – London Transport and its predecessors. Typically, the independent was a small one-man, partnership or family business with a compact network of routes based on their home village and serving the surrounding towns, which provided for the work, school or shopping needs of those in the hinterland. However, some grew quite large and geographically extensive, like Hants & Sussex, Tillingbourne Bus Co., Metrobus Ltd and Compass Travel.

No attempt is made to offer a comprehensive record of the activities of Southdown, Aldershot & District (A&D) or London Transport and their successors. Details are available in several books, with some of the most useful being listed in the bibliography, although these operators must be referred to when they interface with the stories of the independents. A brief chronology is also given in Appendix 1.

Technically speaking, nearly all bus operators in Great Britain have been independent since the break-up of the National Bus Co. in the mid-1980s, but since then there has been a large amount of re-grouping and merger. Three of today's major national bus groups are active in Horsham – Arriva, Go Ahead and Stagecoach. Like their antecedents, they are excluded from the narrative except where necessary to the story, although the case of Go Ahead's Metrobus Ltd is less clear-cut.

The purpose of this survey is to examine the chequered careers of the various independent operators to have served the town of Horsham itself. Of course these operators had, or have, services radiating out into the surrounding area. Thus, for example, places like Cranleigh over the Surrey border get several mentions. The operators featured have been selected by virtue of the fact that they have run stage-carriage services (now termed local bus services) into Horsham at some time. They are dealt with in approximate chronological order of the

LIGHT FIGURES DENOTE A.M. TIMES   HEAVY FIGURES DENOTE P.M. TIMES

" The Roads are Yours . . . Use them ! "

| PRIVATE MOTOR COACHES | 14—20—26 30—31—32 Seaters | PHONE 606 | ANY DISTANCE NUMBER |

OFFICIAL TIMETABLE OF BUS SERVICE BETWEEN
ROFFEY CORNER and HORSHAM

DAILY—Commencing Monday, November 23rd, 1936.

	L L				
ROFFEY CORNER	‡8 30 9 1 9 21 9 41	Then at the following minutes past each hour	L 1 21 41 10 30 50	UNTIL	L 9 1 9 21 9 41 10 1 1021 9 10 9 30 9 50 1010 1030
HORSHAM, Carfax	‡8 39 10 9 30 9 50				
HORSHAM, Carfax	‡8 40 10 9 30 9 50		L 10 30 50 19 39 59		L 9 10 9 30 9 50 1010 1040 9 19 9 39 9 59 1019 1049
ROFFEY CORNER	‡8 49 19 9 39 9 59				

‡—Not Sunday.   L—Via Littlehaven Lane.

Additional journeys may be operated over sections or the whole of the route after the normal timetable service has ceased, in connection with Dances, Theatres, or any special attractions.

GOOD FRIDAY & BANK HOLIDAYS—Sunday Service.   CHRISTMAS EVE—Saturday Service.
CHRISTMAS DAY—No Service.

SEE OTHER SIDE FOR WEEKDAY SERVICE BETWEEN
HORSHAM AND THREE BRIDGES

LET US QUOTE YOU FOR PRIVATE PARTIES

ANY DISTANCE NUMBER   14—20—26 30—31—32 { Seater, Sun-Saloon Coaches

ENCOURAGE PRIVATE ENTERPRISE
COMFY COACHES

(Sole Proprietor : W. F. ALEXANDER)
45 RUSPER ROAD, HORSHAM, SUSSEX
PHONE 606

INDEX PUBLISHERS (Dunstable) LTD.

introduction of their first service into the town. The account of those from further afield, who were, or are, more significant in other areas of Sussex or Surrey – especially those since deregulation – is necessarily abbreviated and others will have to properly chronicle them.

The story of these bus operators is interesting from the transport historian's or bus enthusiast's point of view, but also serves as an indicator of the changing socio-economic circumstances through the years.

It is hoped that this book will bring back memories for those who worked for the operators described and those who travelled on, or knew of, their services. As well as being a reminder of the enterprising spirit adopted by the small proprietor of the 1920s and 1930s, it attempts to document the fortunes and troubles of a sometimes neglected sector of the industry, before records are lost or memories dimmed over time, especially in relation to those operators whose appearance was of a somewhat ephemeral nature. For local people, it is hoped they might find this account interesting within the wider extent of their knowledge and affection for the town of Horsham.

INTRODUCTION

Until the last thirty years or so, Horsham was a medium-sized market town, being situated some thirty-five miles south of central London in the northern part of West Sussex. The surrounding area is largely rural and the town's chief importance for many years was that it supported, and was supported by, agriculture – once the main local industry. Now, all that has changed. Since the last war, much light industry has been attracted to the locality and new housing built in residential areas on greenfield sites, some of it in satellite neighbourhoods like Broadbridge Heath, Southwater, Roffey and Littlehaven. The area is ideally suited to commercial and residential expansion due to its relative proximity to London, as well as Crawley New Town (just eight miles away) and London's second airport at Gatwick. As well as being an important commuter dormitory town, contributing to the current population of more than 40,000, it is home to several well-known organisations such as Royal & Sun Alliance Insurance and the Royal Society for the Prevention of Cruelty to Animals (RSPCA).

This period of residential and commercial expansion has given Horsham new prosperity. There is now an excellent selection of shops and the town is comparable to Crawley as an attractive regional centre. Redevelopment has prevented Horsham from becoming a mere satellite of Crawley and by 1990 it had the unofficial title of 'top boom town in Britain'. However, in the view of some, its character has changed for the worse. Nevertheless, there have been some new opportunities for bus services.

The settlement of Horsham is thought to go back more than a thousand years and there is some evidence of activity during Roman times. In the year AD 947, in King Eadred's reign, Horsham was part of the Manor of Washington and was mentioned in a charter. Even in Norman times, Horsham was important from a communications perspective. Much later, it was to become a pivotal interchange point in the rapid development of strategic inter-urban bus services, which started just after the First World War, while the railways to London, Littlehampton, Bognor Regis and Portsmouth were electrified by the Southern Railway in the 1930s. However, the lines to Guildford and Brighton were never modernised and closed in the mid-1960s, victims of the short-sighted Beeching Report.

Although there were roads which allowed through traffic to avoid the town centre and a north-south bypass to the west of the town was constructed in the mid-1960s to take the A24 London to Worthing traffic, the centre of Horsham at that time was quite congested, especially during peak hours, thus delaying bus services. In the early 1970s, an inner bypass called Albion Way was built to link Bishopric and Springfield Road to North Street/Park Street to the north of the Carfax. The somewhat run-down property adjacent to it was redeveloped as a multi-storey car park and the Swan Walk shopping centre. West Street, a principal shopping area, was pedestrianised. The last few years have seen further road improvements and an expansion of the shopping precinct to the east of the Carfax.

The focal point within Horsham for bus services has always been the Carfax, centrally situated for the shops and the general market. The name Carfax is generally thought to be 'the meeting point of four roads' or similar. Horsham shares the distinction of having such a place with Oxford. For many years, bus stops were situated around the inner ring of the Carfax, as well as some on the outer ring, principally outside the post office. On the inner ring especially, with its narrow pavements in places, the lack of shelters meant that it was a rather inhospitable waiting environment for bus passengers. Today, the Carfax is landscaped and pedestrianised and traffic can only use the south and east sides. Buses still call there, but in the 1990s a small bus station was opened in Blackhorse Way, south of the shopping area, which has now been replaced by a new facility with a covered waiting area adjacent to the junction of Worthing Road and Blackhorse Way, next to a new retail development.

Even before the age of the motor vehicle, people have needed to travel into Horsham for work, school, the market and general shopping. Until the 1920s, transport from rural areas was performed by village carriers, with either horse-drawn carts or motorised vans. Their main task was to carry goods, shopping and parcels and eventually they started carrying a few passengers as well, when the need arose. Some were to metamorphose into providers of scheduled bus services, using proper passenger-carrying vehicles – mirroring a transition seen all over the country. At the same time, forward-thinking entrepreneurs saw the opportunities for establishing regular bus services by concentrating solely on passengers, now that motor vehicles were becoming more reliable. The relatively cheap, easily maintained lightweight van or fourteen-seat bus, like the Ford Model T, allowed many small transport businesses to become established, sometimes funded by the proprietor's demobilisation gratuity from the armed forces after the First World War. In a short space of time, the sight of country folk walking or cycling along muddy or dusty roads from town, laden with shopping, was a thing of the past.

After the constraints of the First World War, the so-called 'area operators' moved swiftly (and sometimes ruthlessly) to establish networks of cross-country services linking the major towns together. Some were taken under the umbrella of larger concerns, such as the British Electric Traction Co. Ltd or the London General Omnibus Co. Ltd, giving them greater power. Using their strength, they monopolised the lucrative interurban routes, leaving the independents to fill the gaps to villages away from the main roads. They soon established agreed territorial boundaries, mainly to protect each other, and Horsham was very much a frontier town on the boundary of the empire of three of them, although their local route network was not that comprehensive. That situation, coupled with some rather unremunerative rural areas of little attraction to large operators who had better fish to fry, lead to the relatively high proliferation of independents filling the niche in the market, just as it did in other boundary towns like Guildford and Woking. However, quite a few of the independents capitulated and sold out to major companies before the Second World War, while those like Hants & Sussex found it very difficult to make any headway with significant expansion plans, which the established operators jointly regarded as threatening.

ONE

JAMES MITCHELL

Southdown Motor Services Ltd arrived in Horsham in 1919 with their service 5 from Worthing and 17 from Brighton, followed by the East Surrey Traction Co. in August 1920 with a circular service covering Dorking, Reigate, Redhill and Crawley. However, the first locally based private enterprise, in terms of motorised passenger transport, appears to have been that of James Mitchell of Warnham, who, with his family, was in business for fifty-two years, giving them the longest tenure of an independent operator running bus services into Horsham.

After his wedding in 1912, Jimmy Mitchell moved to Warnham, about two miles from Horsham, and purchased a shop and off-licence at 1 Station Road, immediately adjacent to the station on the London, Brighton & South Coast Railway main line from London. He subsequently purchased the coal merchant's business of a Mr Warren, with a yard behind the shop. Initially, deliveries were effected with a horse and cart, but by January 1921, one of the ubiquitous Ford Model T one ton lorries had been purchased. Although ostensibly a goods vehicle, it was decided to also carry passengers by fitting it with makeshift seats and a canvas roof. It was used for trips into Horsham from Warnham on Saturdays and to the South Coast on Sundays. To do this, as much of the coal dust as possible had to be removed in order to protect the best clothes of those partaking in what was probably seen as an exciting pioneering experience. Many village carriers made the transition from goods and parcels to human cargo, in a similar fashion.

Late in 1921, a second convertible Ford T appeared and in due course Mitchell introduced an expanded service on Mondays to Saturdays from Horsham to Ockley via Broadbridge Heath, Warnham and Northlands. On Wednesdays and Fridays the service apparently extended beyond Ockley to the alpine-like village of Coldharbour, high up on the North Downs, although this was quite short-lived. Ockley was thus reconnected to the outside world by motor bus, following a diversion for barely six months of certain journeys on East Surrey's Dorking to Horsham service at Beare Green, to terminate at Ockley from 1 July until November. Jimmy Mitchell did not feel it necessary to print and distribute timetables – he simply drove around the villages telling people he met when the bus would be running.

Mitchell's other main service developed from an initial two round trips from Colgate to Horsham via Roffey on Fridays. These were advertised as the Red Saloon Bus Service and commenced on 25 May 1923. As demand increased, the Colgate service expanded to run from Mondays to Saturday, with extensions to Pease Pottage on Fridays and to Faygate and Rusper on Wednesdays, Fridays and Saturdays. The Rusper journeys were soon running six days a week, but those to Pease Pottage disappeared. This increase in bus work resulted in the sale of the coal delivery business. E.W. Webber of the Star Inn, Rusper, is recorded as the owner in January 1921 of a grey Reo fourteen-seat bus, registered BP 1409. This was apparently last licensed in 1925, although it is unknown whether Webber preceded Mitchell in providing a bus service for Rusper.

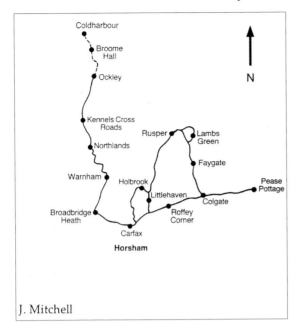

Coldharbour
Broome Hall
Ockley
N
Kennels Cross Roads
Rusper   Lambs Green
Northlands
Faygate
Warnham   Holbrook
Pease Pottage
Littlehaven
Colgate
Broadbridge Heath
Roffey Corner
Carfax
Horsham

J. Mitchell

Opposite: Outside the premises of King & Barnes, the local brewers, is PX 6145, a Dennis 30cwt purchased new by Mitchell in April 1927. The newspaper vendor holding a placard gives the view period charm. (A. Cross/J. Higham)

Two fourteen-seat GMC buses were purchased together in time for them to be used in 1924 on excursions to the British Empire Exhibition at Wembley. Other weekend trips were run to resorts such as Bognor, Worthing, Brighton and Eastbourne, with pickup points at Warnham, Ockley, Rusper, Faygate and Colgate. In July 1925, a twenty-seat Guy BA bus was obtained; it had a body built locally in Horsham by Rice and, with this vehicle and the GMCs on the bus services, the original Fords could be used permanently in lorry form on light haulage duties.

Horsham Urban District Council granted a licence in June 1929 for the use of a second bus on the Ockley service and probably about the same time certain journeys to Rusper were extended on to Hurst Hill, Chennells Brook, Littlehaven and back into Horsham, thus forming a circular route which was worked in both directions.

Spring 1931 saw the first applications from bus operators to the new area Traffic Commissioner, under the provisions of the Road Traffic Act of 1930. This nationally imposed legislation was designed to reduce wasteful on-the-road competition between different companies, in effect quantity control, and included new stringent requirements in terms of vehicle licensing and the fitness of a bus to carry the public, at least comparable in terms of what had been permitted before. Many small operators decided to give up, rather than comply with what they regarded as unnecessary bureaucracy. The new route licensing system replaced the previous, somewhat fragmented arrangements administered through local councils. Some services ran through more than one council area and matters were made complicated by differing views from each council licensing committee.

However, this did not deter James Mitchell and as his services mainly filled gaps in the networks of the major operators, they were allowed to continue. A licence for the excursions and tours was also granted, although not without the usual objections from other operators and a pickup point at Broadbridge Heath was refused.

The 1930s were very productive years for the Mitchell business, with the fleet being improved and augmented by the purchase of several twenty- and twenty-six-seat Dennis and Bedford vehicles. Also in stock for a year was an ADC 416, acquired from Southdown. The GMCs were converted to lorries to replace the Fords. The early vehicles were described as red, maroon or red and black, but this was changed to green or green and cream in the 1930s. During that period, as well as the station stores at Warnham, the Mitchells owned and ran

the Ammabel tearooms and filling station in Guildford Road, Broadbridge Heath. The name was a corruption of Mr and Mrs Mitchell's christian names – James and Mabel. Although the depot was at Warnham, the Southern Railway (as successor to the LB & SCR) imposed a toll on the use of Station Road, which was privately owned. Being the main access route to and from the depot, some of the vehicles were parked at Broadbridge Heath to reduce costs. This arrangement lasted until the Second World War, when the Broadbridge Heath premises were sold as a result of the restrictions on private motoring.

The war put a considerable strain on bus and coach operators and Mitchells were no exception, with the number of passengers on the bus services frequently in excess of the capacity available. Coaches previously used on excursions and private hire were put to work on contracts conveying workpeople engaged in the war effort. Workers were taken from the Horsham area to the Schermuly factory at Newdigate and to construction sites for camps to house Canadian troops in Hampshire. Mabel Mitchell, of small stature, would regularly transport Italian prisoners of war to and from their camp at Billingshurst; initially they were overseen by British guards, but later the only occupants of the coach were Mrs Mitchell and the prisoners. Presumably, the authorities felt that she could adequately cope with an escape attempt!

Wartime vehicle purchases included a Dennis Pike from Yellow Bus Services of Guildford (YBS), with an unusual body designed to the specification of Sydney Hayter, the proprietor of YBS. Any vehicle was in extremely short supply, but eventually some new buses were manufactured to a strict Ministry of Supply utility design. To obtain them, operators had to demonstrate real need in connection with their essential workload, before a permit to buy one would be granted. Single-deckers were based on the Bedford OWB chassis, with bodywork by a small number of suppliers to a standard design, featuring wooden slatted seats for thirty-two people. Mitchells took delivery of their first OWB in April 1944, followed by another in October 1945. Post-war refurbishment meant they were in the fleet until 1955 and 1962 respectively.

In order to cater for residents in the Pondtail Road area of Horsham, an additional service was commenced during the war. At first this was operated under a defence permit, as the normal licensing procedure involving applications, the publication of the document known

Bedford WTB CLY 804 of Mitchell's fleet is seen in the Carfax in Horsham in the late 1930s. The buildings in the background have now given way to the Swan Walk shopping centre. (J.F. Parke)

A wartime photograph, complete with masked headlamps, of FBP 189, another Mitchell Bedford WTB (with bodywork by Willmott), on the 'independents' stand on the west side of the Carfax. (Omnibus Society/J. Parke Collection)

This Dennis Pike (GPF 117), with an unusual body designed by Sidney Hayter of Yellow Bus Services of Guildford, was purchased by Mitchell in 1942. Chart & Lawrence's shop in the background only ceased trading a few years ago. (Omnibus Society/J. Parke Collection)

GBP 555 was a Bedford OWB of an improved utility design. Delivered new in 1945 it was withdrawn from Mitchell service the year after this view was captured in May 1961. (A. Lambert)

as 'Notices and Proceedings of the Traffic Commissioner' and traffic court hearings, had been suspended for the duration. The route ran from Horsham to Rusper via Richmond Road, Pondtail Road and Holbrook Corner before joining the existing Rusper to Horsham via Littlehaven service at Chennells Brook. The new facility ran daily, although the bulk of the weekday journeys only went out as far as Holbrook. In addition, the section of existing route from Horsham to Colgate gained a Sunday afternoon service and additional journeys on weekdays. These routes could be worked with the same bus, as used on the short workings to Holbrook.

With the war over, decent coaches were needed for excursion and private hire activities, which were gradually resumed. Patronage was good, as petrol for private motoring was still initially rationed and people yearned to travel for pleasure, having been restricted to only making 'essential journeys' since 1940. Three new Bedford OB coaches were purchased – two with Duple Vista bodywork, and one with a much less common Whitson body. The latter firm also bodied a Maudslay Marathon in 1949. From the early 1950s, certain coaches carried a cream livery.

Transport of schoolchildren by bus was becoming more common. Indeed, local authorities had statutory duties to this effect through the Education Act of 1944. The county council invited tenders from operators to provide special services to transport scholars from home to school. Among those performed by Mitchells were those from the isolated hamlet of Rowhook to Slinfold Church of England School (previously the children had a lengthy three-mile walk in all weathers, which was now unacceptable), to Horsham High School for Girls and to the Forest boys and girls schools when built in the 1950s.

Around 1951, the Horsham-Holbrook-Rusper service was extended to Muggeridge Hill, although this extension seems to have faded from the timetable by the early 1960s. In February 1952, Mitchell applied to withdraw the Thursday afternoon service on the Ockley route, a reduction observed by some other small local operators due to it being early-closing day in Horsham. Therefore, the service was curtailed at Warnham on that day. Also in 1952, a license was granted for an express service on Sundays from Horsham Station to Warnham Court School, for the benefit of parents visiting boarders there.

Mitchell's first new post-war coach, acquired in November 1946, was this Bedford OB with ubiquitous twenty-nine-seat Duple Vista bodywork. HBP 873 lasted until 1960. (W.J. Haynes)

Above: Here we see Mrs Mitchell driving Bedford OB KBP 749 in Bishopric, Horsham, arriving from Ockley and Warnham. The public conveniences stand in the path of what is now Albion Way, which takes traffic around the town centre. (P. Moth)

Opposite: Acquired in December 1949 from Smith of Fernhill Heath was HUY 521, a Maudslay Marathon with Plaxton bodywork. On 22 May 1965 it was caught on film by Alan Cross. It was withdrawn in 1967. (A. Cross)

Although they had tried, apparently unrewarded, in the past to link Pease Pottage with Horsham, the Mitchells made another attempt from 27 September 1954, when Mabel Mitchell drove the first journey. This was achieved by means of a revised timetable and a bifurcation of the Horsham-Rusper via Colgate circular service. The following month, the various service licences were transferred into the joint entity of J. & M.A. Mitchell. The last new vehicle was delivered to the business in June 1955, being one of the relatively rare forward-control Leyland Comet 90s.

In general, patronage was declining through the second half of the 1950s as car ownership increased and Mitchell operations began to be reduced from 1961 onwards. The Sunday journeys to Colgate and Rusper were withdrawn and the excursion and tour licence was allowed to lapse. The local journeys from Horsham to Holbrook were reduced. Fleet replacement in the 1960s was by means of second-hand Bedford SB coaches. From about 1964, the standard fleet livery became red and grey.

Although unlikely to produce much extra revenue, Mrs Mitchell did agree in Autumn 1967 to divert some journeys travelling between Faygate and Rusper to serve the hamlet of Lambs Green, last covered on a regular basis on 2 October 1965 when London Transport withdrew service 852 from Crawley to Horsham.

By 1968, Mrs Mitchell was considering giving up the bus services. Receipts were still falling, revenue support from local authorities was not yet available and drivers were generally difficult to obtain. An approach was made to London Transport, as they were the major operator north of Horsham, to see if they would be interested in acquiring the services, but the response was not enthusiastic. Mabel Mitchell herself had recently given up coach driving when the last Bedford OB (KBP 749) was replaced by a larger model. The fleet then consisted of the Leyland Comet and three Bedford SBs.

Mrs Mitchell's wish to surrender the licences for the bus services came to the attention of John Wylde of Orpington (to be described in a later chapter). Wylde thought that the Mitchell routes could be developed by the introduction of a minibus operation. Accordingly, his North Downs Rural Transport enterprise took the majority of them over, together with Mabel Mitchell's principal bus service driver, Vernon Brock, from 8 April 1969. The Colgate-Pease Pottage section and the part of the Rusper route between Chennells Brook and Horsham Station via Littlehaven, were not perpetuated.

Leyland Tiger PS1 LPX 729 was bought new in 1950 and is seen here in February 1965. The body was by King & Taylor of Godalming. Note the eagle radiator filler cap embellishment. Goodacres toyshop in the background still exists. (A. Lambert)

This forward-control Leyland Comet with thirty-six-seat Duple bodywork (featuring their 'butterfly' radiator grille of the period) was the last vehicle bought new by Mitchell, in June 1955. It appears to be loading for a trip to Rusper. (R. Marshall Collection)

Seen in June 1964 is LEL 883, one of a pair of Bedford SB coaches purchased by Mitchell in early 1960. Behind is HOT 339, a Bedford OB of Brady's Brown Motor Services. (Author's collection)

This Bedford SB8 with Duple Super Vega bodywork emanated from Fallowfield & Britten, part of the Ewer Group of London N16. Owned by Mitchell from 1964 until 1971, it is seen in the yard at Warnham. (Bill Walker)

In Station Road, Warnham, by the level crossing is a Bedford SB1/Plaxton coach registered 223 JKL. This lasted until the business was sold to R.Stedman of Crawley in 1973. (Author's collection)

The Leyland Comet was disposed of, but Mabel Mitchell retained the Bedfords for use on school contracts and private hire until June 1973, when she sold the business to R. Stedman of Crawley, who had traded as Compact Coaches for about two years previously. The shed and yard at Warnham Station became Stedman's main base. The trading name was changed to Mitchells Compact and initially a livery of white and orange was in use. During the 1970s, a host of second-hand Bedford, Ford and AEC Reliance coaches entered the fleet, some only for a short time. There was also a rare AEC Monocoach with Alexander bodywork, which originated from Alexander (Northern) in Scotland and a former A&D AEC Reliance with Weymann body. These two buses were used on school contracts in a beige and orange livery.

In 1981 the business began trading as Horsham Coaches and the following year became part-owned by the Moon family with Stedman selling his interest in 1984. Dave Moon operated a small fleet of coaches in a yellow and blue livery, as well as some former London Transport Daimler Fleetline DMS-class double-deckers for school work.

From 7 May 1990, Horsham Coaches joined with Colin Brands (trading as Cosy Coaches), who had been running a service from Crawley to Bewbush for about a year in competition with London & Country. Under the name Hopper Bus, Horsham Coaches started some other local services around Crawley. However, this competitive incursion into London & Country's stronghold was not allowed to last long and the larger company acquired the services from 9 July 1990, running their own vehicles 'on hire to Hopper Bus' for a short while, until the service registrations could be cancelled and the status quo restored. London & Country then set up a franchise – Horsham Buses Ltd – to administer some of their local services, being managed by Colin Brands and initially involving a minority financial interest of Dave Moon. The remaining Horsham Coaches vehicles eventually passed to the London & Country group in 1994 when Moon's involvement ceased. The Warnham site was used by Horsham Buses and its successors from 1990 until 1992, and then from 1996.

Mabel Annie Mitchell passed away on 18 January 1985, aged ninety-two. The notice in the *West Sussex County Times* said, 'She will long be remembered for her many years of service to the people of Warnham and the surrounding villages'. Mitchells buses and coaches were indeed a local institution.

TWO

W.H. RAYNER & SON
(HORSHAM BUS SERVICE)

The name Rayner is as synonymous as Southdown in respect to early bus services in Horsham. The family business based at Brookside, Barns Green, not only provided links into town from their home area, but also pioneered local services within Horsham and even ran a regular service to London. Like a multitude of others throughout the British Isles, Rayner was a carrier who expanded and developed regular bus services, as motor vehicles became more reliable and demand for travel increased, including in areas where there was no railway station within easy walking distance from a village.

William Rayner was a farmer in Suffolk who followed up an advertisement for a carrier's business in Barns Green in far-off Sussex. The assets included a large van and two horses, but only a week after Rayner took over in 1919, one horse died. When the other horse expired shortly after, he decided to enter the motor age. An Oldsmobile carrier's van was used to collect shopping and other goods for the inhabitants of Barns Green, Itchingfield and Christ's Hospital on Monday, Wednesday, Friday and Saturday, and also on Saturday for Coolham, Shipley and Southwater. When not full of goods, the vehicle could carry up to ten people instead, having partial canvas sides and rudimentary windows. Saturday evening trips from Barns Green into Horsham were offered. By January 1921, the van had been replaced by another dual-role vehicle – a Ford Model T – which could be fitted with fourteen seats and also had canvas sides and roof.

However, according to one source, it seems that the introduction of a more substantial service into Horsham was at the initiative of a gentleman with the name Horton or similar, although evidence is lacking. He is said to have run a blue fourteen-seat bus from about 1922, from Brooks Green, Barns Green, Itchingfield, Christ's Hospital and Tower Hill. It seems this enterprise did not last very long, as the proprietor is alleged to have shot himself one day in a shed at a local public house, although this cannot be confirmed by contemporary press reports. The bus may have been a Ford Model T registered BP 8394, seen in the accompanying photograph, although at the time of its first surviving mention, in the West Sussex vehicle licensing records in November 1923, it was owned by H. Jones of Horsham. Whether Jones used it on the Barns Green route as well is uncertain.

Christ's Hospital is the name of the famous boys school (lately girls too), which moved to Sussex from the City of London in 1902 and is known to this day for its traditional dress uniform of full-length coat and yellow socks, being steeped in heritage and unusual customs.

Meanwhile, not to be outdone, Rayner was carrying passengers seven days a week over a similar route by Spring 1923, under the name Green Saloon Bus Service. A second service started on 14 August 1923 from Coneyhurst to Horsham via Coolham, Shipley Gate and Southwater on Tuesdays, Wednesdays, Fridays and Saturdays, with Mondays and Sunday evenings being added from 1 October the same year. Then, from 26 November 1923, additional journeys were introduced on the Barns Green service, with some journeys serving Two Mile Ash instead of Itchingfield.

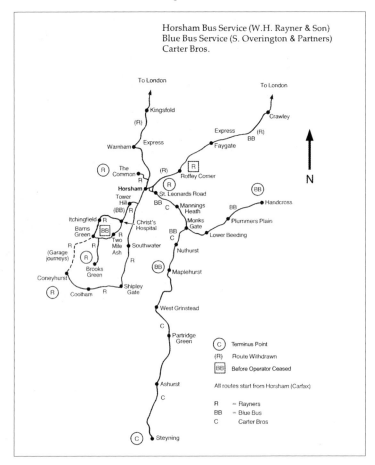

Horsham Bus Service (W.H. Rayner & Son)
Blue Bus Service (S. Overington & Partners)
Carter Bros.

Rayner acquired an eighteen-seat W&G Du Cros Charabanc in April 1924 and by then day trips were being advertised from Barns Green, Itchingfield and Horsham. It is thought that further competition was offered on the Barns Green route by Overington's Blue Bus Co., possibly starting in 1925.

By September 1924, Rayner had applied to Horsham Urban District Council for a licence which was granted to run a town service from Horsham (Carfax) to the Common via Rushams Road, Trafalgar Road and Kempshott Road. Although unclear, he may also have applied for a licence to run to Roffey Corner. This did not proceed, but East Surrey Traction Co. were permitted to run additional journeys from October 1924 on Saturday afternoons as far as Roffey Corner on their established service S5, which linked Horsham with Crawley, Redhill and West Croydon.

From 5 January 1927, Rayner started another town service within Horsham, from the Carfax to St Leonard's Road via East Street and Brighton Road. Like the service to the Common, this ran every half hour, except on Thursday afternoons and on Sundays. From 1 March 1932, it was diverted to run via Horsham Station, Oakhill Road and Clarence Road in order to serve more residential areas. Perhaps to create a local identity, Rayner adopted the trading name of Horsham Bus Service, and concentrated on passenger transport by selling the carrier's business to Mrs Louisa Maynard of Brooks Green in January 1927. By then, a Vulcan eighteen-seat bus was in use on the Barns Green service, a French Berliet was on the Common service and a new eighteen-seat Harrington-bodied Dennis 30cwt bus arrived in March 1927 for the newly started St Leonard's Road service.

This Oldsmobile was believed to be Rayner's first motor vehicle, used as a carrier's van with seating, if required, for ten persons. (Author's collection, courtesy F. Knight)

The fare from Barns Green to Horsham was 6*d*, from Coneyhurst 10*d* and to the Carfax from the Common or St Leonard's Road just 1*d* single! It is recalled that Rayner's son Jimmy drove on the Common service and he knew each passenger by name (usually their christian name) and exactly where they wished to alight from the bus on the way back from town. He was noted for being jovial, with a joke seemingly for every occasion.

In August 1927, Rayner was granted a licence from Horsham Urban District Council for a half-hourly service from the Carfax to Roffey Corner. The East Surrey Traction Co. had renumbered their service S5 to 412 on 1 December 1924 and were none too pleased to learn of the new interloper. Talks between the parties resulted in Rayner agreeing to postpone the introduction of his service until the end of September, pending some negotiations he wished to have with Southdown. These seem to have not reached fruition, as his Roffey service commenced at the beginning of October. East Surrey immediately introduced an additional bus on their service 412 between Horsham and Roffey, in the form of a charabanc which would 'chase' Rayner's bus and then attempt to get in front of it in order to get to his intended passengers first. They also halved their fares and extended their additional journeys beyond the Carfax to the Common. When the council was asked to mediate, it suggested that the two parties came to terms, the result being that Rayner withdrew by the end of October and East Surrey withdrew their chaser and put their fares up to the original level. However, from 9 November 1927, East Surrey introduced extra hourly journeys on service 412 from Roffey Corner to Horsham, which interwove with the original timetable. For the time being, that was that.

A complaint was received by the council in June 1928 from traders in North Street, Horsham, who felt that Rayner's St Leonard's Road service carried potential customers past their shops and on to those in the Carfax and West Street. The council replied that it was unable to interfere, especially in view of the fact that Rayner was providing a good service for the townsfolk.

Always on the lookout for new business opportunities, Rayner commenced a daily Horsham to London (Marble Arch) service via Dorking and Putney, probably from March 1929, when a new twenty-seat Dennis G luxury coach was purchased and this was initially the regular vehicle

The reverse of this photograph is captioned 'first daily bus from Barns Green'. Evidence to confirm ownership of the bus and the people at the time of this view is lacking, but it is not thought to be one run by Rayner. There is a good chance that it is a Ford Model T, registered BP 8394, which by late 1923 was owned by H. Jones of Horsham. (Author's collection, courtesy F. Knight)

Rayner purchased this eighteen-seat solid-tyred W&G Du Cros charabanc (KK 4403) in 1924 for use on private hire and excursions. The road surfaces were indifferent and with a speed limit of 12mph, a trip to the South Coast would have been a gruelling but enjoyable day out, which would be talked about for many a time afterwards. (Author's collection, courtesy F. Knight)

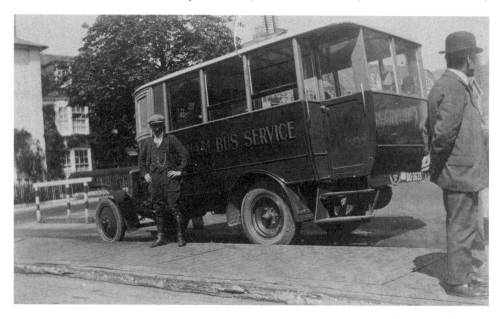

DO 3633 was a French-built Berliet eighteen-seat bus acquired second-hand about 1926. Seen in about 1930, it was used on the local service to the Common. The posing driver is Fred Knight, a long-serving employee of Rayner and Southdown. The bus stands on the former escape lane from the inner to the outer ring of the Carfax. (Author's collection, courtesy F. Knight)

Rayner's Harrington-bodied Dennis 30cwt registered PX 5776 was new in 1927 and used on the local service to St Leonard's Road. It carries fleet number 1 and was the only Rayner vehicle to survive the disastrous fire at the garage. It passed to Southdown with the business. (A. Cross/J. Higham)

This twenty-seat Dennis G coach, PX 9823, was new in 1929 and here it appears to be on one of the rural services into Horsham. (Author's collection)

A fine view of the west side of the Carfax in about 1929. The three vehicles properly visible are, *left to right*, Rayner's Vulcan BO 9512 on the Barns Green service, a Dennis of Lazzell on the Ewhurst service and PX 2414, Mitchell's Guy BA. (West Sussex County Library Service)

The Willmott coachwork on Dennis GL registered PO 1636 had two entrances and a folding canvas roof which could be opened as shown in fine weather. It was new in February 1930. (Author's collection, courtesy M. Rayner)

The pride of the Rayner fleet from 1931 was PO 3840, a thirty-two-seat AEC Reliance coach which was regularly used on the London Express service. Unfortunately it did not survive the fire in 1934. (Author's collection, courtesy M. Rayner)

Purchased second-hand in about 1932 was fleet number 8, a twenty-seat Dennis GL, the complete registration number of which cannot be identified. The Crown Inn (left background) and tree are still there, but the rest of the streetscape is totally altered today. (A. Cross/J. Higham)

on the service. Departure from Horsham was at 9 a.m., returning from London at 6.30 p.m., with pickups en route at Warnham (Corner House), Kingsfold, Capel and Beare Green. This was, however, in competition with four other operators. In 1930, the service ran instead via Crawley, Redhill and Croydon on certain days of the week. Only the Dorking route was used in subsequent years. The coach was licensed to start its run from Barns Green and travel into Horsham via Coolham and Southwater, returning there in the evening. Despite objections from the Southern Railway, the service was granted a licence in the spring of 1931, although fare restrictions were imposed so that Rayner could not undercut the railway, which caused a loss of patronage. The single fare to London was 4s, day return 5s and period return 6s 6d.

In April 1931, the Dennis was replaced with a thirty-two-seat AEC Reliance coach, which became pride of the fleet, for express, excursion and private hire work and compared well with contemporary vehicles of Southdown and the other competitors. From 1 March 1933, the London service was diverted through Warnham village but was withdrawn entirely from 28 February 1934.

Also in April 1931, Rayner's four bus services and his programme of excursions were granted licences with some restrictions under the Road Traffic Act. The Southern Railway and Southdown raised objections in relation to the application for the excursion licence, along with East Sussex County Council, Eastbourne Corporation and Worthing Corporation, who probably did so for reasons that certain roads or stopping points were to be used locally. From 1 March 1933, certain journeys on the Coneyhurst route were extended to Barns Green in service, in order to reach the garage. Rayner was now a well-established and respected operator, popular locally for reliable bus routes and coach private hire, with a reputation for friendly personal service. However, circumstances were fundamentally altered after one disastrous night – 31 July 1934.

When Rayner's Garage at Barns Green was closed at 10.45 p.m., four coaches, two buses and Mr Rayner's car were inside, while Dennis bus PX 5776 was standing outside. By 1 a.m., an outbreak of fire had spread so rapidly that the garage was well ablaze and the breeze began to fan the flames towards the adjacent Rayner family home. The alarm was raised by three girls, who were sleeping outside in the next-door garden on that warm summer evening, and their father raised Mr Rayner. Several other local people arrived on the scene and the bus parked outside was driven to safety, but attempts to rescue the vehicles inside were impossible due to the fierce flames. Efforts were then turned to saving household contents, as streams of burning oil and molten metal, coupled to intense heat, were preventing anyone from approaching the garage. Rayner had called Horsham fire brigade, but as Barns Green was not in their area, the Steyning brigade had to be summoned. They did not arrive until 3.30 a.m., having lost their way, by which time there was not much that could be done. It has since been suggested that the Horsham firemen would not turn out as the Parish of Itchingfield, which included Barns Green, had not paid its dues.

The vehicles were reduced to 'a tangled mass of metal and cinders' – to quote a contemporary report – while a man was injured when corrugated iron roofing sheets collapsed. At the garage entrance was a petrol pump and beneath that, a tank containing 300 gallons of fuel. Fortunately, the flames were controlled so that an even worse conflagration was avoided, although the total damage was costed at £10,000. The cause of the fire was never really discovered, although a popular theory was that a cigarette end was allowed to smoulder on a seat cushion, despite regular checks to prevent this.

The fire was not properly controlled until 6 a.m. on 1 August. All that was left to indicate the existence of the six green-liveried buses and coaches were a few radiators and chassis parts protruding from the general wreckage. Needless to say, the only bus fit for service that day was the Dennis, which had been outside and this ran the service to Horsham via Itchingfield. The good relationship with Southdown meant that the other three bus services were covered from the next day with their vehicles on loan. They were kept at Parker's Yard in Barns Green. Mr W. Albery, a well-known Horsham resident, offered some financial assistance so that Rayner could continue in business on his own account, and there had been no intentions of selling-out to a larger operator. The hire of Southdown buses continued until Rayner sold the remains of his business to Southdown from 2 January 1935.

Rayner's drivers were offered employment by Southdown, while Jimmy Rayner became an inspector at Horsham and went on to have a long career with the larger company. His father retired and returned to Suffolk. The takeover included the surviving Rayner vehicle, however Southdown only kept it for little more than a year, although they ran their own small Dennis buses on the services, with those on the country routes being garaged overnight in a small garage or 'dormy shed', which they had built at Barns Green. Those on the town services were provided by Southdown's existing Horsham depot.

Southdown numbered the bus services from 10 January 1935 when they also revised their local route network, following the acquisition of Rayners and also the service of T. Carter of Monks Gate. The service to the Common became route 72 and extended across town to Highlands Road, while the St Leonard's Road service became 73. After various alterations and extensions through the years to cater for new housing developments, and after being renumbered 290/291 and 292/293 respectively in January 1975, Southdown eventually withdrew their last town service from 25 April 1987, due to post-deregulation cutbacks and they passed to other operators.

The Coolham service was numbered 74 and lasted until just before the Second World War, while the Brooks Green service was numbered 75 and extended to Coolham, Coneyhurst and Billingshurst, originally with a bifurcation to serve Shipley. Service 75 survived until 21 November 1971, when there were extensive cuts to rural services in West Sussex, but since June 1946, in the period of post-war expansion, Southdown had provided service 71, which ran from Horsham to Arundel (and originally Littlehampton) via Itchingfield, Barns Green, Coolham, Storrington and Amberley. Curtailed at Storrington in 1971, renumbered 294 in 1975 and further reduced in 1985, it was not declared as a commercial service at deregulation on 26 October 1986. West Sussex County Council awarded the contract for a replacement service to Tillingbourne Bus Co., so once again the Barns Green bus was run by an independent operator.

THREE

BLUE BUS SERVICES

In the early 1920s, two short-lived bus services ran into Horsham, which seem to have fallen victim to the mighty Southdown's expansion of its territory-breaking cross-country route network. Very little is known and scant evidence uncovered of the details, although there are indications that both were run by a small vehicle in a blue livery.

An influential resident of Slinfold, a Mrs Cumming, is said to have loaned a sum of money to an ex-serviceman to start a bus service for that village. It is remembered that from around 1922, he ran from Billingshurst to Horsham via Five Oaks, Hayes Lane, Slinfold and Broadbridge Heath, two or three times each week. The service probably ceased before or at the time of Southdown's introduction of a trunk route numbered 40 from Chichester to Horsham via Midhurst, Petworth, Billingshurst and Slinfold, which commenced in April 1924, being their third service to link Horsham to the South Coast. The proprietor's name is thought to have been Ashurst or Ashby, the latter being more likely as it appears later in connection with another local enterprise. A fourteen-seat Ford Model T, registered BP 8852 and new around July 1922, may have been the vehicle involved.

In the early 1920s, the village carrier in Wisborough Green, an attractive place between Billingshurst and Petworth, on what is now the A272 road, was Turner & Son, who were running a motor van on Mondays, Wednesdays and Saturdays to Horsham via Billingshurst and Toat Hill. However, by at least August 1923, when an advertisement appeared in the *Horsham & Mid Sussex Guardian*, Cyril Naylor of North View, Wisborough Green, had started a bus service from Petworth to Horsham via Fox Hill, Strood Green, Wisborough Green, Billingshurst, Five Oaks and Broadbridge Heath. Advertised as the 'Horsham-Petworth Blue Bus Service', there were two trips each way on Mondays to Saturdays, as well as an extra round trip from Wisborough Green to Horsham on Wednesday and Saturday evenings. Naylor probably capitulated when Southdown started their service 40 and he subsequently moved to Suffolk where he ran the Halesworth Blue Bus Service.

As a postscript, it can be recorded that Turner sold the carrier's business to J. W. (Jesse) Hunt of Vine Cottage, Petworth Road, Wisborough Green in about 1925, leaving Wisborough Green at 8.30 a.m. and returning from Horsham at 1.30 p.m. He also ran to Guildford via Loxwood and Alfold on Tuesdays and Fridays, departing at 7.30 a.m. and returning also at 1.30 p.m. It is possible these trips continued until about 1936 and Hunt is said to have owned a fourteen-seat bus which was hired by village organisations, although his carrier runs were not licensed in 1931 under the Road Traffic Act.

FOUR

W.F. ALEXANDER (COMFY COACHES) AND PREDECESSORS

Around October 1923, three ex-soldiers, Capt. A. Beaver, Capt. C. Ashby and Capt. H. Jones apparently went into partnership as the Blue Bus Co. It is said they started a service into Horsham from the Crawley direction, serving Ifield, Lambs Green, Faygate and Roffey. The following month saw the opening of the new Capitol cinema in London Road, Horsham, near the Carfax and one of the service's functions was to enable potential patrons to reach it. It seems likely that Mr Ashby was the operator already mentioned as running in to Horsham from Billingshurst. It is recorded that Jones, of 45 East Street, Horsham owned a fourteen-seat Ford Model T, registered BP 8394. Another, registered BP 8852, was thought to be owned and this may have been used by Ashby on the Billingshurst service. It has been suggested that the venture ended in 1925, after an accident involving one of the buses, but it is on record that Ashby & Jones, Omnibus Proprietors of North Street, Horsham had a county court judgement for £38 3s and 1d entered against them on 29 September 1925.

The service passed to Mr J.H. King of Lambs Green in 1925 and he extended it from Crawley to Three Bridges Station on the Southern Railway's main line from London to Brighton. King used the trading name Emerald Green Service and he was part of a family which also had a coach business – W.J.King & Sons Ltd (Emerald Coaches) of Shepperton Road, London, N1. King's house at Lambs Green was named Shepperton Villa.

In December 1926, King sold the Emerald service to Mr T.P. Goodman of Ifield who paid £450 for the route and the vehicle. However, within a month it changed hands again, passing to Mr J.F. Minson of Roffey. The circumstances leading to the arrival of William Frank Alexander in the equation are a little confused. It has been said that he saw an advertisement for the Emerald Service in a London newspaper and also that he went into partnership with Minson, but by October 1927, thirty-eight-year-old Alexander appeared to be the sole proprietor and was living at 107 Crawley Road, Roffey, having fulfilled his ambition of becoming a bus owner.

Before the First World War, Alexander had worked for the Canadian Pacific Railway in British Columbia, where he married in 1914. On returning to Britain he joined the forces and when demobilised he joined the London General Omnibus Co. and drove buses for five years from their Holloway Garage. His exemplary driving record enabled him to win a London Safety First Council diploma for successive years 1924 to 1926 and his colleagues called him 'the gentleman driver of Holloway'.

The Emerald Service ran on Mondays to Saturdays through some extremely rural areas, past isolated hamlets and farms and was not particularly remunerative – passenger receipts were sometimes not enough to cover the cost of the petrol used. The original bus did not have a horn, but had a novelty whistle, which was worked by a wire running back through the exhaust to a valve. The sound of it echoing through the woods could be heard two miles away, and told residents of its approach. At the Gate public house near Ifield, it was usual practice

Alexander's earliest recorded vehicle, possibly the one inherited with the Three Bridges route from J. Minson, was XV 7605 of unidentified manufacture. It waits to leave the Carfax on a short-working to Roffey probably in 1929 or 1930. (West Sussex County Library Service)

The driver of VB 8896 reads a newspaper while waiting for his passengers outside a public house, somewhere in southern England. The coach is a Leyland Tiger TS2, one of four vehicles acquired from Bourne & Balmer of Croydon. (Author's collection)

to put out a Union Jack flag whenever there were passengers requiring the bus. The service had a following of friendly country folk who travelled to Horsham or Crawley for shopping or cinema visits. The Courage family, of brewery fame, lived on the route and were regular customers.

There was a gap in service at lunchtimes, during which Alexander parked the bus outside his house in Roffey. One day he was summoned to the front door by a loud hammering and found a potential passenger on the doorstep demanding to know when his bus would leave for Horsham. The vehicle itself was full of unsolicited passengers! The East Surrey Traction Co. was already running every thirty minutes between Roffey Corner and Horsham Carfax on service 412, but Alexander thought there was scope for a more frequent service. From 8 February 1929 he introduced an additional half-hourly service between those points between 2 p.m. and 5 p.m. In August 1929 he complained to Horsham Urban District Council that irregular running by East Surrey always seemed to result in their bus being just in front of his. A conciliatory meeting was brokered by the council and a supposedly amicable settlement was reached. From 19 March 1930, Alexander was granted an additional licence to run a twenty minute interval shuttle-service between Roffey Corner and Horsham on a daily basis. One journey each hour was diverted to serve Littlehaven. By now he was trading as Comfy Bus Service or Comfy Coaches. From 16 April 1930, East Surrey replaced their service 412 with service 34, running all the way from Horsham to Oxted and Hurst Green in East Surrey via Roffey, Faygate, Crawley, Copthorne, Turners Hill, East Grinstead, Dormansland, Edenbridge, Crockham Hill and Chart, with additional short workings to Roffey Corner. Certain journeys were numbered 34A and diverged at Crockham Hill, to terminate at Westerham in Kent. In addition, Mitchell served Roffey on his Colgate and Rusper service. By the end of the year, relations had become strained again and the Minister of Transport was obliged to intervene to achieve harmony.

When Alexander made his first applications for Road Service Licences under the Road Traffic Act of 1930, there were the predictable objections from East Surrey Traction Co. and the Southern Railway, but the Traffic Commissioner felt obliged to respect the smaller operator and granted a licence so that Alexander's services could continue, as well as a licence for excursions and tours from Roffey and Horsham to places like Brighton, Worthing, Bognor Regis, Littlehampton as well as to race meetings and the Aldershot Military Tattoo. The fleet had grown in size and included vehicles of Chevrolet, Vulcan, Star, GMC and Dodge manufacture. A red and cream livery was used and garage premises were obtained at Sendall's Yard, just off the Crawley Road near Roffey Corner. Here there were sheds offering covered accommodation. During 1931, the Alexander family moved to Glenhurst at 45 Rusper Road, Horsham, where vehicles were also kept.

East Surrey Traction Co. had for some years run a fair proportion of its services on behalf of the London General Omnibus Co. (LGOC), and ran many vehicles and used premises owned by that concern. It had effectively become a subsidiary of LGOC in the country area, south of the River Thames and it was now proposed to transfer to it those country services north of London, which had been run by the National Omnibus & Transport Co. under similar arrangements. The name East Surrey was no longer appropriate, so the enlarged undertaking was renamed London General Country Services Ltd from 20 January 1932. This was soon to be overtaken by the passing of the London Passenger Transport Act in 1933, under which the company was compulsorily acquired by the new London Passenger Transport Board (London Transport) from 1 July 1933, thus forming the country bus department, managed as before from Reigate. In a grand renumbering scheme on 3 October 1934, services 34 and 34A were renumbered 434 and 464, before being consolidated as far as Horsham was concerned into just one service, the 434, which ran as far as Edenbridge and still encompassed the shuttle service to Roffey Corner. If the latter was running late, this had a predatory effect on the Comfy service, which received much local loyalty.

While Alexander was fighting his corner in terms of the bus services, he was building up a good clientele for his excursions and private hire activities. Comfy Coaches could be seen

Two Dennis Arrows with thirty-two-seat bodywork by London Lorries were bought by Comfy Coaches from Bourne & Balmer in 1936. OY 1060 stands inside the depot on a sunny day. (A. Lambert)

over large areas of southern England on such work or contract duties. Good relations were maintained with other coach operators in Sussex, Surrey and south London and Comfy Coaches were often sub-contracted to firms such as Surrey Motors of Sutton. In January and February 1933, Comfy Coaches were granted one-day licences for special services to social functions held at Slinfold and Holmwood, highlighting the potential for such transport before the advent of private motoring and television set ownership in significant volume. However, an application to run express services from Horsham to villages up to ten miles away, to carry dance bands and friends, was refused, although such activities were later authorised as an addition to the excursion license. In the summer, mystery tours were run on Sundays, the most popular being to Ashdown Forest and Balcombe High Beeches. Every year, a titled gentleman would hire a fourteen-seat coach to take his servants and luggage to his holiday residence in Sandwich, Kent. On 15 March 1935, Southdown paid £200 to Comfy to acquire the goodwill of certain coach excursions, but this activity was still continued by Alexander.

In 1936, the original service to Crawley and Three Bridges had around three journeys during the day. On Thursdays there were extra trips between Crawley and Three Bridges, and fewer to Horsham as it was early closing day, while additional journeys were run on Saturday evenings, for late night shopping in Horsham and the Imperial cinema at Crawley. This timetable saw little change from then on. The single fare from Horsham to Roffey Corner was 2*d*, to Crawley 10*d* and to Three Bridges, 1*s*. From Horsham Carfax to the corner of Kings Road/Rusper Road it was 1*d*; some people in Roffey got off there and walked the rest of the way, to save money.

This Dennis Ace twenty-seat bus BBP 339 new in September 1935 was sold by Alexander to Newbury & District Motor Services who operated a number of the type. Eventually it ended up with Loudwater Estates near High Wycombe where it was photographed. (J.F. Parke)

The other former Bourne & Balmer Dennis Arrow was OY 3291, seen in the Carfax in the late 1930s. The buildings behind it (King & Barnes offices and the post office) have long been demolished. (Author's collection)

One of two twenty-seat Dennis Ace buses bought second-hand in 1939 was RV 5736 acquired from T.R. Lee of Winterbourne Gunner. The Ace's protruding bonnet which looked like a snout earned them the nickname of *Flying Pig*. (J.F. Parke)

Standing in the Carfax is one of several Gilfords bought by Alexander in the 1930s and early 1940s. They had American Lycoming engines and could be identified by the bulbous Gruss air springs either side of the radiator. (A. Lambert)

Bought new in 1945 was Comfy's Bedford OWB utility model with thirty-two wooden-slatted seats in the Duple body. GBP 292 passed to Hants & Sussex along with the business in October 1946 and is pictured some years later repainted in Hants & Sussex livery and was transferred away from Horsham for use on workers transport contracts. (A. Lambert)

During the 1930s a large number of vehicles was purchased, some of which did not remain in the fleet for long. There were thirteen Dennis vehicles of varying types, six Gilfords, as well as a Leyland Tiger TS2, an AJS Pilot, a Renault, a Thornycroft A6 and an AEC Regal. Only two were bought new – a twenty-seat Chevrolet coach in April 1930 (PO 1977) and a twenty-seat Dennis Ace bus (BBP 339) in September 1935. In 1939, there were twelve vehicles in stock.

The drivers were well-respected for their friendly, reliable service and were smartly attired in dark navy blue uniforms, with peaked caps, to which were added white covers in summer. The driving staff included Ted Frost, George Burchett, Fred Scutt, Tom Merritt, and Mr Sopp. Jimmy Wells and Mr Hunt worked part-time, while Reg Heavens was a conductor. Arthur Monk was chief mechanic and was assisted by Fred Scutt. At times, they worked all through the night to make the buses ready for use next day. At one point, Tom Merritt who had previously worked for Mitchells from 1924 until joining Comfy Coaches in 1936, became unhappy with his working conditions. He got a job with Southdown and gave his notice to Alexander. The latter got on his bus and took over his shift, telling him to come to Glenhurst later to see him. When he got there, Bill Alexander got out the sherry and asked Merritt what the problem was. As a result of the conversation, a staff rest day was introduced and Merritt got a 10s a week rise, so he stayed with Comfy!

Any thoughts of business expansion faded away with the outbreak of the Second World War in September 1939. Alexander managed to get most of his regular drivers exempted from war service although his nephew, Francis Maundrell, who assisted with the business, did join the forces and later received a Military Medal for Gallantry prior to the evacuation of Dunkirk. Alexander's daughter Evelyn took her public service vehicle driving test in early 1940, as soon as she was old enough and was the youngest woman bus driver in Horsham, and one of the youngest in the country. She remembers the surprise of the boys at Lancing College on seeing a female driver when she took them to cricket matches and recalls taking nurses at 5.30 a.m. to

CAR HIRE—WEDDINGS, DANCES, &c.   ANY {TIME. / DISTANCE.

THE "COMFY" BUS SERVICES.

ROFFEY——HORSHAM.–DAILY SERVICE.

	a.m.				THEN				p.m.	
ROFFEY	x 8.31	9.1	9.21	9.41	1,	21	&	41	10.1	10.21
HORSHAM	x 8.40	9.10	9.30	9.50	minutes past each hour until				10.10	10.30
HORSHAM	x 8.40	9.10	9.30	9.50	10,	30	&	50	10.10	10.40
ROFFEY	x 8.49	9.19	9.39	9.59	minutes past each hour until				10.19	10.49

X—NOT SUNDAYS.

PLEASE NOTE—Littlehaven Service TO HORSHAM is - 1 minute past the hour.
　　　　　　　　"　　　"　　　"　　FROM HORSHAM is 30 minutes past the hour.

Fares :   Horsham—Roffey Corner, 2d.; Horsham—Rusper Road, 1d.; Horsham—Fountain (Littlehaven Lane), 1½d; Littlehaven Lane (Fountain) to Roffey Corner, 1½d.

Private Parties catered for, 14, 20, 26-seaters. Lowest terms on application to

W. F. ALEXANDER, 45, RUSPER ROAD, HORSHAM, SUSSEX.   'Phone : Horsham 606.   [P.T.O.

Fred Holmes, The Printer, Horsham.

Roffey Park when it became a hospital. During periods of frequent air raids she would sleep in the pit in the garage at Glenhurst, which was covered over and surrounded with sandbags, so that if the house was hit by a bomb, she would be able to carry on her essential driving duties. Three vehicles were requisitioned by the forces and it was understood that some ended up in France after D-Day. Wartime vehicle purchases included some elderly Gilfords, a Morris Viceroy and a Reo Pullman.

The fleet was kept very busy; the bus services, despite the ten minute interval service to Roffey, provided by Comfy and London Transport, became very overloaded at peak periods, while contracts were undertaken for transporting, among others, troops and munitions workers, to places such as the RAF base at Faygate and the Schermuly factory at Newdigate. Spare parts for the vehicles were hard to obtain and much 'make do and mend' had to be employed to keep the elderly and somewhat tired buses and coaches fit for service. Some relief was given when Alexander obtained the necessary permit from the Ministry of Supply to take delivery in March 1945 of GBP 292, a utility specification Bedford OWB with thirty-two-seat Duple bodywork.

By the end of the war, Alexander was in poor health and relied on his wife and family to administer the day-to-day operations. He was advised by his doctor to retire on medical grounds and an approach was made to Southdown in April 1946 to ascertain if they were interested in taking the business over, but they were advised that another bidder was in the frame. Southdown, who rightly guessed that the other bidder was Hants & Sussex, alerted London Transport, as the bus services were primarily in the latter's territory north of Horsham and they did not wish to run services into the Board's area.

Despite their concern at the potential expansion of the Hants & Sussex group, the London Transport Board were not minded to acquire any more small operators in their area, due to the threat of nationalisation of the industry on the horizon. So, Alexander agreed terms with Basil Williams and the latter's application to transfer the Comfy licences to his F.H. Kilner (Transport) Ltd company was not contested. The takeover occurred on 3 October 1946 and there was optimism that being part of a larger organisation with supposedly more resources, would be beneficial. However, matters were to progress rather differently in due course.

FIVE

A.T. BRADY
(BROWN MOTOR SERVICES)

Forest Green is an attractive village in Surrey, south-west of Dorking and near the slopes of Leith Hill on the North Downs. Apart from agriculture, there is no real industry in the village and thus it remains relatively unspoilt and undeveloped. The first public transport is thought to have been the Mail Coach service which passed through on its way from Dorking to Horsham. Its route mainly followed the upland trackways so as to avoid the more waterlogged land of the flatter areas below, especially in winter.

The first local enterprise is believed to have been a donkey cart running from the village to Ockley, to connect with the trains. The London, Brighton & South Coast Railway opened their line from Dorking to Horsham via Ockley in May 1867 and this was the closest that the railway was to get to Forest Green. However, as was the case of many rural areas, it was not until the 1920s that a motor bus operation became established.

In February 1923, with the aid of his demobilisation gratuity from the Royal Flying Corps, Mr Alfred Thomas Brady became a partner to A.G. Baxter in the local carriers business, which operated a converted Buick military ambulance. A Ford one-ton truck was purchased and as well as the carriage of goods, this vehicle was used for conveying a few passengers into Horsham on Wednesday mornings and in summer for Sunday trips to the South Coast.

In Summer 1924, Brady and Baxter saw the potential of a regular bus operation and had a fourteen-seat bus body supplied by a firm from Newbury and put on the Ford Model T chassis. In September of that year, a licence was granted by Horsham Urban District Council for a service into the town, all the way from Gomshall Station. It ran via Abinger Hammer, Holmbury St Mary, Forest Green, Walliswood, Oakwoodhill, Northlands, Clemsfold and Broadbridge Heath on Mondays, Wednesdays and Fridays, with additional journeys diverted between Forest Green and Northlands via Ockley on Wednesdays and Saturdays. At Gomshall the bus connected with the trains of the Southern Railway.

By 1925, Baxter had decided to emigrate and departed for Australia in March. The carrier's business passed to Mr H. Francis, while Brady became the sole proprietor of the Forest Green & District Bus Service, as it was then known. Meanwhile, Bob Mathews, the owner of Forest Green Garage had also been conveying passengers. He had started the first school contract in the district from Forest Green to Walliswood, initially with a horse-drawn wagonette, but by 1925 he also owned a Ford Model T, as well as a Daimler lorry mainly used for haulage work, but on Saturdays for a trip into Horsham and back, with the aid of detachable seats, canopy and steps. However, these passenger-carrying activities are thought to have ceased as Brady's services became more established.

Brady's journeys via Ockley were detached from the main service in 1926, when a separate route from Capel to Horsham via Ockley and Northlands was introduced following requests from Ockley villagers for a link to the station and also Capel for connections with the East Surrey Traction Co. service 414 to Dorking. Three round trips were run on Mondays,

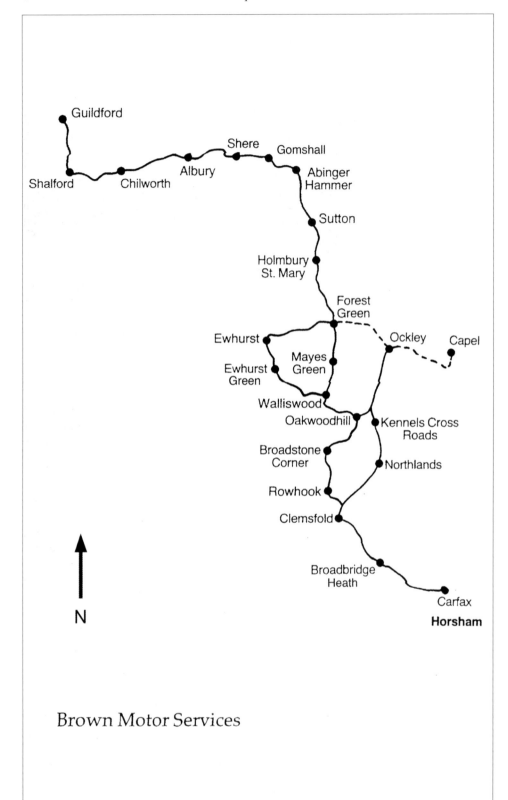

Brown Motor Services

The earliest vehicle owned by Tom Brady for which a photograph has been found is Chevrolet LQ/ London Lorries fourteen-seater PG 5063. Delivered in late 1929 it is believed to be outside the Parrot Inn at Forest Green. (Author's collection, courtesy Frank Brady)

Wednesdays and Saturdays and an extra one on Saturday evenings. The bus was scheduled to run in service between Forest Green and Ockley at the beginning and end of the day. A Chevrolet fourteen-seater was bought second-hand and also another Ford Model T. The body of the latter was in quite good condition, so it was transferred to a new Chevrolet chassis in 1927. The original Ford was green, but these acquisitions were given a brown and cream livery and the trading name of Brown Motor Services was adopted.

In November 1927, an application was made to Guildford Corporation's watch committee for a new service from Forest Green to Guildford via Holmbury St Mary, Sutton, Abinger Hammer, Gomshall, Shere, Albury, Chilworth and Shalford. Connections were to be made at Forest Green with the main Horsham service which would be withdrawn between Gomshall and Holmbury St Mary. The Holmbury to Horsham service was then running daily, except Thursdays, although on Sundays there was only an evening trip from Forest Green to Horsham and back. The daily service to Guildford every two hours was a bold venture as it was in competition with the joint East Surrey/A&D service 25 between Abinger Hammer and Guildford, as well as with Tillingbourne Valley between Albury (Park Gates) and Guildford, and East Surrey/A&D 44, Tillingbourne Valley and Magnet Omnibus Service between Gomshall and Silent Pool. Brady's Chevrolet bus PH 6304 was inspected by Guildford's chief constable in January 1928 and the new service probably commenced about that time.

In 1928, Brady had a bus garage built adjacent to Bob Mathews' premises in Horsham Road, Forest Green. Until then, the buses had been kept at stables at Tillies Barn. In 1929 and 1930 the fleet was modernised with two new Chevrolets and two GMCs, the second of which in November 1930 was the first twenty-seater. From 24 February 1930, a co-ordinated timetable was introduced by all the operators running between Albury and Guildford.

The three bus services were granted licences by the Traffic Commissioner in 1931. However, the Capel service was unremunerative and was withdrawn in May 1932, being replaced by a diversion of the main Horsham service from Oakwoodhill up to Ockley and then back to rejoin the original route at Kennels crossroads. In 1933 Brady had a house built, later to be

This photograph shows CPL 18, probably not long after it was delivered in 1935, Brady's second Bedford WLB with twenty-seat Duple bodywork. It is loading in the Carfax for Ockley, Oakwoodhill and Forest Green. It seems to have already gained some collision damage to its mudguard. (J.F. Parke)

The last Brady vehicle delivered before the outbreak of war in 1939 was HPL 700, a twenty-seat Bedford WTB. Complete with masked headlamps, it is seen in Guildford during the war before departing for Holmbury St Mary. (J.F. Parke)

The poster behind Brady's Bedford OWB JPK 817 suggests that female members of the forces enjoyed their Ovaltine. This was the first of two such utility vehicles and was delivered in 1943. This is another wartime view in Guildford. (J.F. Parke)

called Motena (a derivation of Tom and Ena, his wife) next to his bus garage. Previously he had operated from his parents' house in New Road, Forest Green. During the 1930s the Chevrolets and GMCs were replaced with new twenty-seat Duple-bodied Bedford WLBs and WTBs. The bus services were doing reasonably well and private hire business was increasing.

In 1934, Mr A.W. (Archie) Charman moved his Felday Coaches business from Sunnyside, Holmbury St Mary to Forest Green, where he became the proprietor of the garage in succession to R.A. Mathews and in so doing he beat off the rival interest in the garage by Arthur Beaver. Charman ran a service in competition with East Surrey between Holmbury St Mary and Dorking via Abinger Common and Westcott from January until October 1931, but was not permitted to continue it, being a casualty of the new licensing legislation. He operated a twenty-seat Duple-bodied Bedford WLG bus bought new in January 1931 for the service as well as a fourteen-seat Chevrolet coach. These were kept at Keeble's Yard in Holmbury. He subsequently tried again in 1932 to gain a licence for a service to Dorking, but was unsuccessful.

Having moved to Forest Green Garage in 1934, Charman never again ran bus services. The garage changed hands several times after the war and the new owners also ran a couple of buses or coaches for private hire and school contracts, under the name Forest Green Coaches. Felday Engineering, Reg Burrows and J. Charles were all owners, latterly under a limited company, Forest Green Garages Ltd, until the early 1960s. The two Brown Motor Services GMCs and Bedford WTB EPC 47 were sold to Charman next door, while a Bedford OWB and an OB were later to pass to Forest Green Garages Ltd.

When the Second World War started, Brown Motor Services found itself under various pressures and replacement vehicles were impossible to obtain. No contracts could be undertaken for civilian workers or the military, as the four small Bedfords were coping with the demands of the bus services, which were busier than ever. Some relief was derived from the acquisition of two utility thirty-two-seat Bedford OWBs with wooden slatted seats – JPK

In April 1949 the other Bedford OWB in the Brady fleet is seen at the Scarlett Arms in Walliswood, collecting passengers for Horsham. (J.Gillham)

Brady's first post-war coach was MPE 59, a standard Bedford OB with Duple Vista twenty-nine-seat bodywork. It is at the Farnham Road Bus Station in Guildford waiting to leave for Forest Green. (R.H.G. Simpson)

Lasting exactly ten years with Brady from 1949 was NPC 430, a Bedford OB with attractive bodywork by Mulliner. When seen in Guildford, its radiator was well-protected at night from winter frosts. (Supplied by M. Rooum)

Many people remember Brown Motor Services for its Leyland Comet, which in September 1964 is at the Bulls Head in Ewhurst taking a rest before leaving for Horsham. New in April 1950, it was sold with the business to North Downs Rural Transport in 1970 and was subsequently sold to Allen Whitehart for preservation. Today it belongs to a coach firm in Sheffield. (P. Wallis)

Once owned by Graceline Coaches of Alresford, Hants, Bedford OB HOT 339 was the last petrol-engined vehicle in the Brady fleet when sold in 1968. Seen in the Carfax at Horsham. (A.G. Newman/ PSV Circle)

817 in May 1943 and JPL 582 in April 1944, although a formal application to increase the authorised seating capacity of vehicles on the bus services from twenty to thirty-two was not lodged until September 1947.

After the war, a contract was obtained to take children to the new school, which was opened at Beare Green and it was not until 1948 that Brady managed to take delivery of his first new post-war vehicle – a Bedford OB coach with twenty-nine-seat Duple Vista bodywork. In both 1948 and 1949 Brady applied for a licence to run a service from Ewhurst to Dorking via Forest Green, Ockley, Capel, Beare Green, South Holmwood, Holmwood Common and Blackbrook but his applications were refused following objections from London Transport, who then started their own service over this route from 1 March 1950, numbered 449, using initially twenty-seat Leyland Cubs of their C class, and then the well-known twenty-six-seat Guy Special GS class, with attractive ECW bodywork.

In April 1950 Brady purchased what was probably his best-known vehicle, a thirty-two-seat Leyland Comet registered OPB 536, which introduced the diesel engine into the fleet. The Comet was more popularly used as a lorry chassis. In 1951, an application was granted to run summer excursions to coastal resorts from Forest Green, Holmbury St Mary, Abinger Common, Walliswood and Oakwoodhill and these trips were advertised until around 1964, when they were no longer worthwhile.

Brown Motor Services had shared the traffic from Walliswood and Oakwoodhill into Horsham with Lazzell's service, and latterly Hants & Sussex's service 34. When the latter went into receivership in late 1954, service 34 passed to London Transport on a short-term licence. They operated GS-type vehicles on a service 852 from Ewhurst to Crawley via Walliswood, Oakwoodhill, Rowhook, Clemsfold, Broadbridge Heath, Horsham, Roffey, Faygate, Lambs Green, Ifieldwood and Ifield, which actually combined two former Hants & Sussex services. Tom Brady submitted an application in January 1955 for the Ewhurst to Horsham section when the time came to award substantive three-year licences. The Licensing Authority (as

This neat Albion Nimbus with Willowbrook bodywork (335 KPL) was a regular visitor to Horsham.
Having been sold to North Downs it inspired them to purchase further examples of the type.
(R. Marshall Collection/East Pennine T.G.)

the Traffic Commissioner was known from 1948 to 1956) found in Brady's favour, as the latter was prepared to integrate the new service with his existing one to Horsham, despite various objections from London Transport, Southdown and A&D, who were concerned about expansion by small operators, and from Basil Williams who was trying unsuccessfully to get his own services back. From 18 May 1955 Brown Motor Services duly introduced a service from Forest Green to Horsham via Ewhurst, to replace part of London Transport route 852, with four journeys on weekdays and an additional one on Wednesday and Saturday evenings.

London Transport service 449, which had been developed as a local service around Dorking serving the Goodwyns and Chart Downs Estates, was curtailed from 29 October 1958, after a long labour dispute, so that it only ran out from Dorking as far as Holmwood Common (Four Wents Pond). Brady duly applied again for a service from Ewhurst to Dorking, this time routing it between South Holmwood and Dorking via the main London Transport service 414. The latter objected on the grounds of passenger abstraction between Capel and Dorking and the application was frustratingly refused, such was the protectionist way that the licensing system then worked in favour of large and established operators.

Three second-hand Bedford OB coaches were purchased by Brady in the 1950s, while in July 1959 he replaced his 1949 Bedford OB bus with a new thirty-one-seat Willowbrook-bodied Albion Nimbus – an unusual make for a small southern independent operator. This neat, light, little bus worked on all the bus services, although it had a tendency to slide around on icy roads unless weighed down with something suitably heavy inside at the rear. By 1960, the growth of car ownership had made a dent in bus service patronage. Two separate routes to Horsham could no longer be justified, so the original one via Ockley was withdrawn after 18 March 1961. Latterly, it had not run on Mondays and the outer terminus had been at Forest Green for some time; passengers for Holmbury St Mary were required to change onto the Guildford service at the bus garage. Some of the route was covered by the other Horsham service, to which was added an additional round trip as part of a revised timetable,

Brady's last new vehicle was 3255 PJ, in 1963. Used mainly on the Guildford service and seen here at Holmbury St Mary, it was a Bedford VAS with Marshall Cambrette bodywork. It still exists in private ownership as a mobile caravan and may soon be repainted in its original livery. (R. Marshall Collection/East Pennine T.G.)

while Ockley was still served by Mitchell's service. Also by 1961, the Guildford service was not running on Sunday mornings, being withdrawn entirely on that day of the week in Autumn 1969.

In 1963 a twenty-nine-seat Bedford VAS1 bus with a somewhat flimsy Marshall Cambrette body was purchased for the Guildford service, and was rarely seen in Horsham. There was then no change to the fleet until September 1967, when a forty-one-seat Bedford coach had to be purchased to cater for the larger number of children using the school contract service. The last petrol-engined vehicle, Bedford OB HOT 339, was sold for preservation in March 1968.

During 1970, Tom Brady was turning his thoughts to retirement and, knowing that John Wylde and partners had already taken over Mitchell's services, Brady concluded negotiations with them to buy the business, including the bus garage, services, school contract, four vehicles and his house. The Brown Motor Services ran for the last time under Brady auspices on 31 October 1970, with North Downs Rural Transport Ltd taking over from 2 November. Thus, one of the oldest independent operators disappeared after forty-seven years in the hands of one owner.

The Brown Buses had become a household name in villages along the Sussex/Surrey border north of Horsham and west of Dorking, and Brady was the epitome of the village operator. The drivers, like Tommy Muggeridge, Bert Short and Charlie Bowler, were mainly local and knew all their regular passengers by name as well as their travelling habits. If a person was not at the roadside to catch the bus at a certain time on a certain day, the bus would wait until they appeared. If people were missing when it was time to leave Horsham, the bus would likewise be held back. In a village like Forest Green, the driver would know virtually everybody, whether they used the bus or not, and much village news could be swapped during the course of a journey. The Brown Buses provided a friendly, regular and reliable service, with sometimes no changes to schedules for several years, and were much appreciated by those who relied on the bus as their sole means of transport for work, school, shopping or social outings. Tom and Ena Brady moved to Cornwall and enjoyed a well-earned retirement, while the varying future fortunes of the bus services are described later under the North Downs heading.

SIX

OVERINGTON, CAREY & GLAZIER (BLUE BUS CO. – HORSHAM MOTOR COACHES)

Sid Overington had been stationed at Bulford Camp in Wiltshire when he was in the forces during the First World War. His parents ran a garage at Ockley and it is there that he may have gained engineering experience. After the hostilities ceased, Overington remained in Wiltshire and bought a new Ford Model T fourteen-seat bus in November 1921. With his business partner H. Stinchcombe, they operated on the Bulford-Salisbury via Amesbury route, from A. Lines Garage, Bulford. This venture ended in June 1923, but Overington bought a second-hand twenty-two-seat Dennis Charabanc in January 1924, but it was sold in July of that year.

By 1925 he had moved to Sussex and started a business, which perpetuated the name Blue Bus Co., a title previously used by Messrs Jones and Ashby for their service from Horsham to Crawley. He started running a fourteen-seat bus on the Horsham to Barns Green route in competition with Rayners for a time, as described under the latter heading, but details are lacking. This may have been a Guy, registered PX 2017.

By Spring 1927, coach excursions departing from Horsham (Carfax) were being advertised under the name Red Coach, at a time when the market for such leisure travel by charabanc or saloon coach was rapidly increasing. At this stage he had been joined in partnership by Charles Carey. Subsequently, the name Horsham Motor Coaches was adopted for coaching activities. Overington's base was Crown Garage in Linden Road, quite near the Carfax. Petrol and oil were also sold, motor repairs carried out and taxi work undertaken. In due course, Overington and Carey were joined in the business by A.S.Glazier – little is known about Carey and Glazier.

Horsham Urban District Council had imposed a waiting limit of fifteen minutes for excursion vehicles standing in the Carfax. This was objected to by several firms, Blue Bus included. Overington registered his protest forcefully with the council, but the by-law remained operative. The Carfax was becoming something of a traffic bottleneck, so a one-way clockwise traffic circulation around both the outer and inner rings was introduced on 15 August 1927. Ultimately, the cut through from the inner to the outer section, allowing access for buses heading off along the London Road, was abolished.

The Blue Bus Co. started two daily bus services in the summer of 1927, possibly in September, when PX 7123, a twenty-seat Reo Sprinter, arrived, having been used for the previous two months as a demonstrator for Harris & Hassell of Pentonville Road, London N1. One service was from Horsham to Maplehurst via Mannings Heath, Monks Gate and Nuthurst and the other from Horsham to Balcombe via Mannings Heath, Monks Gate, Prongers Corner, Plummers Plain and Handcross. These competed with Southdown service 17 over the first part of their journey, and in 1928 Southdown started their own service (82) between Horsham and Handcross over the same route as Blue Bus, but continuing on to Staplefield, Slough Green, Cuckfield and Haywards Heath. While this competed to a degree, the timetable was reasonably co-ordinated with that of Blue Bus Co. and return tickets from Horsham to Handcross were

The crew (including dog) of Sid Overington's twenty-seat Reo Sprinter PX 7123 pose before making a journey on Blue Bus Co.'s Horsham to Balcombe service. New in 1927, the bus displays advertising for the Capitol cinema in Horsham which was showing *Two Lovers* and *Luck of the Navy*. (Author's collection, courtesy B. Overington)

Sid Overington with the *Horsham Belle*, a Dennis 2.5 tonner with twenty-five-seat Duple bodywork featuring a folding canvas roof. Registered UF 1832, it was once in the Southdown fleet. (Author's collection, courtesy B. Overington)

inter-available between the services of the two operators. Similarly, there was a degree of co-ordination on the Maplehurst service with that of T.W.Carter's between Horsham and Steyning.

In 1929, Blue Bus Co. inaugurated an express service from Horsham to London, departing daily at 9.00 a.m. from the Carfax and returning from Marble Arch at 7.00 p.m. It ran via Roffey, Faygate, Crawley, Redhill, Croydon and Victoria, with picking up allowed as far as Crawley only. The populace of Horsham then had no fewer than five different companies' services to take them to London, namely Blue Bus, Rayner, Southdown,

Fairways and Grey Coaches. During the late 1920s, Southdown had been consolidating a network of express services to London (Victoria) from various South Coast towns, and the service from Worthing passed through Horsham.

By July 1928, Fairway Coaches Ltd of Maida Vale, London W9 and Chandon Garage, Broadwater in Worthing were running three times daily from London (Strand) to Worthing via Leatherhead, Dorking and Horsham. In 1929 the number of journeys doubled, with a split in the route between London and Leatherhead via either Putney, Kingston and Hook or Clapham, Tooting, Merton and Epsom. By 1931 all journeys ran via Putney. Fares could be paid to the driver without pre-booking for local journeys outside of the Metropolitan Police area. To consolidate its position, Southdown persuaded Fairway to sell them their service and it was acquired from 18 December 1933 along with the five Maudslay and three Dennis Lancet coaches used on it. Grey Coaches Ltd, of London SE1, had started an express service from Horsham (Bishopric) to London (Trafalgar Square) by 23 November 1928, running via Dorking, Reigate, Sutton and Brixton with four return journeys daily. Tilling-Stevens coaches were used.

Perhaps to endorse the fact it was a local enterprise, Overington had *Horsham Belle* painted in large letters on the side of his Dennis coach UF 1832. Other vehicles used by Blue Bus Co. included two twenty-seat Thornycrofts, a fourteen-seat Chevrolet bus and a twenty-six-seat Reo coach. There may have been other vehicles, details of which have not come to light.

Southdown strengthened their services from Horsham to Haywards Heath in January 1931, when they started service 83 via Monks Gate, Plummers Plain, Warninglid, Slough Green and Cuckfield. At the time of licence renewal for the Blue Bus Maplehurst service, an application was made by Overington in October 1932 to divert it within Horsham via Clarence Road on the eastern side of the town. By this time, Sid Overington, once again the sole proprietor, had probably received overtures from Southdown about selling his bus services. This eventually occurred from 1 January 1933 for a consideration of £450, which included the withdrawal of the London service. No vehicles changed hands and Overington continued his excursion and private hire activities until about 1935, after which the Crown Garage premises were sold to a Mr A.C. Collins.

Southdown numbered the Maplehurst service as 80 and amalgamated the Blue Bus Handcross workings with their service 82, which then ran from Horsham to Balcombe. From 10 January 1935 service 82 was replaced by services 78/79 which also ran from Horsham to Slinfold until January 1945. From June 1947 all journeys were numbered 78, and this service lasted until 1971, although it was truncated at Handcross in 1969.

SEVEN

A. LAZZELL (EWHURST & DISTRICT BUS SERVICE)

Having been the focus of pioneering operations by George Readings' Surrey Hills Motor Services, by 1927 Ewhurst's bus services were in the hands of two major concerns. A&D were running services to Guildford either via Cranleigh or the villages along the Tillingbourne Valley, while the East Surrey Traction Co. had extended their service 26 from 4 June 1927 to run from Reigate to Ewhurst via Irons Bottom, Charlwood, Newdigate, Beare Green, Capel, Ockley and Forest Green, although operation as far as Ewhurst only lasted until 31 October 1928. However, it was left to local initiative to provide a service into Horsham, through potentially unremunerative territory on the boundary of the two major operators.

Arthur Lazzell was the proprietor of Ewhurst Garage, situated in the main street, not far from the erstwhile Surrey Hills bus garage. In October 1927 he applied to Horsham Urban District Council for a licence, which was soon granted. He started the Ewhurst & District Bus Service from Ewhurst to Horsham via Walliswood, Oakwoodhill, Rowhook, Clemsfold and Broadbridge Heath. A licence for the use of a second bus on the route was granted in June 1929.

By the time of the first application for licences from the Traffic Commissioner in 1931, Lazzell was operating some coach day trips from Ewhurst and a scheduled express service to London on Mondays to Saturdays, picking up at Ewhurst, Peaslake, Shere and Clandon, for which a licence was granted, despite opposition from the Southern Railway. However, in Spring 1933 the London service was dropped in favour of an authorisation on the excursion licence for periodical trips to London (Regents Park). This licence also permitted day trips to the usual selection of coastal destinations and race meetings. Also, a feeder service was included from Rowhook, Oakwoodhill and Walliswood.

A revised timetable was introduced on the bus service from 14 November 1935, giving a morning return journey to Horsham and a roughly two-hour interval facility in the afternoon. On Thursdays, only the morning trip ran, while on Sundays, operations commenced at 1.10 p.m. At weekends there were evening journeys for the benefit of late shoppers and cinema patrons, while during the day the main custom came from those going to the shops or market. The route was very rural and meandered through the country lanes. From Clemsfold Corner into Horsham, it followed the services of A&D (33), Weller, Brady and Kilner. The rest of the service's life under Lazzell administration seems to have been fairly uneventful.

The initial vehicle operated has not been identified, but a Dennis G was purchased in 1928, followed by a ubiquitous Chevrolet, and then another Dennis G. In July 1935, a new Bedford WLB with twenty-seat Duple bodywork was purchased – CPL 91 – and, in February 1939, Lazzell obtained Bedford WLG PL 7696 from Charman of Forest Green. Unlike some other local firms, Lazzell did not obtain a utility Bedford OWB during the war and had to utilise his pre-war vehicles, CPL 91 being the usual bus on the Horsham service.

Arthur Lazzell purchased this Chevrolet with canvas-roofed fourteen-seat Willmott body in May 1929. Here it waits in Horsham Carfax between journeys on the Ewhurst service. The white building in the right background is the Capitol cinema which opened in November 1923 and has been replaced by the Swan Walk shopping centre. (A. Cross/J. Higham)

Dennis G-registered UA 6571 on Lazzell's service in the Carfax during the 1930s, loading for Rowhook, Walliswood and Ewhurst. (J.F. Parke)

This Bedford WLB (CPL 91) was bought new in 1935 and is seen during the last war. When the bus route passed to Hants & Sussex in 1946 the vehicle was retained by Lazzell for further work. (J.F. Parke)

Representative of the Lazzell fleet when he was solely a coach operator is BSC 878, a Bedford WTB with Duple bodywork acquired in 1948. In October 1956 it was parked outside the Ewhurst Bus Garage built in the 1920s for George Readings (Surrey Hills Motor Services) and then used by Aldershot & District, London Transport and Hants & Sussex. (A. Cross)

A selection of tickets issued by J. Mitchell in the 1930s.

Having established bases at Loxwood and Roffey, Basil Williams made his final purchase for his Horsham area Hants & Sussex operation in November 1946. He only acquired Lazzell's bus service, the licence for which was granted with the stipulation that there should be only one stop permitted at Broadbridge Heath, to appease Southdown and A&D, who took the opportunity to object on the grounds of abstraction of passengers. Lazzell retained his two Bedford vehicles and also acquired another from Williams's Sunbeam company at Loxwood, which no doubt was part of the financial transaction. Trading as Ewhurst Coaches, the private hire work and the excursion programme was continued by Arthur Lazzell, who began to use the old Surrey Hills Motor Services (later A&D and London Transport) depot building in Ewhurst. A small fleet of Bedford coaches in a two-tone green livery was maintained, firstly WTB models, progressing on to OBs and finally SBs in the 1960s.

Following Arthur Lazzell's death, the transfer of the excursion licence to Mrs Dorothy Lazzell was granted in September 1955. She was assisted by her son Jim, who subsequently became sole proprietor. The business ceased in August 1971 when the three coaches were sold. One of them passed to Gastonia Coaches Ltd of Cranleigh, together with the goodwill of the work. As Gastonia did not wish to use Ewhurst Garage, it remained empty until 1975, when it was bought by the proprietor of Tillingbourne Bus Co. as a maintenance base for their expanding fleet. Apart from a brief period in the mid-1950s when it fell under London Transport jurisdiction, the bus service remained in the independent sector and is covered in no less than eight subsequent sections of this book.

EIGHT

CARTER BROTHERS

About Summer 1928, Carter Bros of Monks Gate Garage began to advertise a fourteen-seat saloon bus for hire, as well as cars. The bus was believed to be a Ford Model T and the proprietors were T.W and E.J. Carter. The latter was Ernest, also known as 'Bunny'. Monks Gate is a hamlet on the Brighton road, some four miles south-east of Horsham, and was served by Southdown service 17 and by the Handcross and Maplehurst services of Blue Bus Co.

The Carters started a bus service from Horsham to Steyning via Mannings Heath, Monks Gate, Nuthurst, Maplehurst, West Grinstead, Partridge Green and Ashurst. On Mondays to Saturdays there was a basic service of five journeys each way, while on Sundays the service only ran during the late afternoon and evening. Between Horsham and Maplehurst it supplemented Blue Bus Co. and it was the first road-passenger transport link between Horsham and Steyning, although the Southern Railway ran that way on its line between Horsham and Shoreham. The through fare by bus from Horsham to Steyning was 1s 6d for a single and 2s 6d a return.

By March 1929 it appears that Bunny Carter had a disagreement with his brother and set up on his own as Reliance Safety Coaches of Oak House in Monks Gate. He wished it to be known that Reliance Safety had 'no connection with Carter Bros Garage', and the two competed for coach business. Bunny bought a new twenty-seat Chevrolet LQ coach, registered PX 9802, and relocated to a garage at Plummers Plain, not far from Monks Gate, and ran excursions from Lower Beeding and also from Warninglid from 1933.

T.W. Carter maintained the bus service and ran excursions from Monks Gate, which were granted the appropriate Road Service Licences in 1931. Excursion pickups at Nuthurst and Maplehurst were licensed in 1932 and from Partridge Green from 1934. In Summer 1929 he acquired two new Chevrolet twenty-seaters, registered PO 413 and PO 581, which were painted two shades of blue. The original Ford was converted into a furniture van. PO 413 was replaced in 1931 by a new Commer Invader.

Following their acquisition of the bus service licences of Blue Bus Co. in January 1933, Southdown consolidated their position on the route out of Horsham towards Mannings Heath and Monks Gate by acquiring T.W.Carter's service and excursion licence for £450 from 10 January 1935, but no vehicles changed hands. Southdown amalgamated the Carter service with their own service 80, which was extended from Maplehurst to Steyning. Carter's Garage at Monks Gate was sold and he became a driver for Southdown in the Worthing area. Service 80 was extended from Steyning to Bramber and Shoreham in April 1965, and then right through to Hove and Brighton from 6 March 1966, when it formed part of a package of services designed to replace the train service when the line was closed. It finally disappeared from 2 September 1973 when it was replaced by the 107, which was a variation of Southdown's main service 117 from Horsham to Brighton via Henfield. The 107 followed route 80 from Horsham to Partridge Green, where it turned east to join the 117 at Shermanbury.

Commer Invader PO 3551 with twenty-seat bodywork was bought by T.W. Carter in February 1931 to replace a Chevrolet. It was likely to have been used on the Horsham to Steyning bus service until the licence was sold to Southdown. (A. Lambert)

To illustrate Ernest Carter's post-war coaching fleet, here is Bedford OB LPX 672 with standard Duple Vista bodywork. (Author's collection)

Various changes and reductions have occurred since then. Today, there is only a Wednesday shoppers' bus into Horsham over Carter's route, Compass Travel service 108, supplemented by a Postbus between Maplehurst, Nuthurst and Horsham.

Ernest Carter continued in business trading as Carter's Coaches, for private hire and excursions, running a small fleet of coaches, mainly of Bedford manufacture, which included OB models purchased new in 1946, 1949 and 1950 and SB models new in 1951, 1952 and 1955. In May 1961 the business was acquired by Panther (Coaches) Ltd of Haywards Heath, the proprietors of which were haulage contractors Andrews Brothers. Two Bedford SBG coaches changed hands.

NINE

G. WELLER (GASTONIA MOTOR SERVICES) & J. WISE

Aldershot & District reached Horsham on 9 April 1923 when they introduced their service 33 from Guildford via Bramley, Nanhurst Corner, Alfold Crossways, Bucks Green and Broadbridge Heath. They later acquired services from Ewhurst to Guildford via Cranleigh when they took over the business of George Readings of Ewhurst (trading as Surrey Hills Motor Services) on 16 January 1926. For the following five months they operated Readings' services separately, still under the Surrey Hills name, and it was during that period that they commenced a very short-lived service, eventually numbered 38, between Cranleigh and Horsham, probably via Ellens Green and Rudgwick, before joining service 33 near Bucks Green. Readings had previously applied in May 1925 to the Guildford Watch Committee for a service every two hours from Guildford to Horsham via Bramley, Cranleigh and Rudgwick, but this does not seem to have reached fruition.

It was therefore left to a small local operator in Cranleigh to develop a bus service from there to Horsham, and to compete with the Southern Railway line from Guildford to Horsham via Cranleigh, Baynards, Rudgwick and Slinfold. Although the available pieces of information are somewhat contradictory at times, it is necessary to attempt to chronicle the complex chain of circumstances and domestic intrigue that surrounded the operations of the Weller family, and others.

George Weller Sr started a steam threshing business at Ewhurst in 1894, later relocating to Cranleigh. His sons George Jr and Stanley served with the Army Service Corps as drivers in Egypt during the First World War. After his death in January 1921, the agricultural activity was carried on by his youngest son Ronald and daughter-in-law Mary. However, George Jr started running a Charabanc in about 1921 on trips to the seaside. It was known as *Bluebird* and Weller had a body made by Cranleigh builder Frank Gardner, which was then placed onto a chassis. The date of introduction of Weller's first bus service, from Cranleigh to Guildford, is given as 23 December 1926, using the trading name Gastonia Motor Services, derived from the name of the location of Weller's premises – Gaston Gate Garage – just outside Cranleigh.

The Gastonia service started at the corner of Grove Road and Horsham Road in Cranleigh and then through the village and across Smithwood Common (unlike the A&D service which went via Rowly) and on to Guildford via Gaston Gate, Shamley Green, Wonersh and Shalford. It ran daily, except for Sunday mornings, on an hourly interval requiring two buses.

In June 1929, a licence was granted by Horsham Urban District Council for a service from Cranleigh to Horsham via Hazlewood, Baynards, Rudgwick and Broadbridge Heath, which ran daily except Sunday mornings every two hours with one bus. By about that time, another service was operated from Loxwood to Horsham via Alfold, Alfold Crossways, Bucks Green and Broadbridge Heath. This competed with A&D service 33 between Alfold Crossways and Horsham.

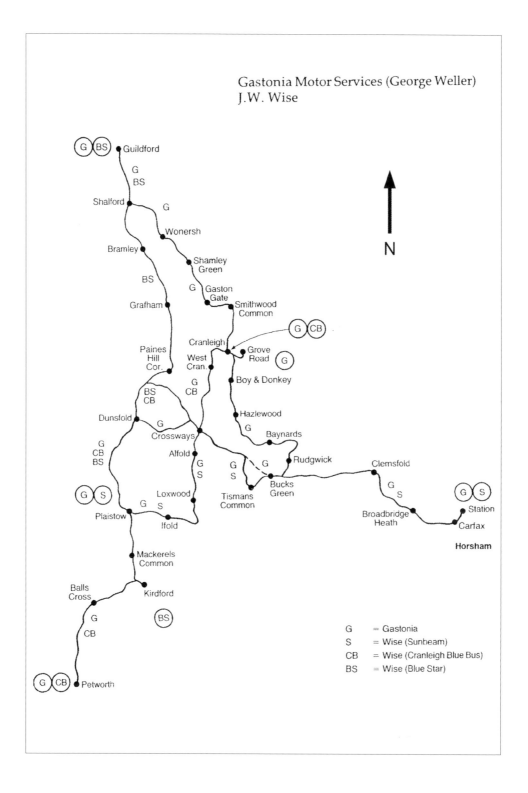

Gastonia Motor Services (George Weller)
J.W. Wise

G   = Gastonia
S   = Wise (Sunbeam)
CB   = Wise (Cranleigh Blue Bus)
BS   = Wise (Blue Star)

Loxwood is a rural community in Sussex known for its Cokeler religious sect, which had several local business interests including the village stores and is located about a mile south of the Surrey border, which is at a point on the road to Guildford known as Alfold Bars. The local carrier, William Powell of Aylward, Smith & Co. Ltd of the Combination Stores was running a maroon fourteen-seat Ford van/bus registered BP 5063 by January 1921. He was licensed by Guildford Corporation by June 1923 to carry passengers into that town. Another vehicle was registered BP r9444 and this was still running in March 1928 when T. Moore of Shalford also applied to run from Loxwood to Guildford. No more was heard of the latter and it appears that Powell ceased running (at least for passengers) when A&D started their service 49 from 22 March 1928 from Wisborough Green to Guildford via Loxwood, Alfold, Nanhurst Corner and Bramley.

Also in the late 1920s, Ralph Mann of Westlea, Elmbridge Road, Cranleigh was running his Pioneer Bus Service from Cranleigh across country to Petworth via Alfold Crossways, Dunsfold, Plaistow, Kirdford and Balls Cross. Even then, this rural service was not very remunerative. With the introduction of road service licensing, under the Road Traffic Act, Mann applied in July 1931 for permission to continue his service but this was refused in the following December. The reason for this is not known, but it has been said that Mann got into trouble for displaying an out-of-date tax disc on his bus, which he had tried to change the colour of, to correspond with that for the appropriate year, by leaving it out in the sun!

Weller obtained licences for his bus services in 1931 and one for excursions from Cranleigh and Shamley Green to various coastal resorts, race meetings and to London on Tuesdays and Thursdays. The granting of the licence for the Loxwood service in December 1931 included an extension onwards to Ifold and Plaistow and a diversion from the main A281 road into Bucks Green to run via Tismans Common. In April 1932 his application for a licence to run a service from Cranleigh to Petworth on Tuesdays, Thursdays, Saturdays and Sundays was granted over Mann's erstwhile route.

George Weller found that the Plaistow-Horsham service was not a good financial proposition, especially as it was inconveniently situated in relation to his base at Cranleigh. His drivers included Jack North, Rex Chapman, a Mr Skilton and Jesse Wise. The latter lived at Grafham, on the other side of Run Common, not far from Gaston Gate, and he offered to take the service over by setting up in business on his own account, the licence being transferred in August 1932. Previously, certain journeys had only run between Horsham and Tismans Common and these were extended to Loxwood. There was then a two-hourly headway with daily operation. One of Weller's vehicles, a fourteen-seat Dodge bus registered PL 4707, was acquired by Wise with the service still being garaged at Weller's premises. The trading name Sunbeam was used.

As an owner and driver of an unremunerative rural service, Jesse Wise seems to have got into difficulties and A&D made complaints about Wise running erratically and earlier than timetabled, no doubt in an attempt to cream off patronage from A&D's service 33 between Bucks Green and Horsham. The latter service had been diverted between Nanhurst Corner and Bucks Green via Cranleigh, Ellens Green and Rudgwick in 1931, offering significant competition for the Gastonia Horsham service. Cash problems seem to have prompted the sale of Wise's service to Fred Kilner in 1933 for the sum of £450. Undaunted, Wise applied for a service from Cranleigh to Petworth, granted in September 1933, to run daily except Mondays, with a basic four journeys each way and an extra departure from Cranleigh to Plaistow at 10 p.m. on Saturdays and Sundays. The through fare was 1s 9d single, 2s 3d return. Whether the Gastonia Petworth service was still operating is unclear – certainly two competing services would have been hard to sustain. To complicate matters, an undated timetable exists for yet another service over the same route between Cranleigh and Petworth, running daily except Wednesdays and titled Cranleigh Blue Bus Service. Whether this was Wise or somebody else is unclear. A member of the Weller family has said that at one point, money had to be found to 'buy Jesse Wise off', and this may have been to facilitate his agreement to end his Petworth service.

Photographs of the vehicles of Weller's Gastonia Motor Services and Jesse Wise's ventures are particularly elusive. Here in Guildford in the mid-1930s is Weller's Graham Dodge XV 3508 on the service to Cranleigh. Behind it, the other vehicle could be APD 387, a Bean bought new in 1933. (A. Cross/J. Higham)

In any case, Wise was granted a licence in September 1935 for a service from Kirdford to Guildford via Plaistow, Dunsfold, Paines Hill Corner, Grafham, Bramley and Shalford, with three return journeys on Mondays to Saturdays and two on Sunday afternoons. There was a restriction on the carriage of local passengers between Paines Hill Corner and Guildford to offer protection to A&D and this time, Wise ran under the title of Blue Star Bus Services, probably using a fourteen-seat Chevrolet LQ registered PG 5063, which he acquired from Tom Brady of Forest Green. The venture was short-lived and was his last as a bus operator.

The Gastonia fleet was varied and in the late 1920s included vehicles of Ford, Reo, Dodge and Chevrolet manufacture. Three small Morris 12cwt vehicles were purchased in June 1930, followed by a Citroën in 1931, a Bean in 1933 and another Dodge in 1934. Unfortunately, many of the details – including dates of ownership – are now lost.

In order to achieve a monopoly on the services from Cranleigh to Guildford, it is likely that A&D made an offer to acquire the Gastonia service. This was achieved on 5 May 1937 for a consideration of £1,750 when the licence was transferred, with A&D numbering it service 25. Weller's driver Jack North continued to drive on the service for A&D, having driven the first journey in 1926. In June 1937, somewhat astonishingly after previous activities, Gastonia restarted the Cranleigh to Petworth service, with three return journeys on Fridays, Saturdays and Sundays and an additional evening trip on Saturdays. How long it lasted is still unclear.

By some accounts, George Weller was something of a character, a real smooth talker who was adept at extracting finance from his own family and that of his in-laws for his various ventures. He hoped these ventures would make a far better return than they actually did. It is alleged that he got the nickname Gentleman George and had other qualities not relevant when describing the history of a bus service. His brother, Stanley, was also involved in the business and for some reason, when the application was made in December 1936 for the continuance of the licence for the Horsham service, it was in his name. At the time of the next renewal a year later, the application was made in the name of Edith Weller, George's wife.

This 3*d* bell punch 'stock' ticket (without an operator name on it) was issued on 17 April 1937 for a journey from Shalford to Guildford, just before the Gastonia Guildford service was acquired by Aldershot & District.

In April 1938, George Weller apparently disappeared in a mysterious fashion, leaving behind his wife, the Gastonia business and many who were owed money – he did not return for the creditors' meeting! Rumour has it that he went to Canada. Stanley Weller carried on the business in partnership with Sid Warren until about August 1938, when the licence for the Horsham bus service was surrendered and Warren acquired the coaching work, together with some of the vehicles and the Gastonia name. Stan Weller moved to Graffham in Sussex and various members of the family worked for Hants & Sussex Motor Services in the Midhurst area. He later started his own coach operation there, Weller's Coaches, which was carried on by his son Gerald.

Another branch of the Weller family was subsequently involved in the passenger transport business. Ronald's wife, Mary, and her sons, Maurice and Lionel, bought a thirty-three-seat Plaxton-bodied Seddon coach in July 1956 for private hire. They gave up a year later and sold it back to the dealer as they became disenchanted with the rowdy behaviour of some of their customers on outings involving stops at public houses.

Sid Warren continued the Gastonia business until 1964 and later in partnership with none other than Ralph Mann, running mainly Bedford coaches, but also an Austin CXB and a Commer Commando during the 1950s. He sold out to Reg Noakes who formed Gastonia Coaches Ltd, operating from Wakehurst, the Common, Cranleigh. By 1974 the Noakes family had built up the fleet to around thirty coaches, mainly used on private hire and school transport contracts over a wide area. The expansionist activities of Gastonia in the 1970s and 1980s are really another story, but to round off this account, it can be recorded that the business ceased operating coaches and buses in its own right on 31 December 1984. Four coaches were leased until June 1987 to Stuart Mathis, who had been Gastonia's last traffic manager. Reg Noakes's son, Martin, continued to run taxis and minibuses under the name Gastonia Chauffeur Cars and later formed Carlone Ltd to run coaches and minibuses. This venture is described in a later chapter. Gastonia Coaches Ltd remained in the ownership of the Noakes family and from 1991 to the present day has run minibuses and taxis from Cranleigh under the direction of Josie Bicknell, Martin Noakes's sister. Thus, these current enterprises can be traced back indirectly to George Weller, over eighty years ago.

TEN

F.H. KILNER (SUNBEAM BUS SERVICE)

During the years leading up to 1933, Fred Henry Kilner and his wife Mary had owned the Woodlea Garage at Clemsfold on the A281 Guildford to Horsham road. Jesse Wise's Sunbeam service passed by and he would obtain petrol and tyres from the garage. Over a period of time, the money he owed on account increased and he told Kilner that he would get paid when the bus service was sold. By chance, Kilner had a potential buyer for the garage so he bought Wise's service and the green-liveried 1930 Dodge bus that ran on it, in April 1933, and sold the garage to Mr E. Barnard. The trading name Sunbeam Bus Service was retained.

Kilner made an application to take over the licence without change to timetable or fares for the daily bus service from Plaistow to Horsham via Ifold, Loxwood, Alfold, Tismans Common, Bucks Green, Clemsfold and Broadbridge Heath. A decision in his favour was given by the Traffic Commissioner on 24 May. Kilner was living at his mother-in-law's house, Burnleigh, on Station Road, Loxwood. The station referred to was at Rudgwick, three miles away. The bus was kept in William Cole's yard in Guildford Road, Loxwood. Cole, a coal merchant, had previously owned a fourteen-seat Chevrolet LQ, registered PO 1862, for a period from March 1930.

In July 1933, Kilner took delivery of a new Duple-bodied twenty-seat Bedford WLB coach, registered PO 7943, and a grey and green livery was adopted. Private hire was undertaken and a contract was obtained to take local Roman Catholics to a church in Pulborough every Sunday. School transport contracts were undertaken for West Sussex County Council to schools at Wisborough Green and Billingshurst. In April 1934, an application was made for an excursion and tour licence, picking up at Loxwood, Alfold, Plaistow and Tismans Common, allowing day trips to Bognor Regis, Littlehampton, Worthing and Brighton. Subsequently, Hastings, Eastbourne and Southsea were added as well as London (Regents Park).

Kilner's brother-in-law, W.B. Hempstead, had been a goods carrier and ran into Horsham on Mondays, Wednesdays and Fridays, departing Loxwood at 7 a.m. and returning at 2 p.m. Willy Powell of Loxwood and Jesse Hunt of Wisborough Green were the carriers who ran from Loxwood to Guildford. Hempstead had purchased Cole's Chevrolet by March 1933. After moving to The Laurels in Bucks Green, he also applied in April 1934 for an excursion licence to similar destinations as served by Kilner, picking up at Loxwood, Plaistow, Northchapel, Kirdford and Alfold. This was thought to be complementary to Kilner, rather than competitive. He also operated another fourteen-seat Chevrolet, registered VW 9276, and when he ceased operations in 1937 it passed into the Kilner fleet for a short time.

Some statistics relating to the bus service for the year 1935 have survived. A total of 39,142 tickets were issued, and this figure was declared as the number of passengers carried. It is recorded that 4,276 journeys were operated and 57,800 miles run in service. Revenue was about £1,092 and the average receipt per vehicle mile was 4.52 old pence. Between Bucks Green and Horsham return tickets were inter-available between the Sunbeam service and that of Gastonia.

Outside Horsham post office is PO 7943, Kilner's Bedford WLB with Duple twenty-seat bodywork.
This arrived in July 1933, not long after he took over the Plaistow to Horsham service from Jesse Wise.
(A. Cross/J. Higham)

There are usually some amusing anecdotes surrounding a country bus service. One day, Fred Kilner had to prevent a man boarding a bus at Plaistow as he wished to travel with his live calf. Chickens in baskets were one thing, calves were another. On another occasion, Fred found an A&D conductor by the roadside one night. He had 'taken a parcel into a pub', when a passenger had rung the bell and the bus had departed, leaving him stranded. The Sunbeam bus was timed three minutes behind the A&D service, so Fred easily caught it up and reunited the conductor with his bus.

The Loxwood to Horsham section of the service loaded well, the busiest journeys often requiring duplication. The police regularly complained about overloading of Kilner's buses between Broadbridge Heath and Horsham. Busy journeys would sometimes need two duplicate vehicles and one conductor would collect fares on all three, by changing bus as the trip progressed. However, the Loxwood to Plaistow part was less remunerative and was reduced to run only on Wednesdays, Saturdays and Sundays from Spring 1936. Thursdays were especially quiet and sometimes Mrs Kilner would use an eight-seat Morris on the service. A revised timetable was introduced in May 1938, which reduced the whole service on Thursdays to only two round trips, giving an 8.55 a.m. arrival in Horsham, and a 4.40 p.m. return. Daily running was extended beyond Loxwood to Ifold, except for on Thursdays, to cater for new housing development there.

Kilner expanded his business so that the normal fleet strength reached about eight vehicles and the coal merchant's premises in Loxwood were then mainly used for buses and coaches. In 1938, Kilner moved in to a new house called Gaywood, which was built next to the yard, having lived in a house called Haltings, also in Guildford Road, since 1934. The fleet was quite varied and, up to 1939, contained Chevrolet, Morris Commercial, Dennis, Tilling-Stevens, Ford, GMC, Bedford, Bean and Gilford vehicles. During the 1930s, a good relationship was established with dealer H. Lane of Chelsea, which was later to prove useful during the war when any sort of vehicle was scarce. Taxi work was also undertaken and Mary Kilner drove

Another view of PO 7943, this time on a private hire outing where women were definitely off the agenda. Caps were predominantly *de rigeur*. This coach passed to Hants & Sussex in 1946 and was sold to Bill Potter of Stedham, Sussex, just before Basil Williams bought the Potter bus services in 1947. (Author's collection)

Fred Kilner with his GMC twenty-four-seater, which he acquired in September 1936. When sold in July 1941 to Crayford Urban District Council, it was converted to an ambulance. The location is probably the Loxwood depot in Guildford Road. (Author's collection, courtesy F. Kilner)

With a makeshift destination board, Kilner's Chevrolet LQ (VW 9276) with fourteen-seat Eaton bodywork is parked in the Carfax about 1937. He acquired it from Wesley Hempstead, his brother-in-law. (J.Higham)

the cars and was also one of the first lady public service vehicle drivers to obtain a licence in the South Eastern Traffic Area. Kilner's daughter also obtained PSV drivers' and conductors' licences.

After the outbreak of war in September 1939, one of Kilner's drivers was conscripted, while there was an influx of military personnel and civilian workers into the area. None of the vehicles were requisitioned, as they were in great local demand for contracts for troop transport and the movement of workers to firms engaged in activities of national importance. Work included the transport for the City of London Yeomanry at Rudgwick Camp, military staff based at Alfold and food rationing officers working at Harsfold Manor in Wisborough Green. Bus drivers were hard to obtain but Kilner arranged for a former London Transport man, Harry Edwards, to come to Loxwood and work for him. Edwards's son Tom later ran his own coach business – Primrose Coaches – from a garage in Station Road, Loxwood.

Vehicles were also difficult to come by, but Kilner was fortunate to be able to buy in 1941 three Bedford WLB twenty-seaters which London Transport had previously acquired from various independent operators that had been absorbed. A second-hand twenty-seven-seat Opel arrived in 1942 and on 26 May 1943 a new Bedford OWB with utility Duple thirty-two-seat bodywork was delivered. These vehicles could only be purchased by hard-pressed operators who could demonstrate need; Kilner had wanted two but only got one new bus, registered FPX 747, although a second-hand specimen was obtained in the following year.

In Summer 1944, rival applications for bus service defence permits were received by the South Eastern Regional Transport Commissioner, who held a hearing, a rare occurrence in wartime. Under the emergency situation, normal licensing procedures had been abandoned, together with the issue of Notices and Proceedings. Operators relied on the latter to warn them of potentially hostile applications in their area, but during the war they should have been advised individually by the Commissioner when their interests were thought to be involved. Petworth Rural District Council were wishing to see bus services link Balls Cross, Kirdford,

This very smart Bedford WLB had a low mileage when acquired in 1938, making it quite a bargain, according to Fred Kilner. It had bodywork by East Lancs. (Author's collection, courtesy F. Kilner)

Looking somewhat the worse for wear is Kilner's Bedford WLB AKE 725, acquired in 1940 after use by London Transport. It passed to Hants & Sussex in February 1945. The location of the view is not known. (D.A. Jones)

APC 55 was another Bedford WLB formerly used by London Transport. New to Sunshine Saloon Coaches of Kingston upon Thames, it passed to Hants & Sussex with the Kilner coach business in 1946 and was sold to Ernest Carter of Plummers Plain in July 1947. (S. Newman)

Wisborough Green and Plaistow with Petworth and Haslemere, but had received a negative response from Southdown and A&D. The council then contacted the Commissioner for his assistance, so the latter wrote to Fred Kilner suggesting that he might provide some new facilities. Kilner declined, as he felt the territory to be unremunerative, perhaps recalling the previous efforts of Messrs Mann, Weller and Wise.

In June 1944, new services were applied for by Basil Williams of Emsworth, Hants, with the support of the council. One was to run from Wisborough Green to Haslemere via Kirdford, Plaistow and Fisher Street and another from Kirdford through Balls Cross to Petworth. A&D counter-proposed an extension of their service 60 (Godalming-Dunsfold) to Plaistow, Kirdford and Petworth and also a brand new service from Haslemere to Horsham via Fisher Street, Plaistow, Loxwood, Tismans Common and Bucks Green. The latter covered all of Kilner's service though it did not serve Alfold, but he was unaware of these proposals, as was Basil Williams since the Commissioner had not advised them.

At the hearing, the Commissioner said he had not invited Fred Kilner as the latter had previously given in writing his view that the routes would not be worthwhile. The only application granted was the extension of A&D service 60. When Kilner heard about these developments he was very angry and offered to extend his service, if it was thought necessary, from Plaistow to Fisher Street, in order to connect with A&D's existing Petworth to Haslemere service. However, to safeguard his interests, he applied to increase the frequency of his existing service and, despite objections from Southdown and A&D, this was granted. This service would involve a premium fare structure between Bucks Green and Horsham, to protect the objectors.

The aforementioned Basil Williams was effectively the architect, majority shareholder and managing director of a concern called Hants & Sussex Motor Services Ltd, which he had registered on 30 April 1937. By 1944, Williams was running bus services in the Emsworth, Havant, Midhurst and Petworth areas. The full story of the Basil Williams empire has been

Kilner's utility Bedford OWB registered FPX 747 waits to leave for Horsham and has headlamp masks that would almost prevent any useful illumination escaping. This view was taken by Charles Klapper – a well-known transport journalist of the time and a founder member of the Omnibus Society in the early 1930s. As an aside, there were no kerbstones in this part of Loxwood in 1944. (C.F. Klapper collection/ Omnibus Society)

admirably told already elsewhere and a description of the activities of Hants & Sussex in the Horsham area is given later in this book. However, it should be recorded that in January 1944, Williams had formed Silver Queen Motor Services Ltd as part of his attempt to acquire the business of Cecil Walling of Eastergate, Sussex, which included a bus service from Bognor Regis to Slindon. The transfer of the permit for this service to the new company was objected to by Southdown and the application was refused by the Transport Commissioner. Southdown acquired the Walling business themselves from 21 December 1944, leaving Williams with a company which had no purpose.

Williams had accrued some capital earned from lucrative contract work during the war and he found that buying small bus operators in southern England was the easiest way of expanding his territory. He may have become acquainted with the Kilner business during the attempt to introduce routes around Plaistow and Kirdford and it seems he visited Loxwood and made a tempting offer to Fred Kilner to buy into his business in two stages. This was possibly seen as beneficial by Kilner, as the fleet needed some investment and running a bus company in wartime was a great strain on his family.

In January 1945, Silver Queen Motor Services Ltd had its name changed to F.H. Kilner (Transport) Ltd and Fred Kilner became a director in place of Williams on 28 February 1945, when the company took over the operation of the bus service and three vehicles – a Bedford WLB and the two OWBs. The management of the service came under the control of Hants & Sussex. Mary Kilner was also made a director from April 1945 until April 1946, after which Basil Williams and his father acquired the Kilners' shareholding in stages. Fred Kilner ceased to be a director in June 1948. To the outside world in 1945, it appeared that Kilner had formed a limited liability company so there were no objections to the transfer of the permit for the bus service. For various reasons, the coach aspect of the Sunbeam business – private hire, contracts and the excursion and tours licence – remained with the Kilner family until 21 March 1946 when Williams formed Sunbeam Coaches (Loxwood) Ltd. Kilner was the

SUNBEAM BUS SERVICE.

Proprietor : F. H. KILNER, LOXWOOD.   'Phone Loxwood 318.

	A.M.	N.S.	P.M.				S.O.
Plaistow (The Sun) w.s.s.o.		10.27		2.27		6.27	8.27
	N.S.	N.S			N.S.	N.T.	S.S.O.
Loxwood P.O.	8.35	10.35	12.35	2.35	4.35	6.35	8.35
Alfold (Crown)	8.40	10.40	12.40	2.40	4.40	6.40	8.40
Alfold Cross Ways	8.45	10.43	12.45	2.43	4.45	6.43	8.43
Tismans Cross Roads	8.52	10.52	12.52	2.52	4.52	6.52	8.52
Bucks Green	8.55	10.55	12.55	2.55	4.55	6.55	8.55
Woodlea	9.2	11.2	1.2	3.2	5.2	7.2	9.2
Broadbridge Heath	9.10	11.10	1.10	3.10	5.10	7.10	9.10
Horsham Station	9.18	11.18	1.18	3.18	5.18	7.18	9.18
	N.S.	N.S.			N.S.	N.T.W.	W.S.S.O.
Horsham Station	9.22	11.22	1.22	3.22	5.22	7.22	9.22
Broadbridge Heath	9.30	11.30	1.30	3.30	5.30	7.30	9.30
Woodlea	9.37	11.37	1.37	3.37	5.37	7.37	9.37
Bucks Green	9.45	11.45	1.45	3.45	5.45	7.45	9.45
Tismans Cross Roads	9.48	11.48	1.48	3.48	5.48	7.48	9.48
Alfold Cross Ways	9.57	11.55	1.57	3.55	5.57	7.55	9.57
Alfold (Crown)	10.0	12.0	2.0	4.0	6.0	8.0	10.0
Loxwood P.O.	10.5	12.5	2.5	4.5	6.5	8.5	10.5
				SUNDAY			
Loxwood P.O.				6.0			
Plaistow (The Sun) w.s.s.o.	10.13		2.13	6.13	6.13		10.13

N.S.—Not Sundays.   S.O.—Saturdays only.   S.S.O.—Saturdays and Sundays only.   N.W.—Not Wednesdays.
W.S.S.O.—Wednesday, Saturdays and Sundays only, also Bank Holidays.   N.T.—Not Thursdays.
Wednesdays, Saturdays and Sundays only to Plaistow.

20-SEATER COACHES FOR HIRE.   Enquiries Solicited.

majority shareholder in this company and the other directors were Basil Williams and Mrs Irene Williams. Three Bedford WLBs and the Opel were transferred.

The Kilners continued to live at Gaywood until late 1947, but they had no control over the day-to-day running of the businesses. Their good reputation was not maintained by the replacement local Hants & Sussex management. Therefore, the Kilners found themselves in the front line and having to answer public complaints about unreliable and erratic operations and allegations of financial impropriety by conductors, over which they had no effective control. They also had to endure noise at night due to the maintenance work being carried out on the vehicles in the adjacent yard. In hindsight, the Kilners wished they had never entered into any arrangement with Williams and ultimately Fred Kilner lost a considerable investment when the Hants & Sussex group of companies largely collapsed in 1954.

ELEVEN

F.H. KILNER (TRANSPORT) LTD (HANTS & SUSSEX MOTOR SERVICES)

The Hants & Sussex group was made up of several operating units spread over a wide area of southern England and the one responsible for bus service activities around Horsham was F.H. Kilner (Transport) Ltd. It was active in the district for just under ten years and unfortunately became wellknown for its failures rather than its successes. As has been recounted already, this company was engineered by Basil Williams to take over Fred Kilner's bus service on 28 February 1945, in such a way that little was apparent to the travelling public and more importantly, to other local operators like London Transport, Southdown and A&D, who were concerned at Basil Williams's potential ability to take over small operators and to then strengthen their services so as to effect a more significant challenge to the larger companies. They did not expect the services to be particularly remunerative – they were more concerned about the nuisance value that Williams's involvement could cause and felt that their absorption by one of the larger operators would create better co-ordination and efficiency. They agreed a policy of mutual co-operation to progress takeovers if the opportunity arose. Southdown had already had experience of Williams's acquisitive tactics in terms of the Silver Queen affair.

It seems that Fred Kilner had not exercised his receipt of permission to increase his Plaistow-Horsham service in 1944, but from 9 July 1945 the service was effectively doubled in frequency to operate hourly throughout. The publicity for this change showed the trading name to still be Sunbeam Bus Services, with Fred Kilner as managing director, thus perpetuating the illusion that this was nothing to do with Basil Williams, especially as Kilner was still running coaches from Loxwood in his own right under the Sunbeam name. Williams decided to increase the service, despite Fred Kilner feeling that at that time, it would not be particularly remunerative, when the increased costs were equated with potential extra revenue. The new timetable required fairly tight turnarounds at the termini using two vehicles. As only three buses were technically available at Loxwood for the service and spare cover, others were drafted in on loan from elsewhere in the Hants & Sussex empire when required, and it was not long before a London Transport inspector noted a 'red thirty-seat coach' in Horsham 'on hire to Kilner'. This may have been LJ 1533, an elderly Daimler CF6, which Williams had acquired second-hand during the war for contract duties.

Hants & Sussex had obtained a contract from the Ministry of Works to provide the transport for workmen engaged in clearing and repairing buildings in the London area which had been damaged by flying bombs. This required the hiring of a large number of vehicles. Three of these were diverted at various times from Autumn 1945 until Autumn 1946 to supplement the fleet available at Loxwood, being utility thirty-two-seat Bedford OWBs with Duple bodywork, registered FYD 569/570 (owned by Mid Somerset Coaches of Shepton Mallet) and CWV 846, owned by E. Dennis of Trowbridge. Also used at Loxwood was ARV 920, a Bedford WTB, which Williams had acquired with the Liss & District Omnibus Co. business.

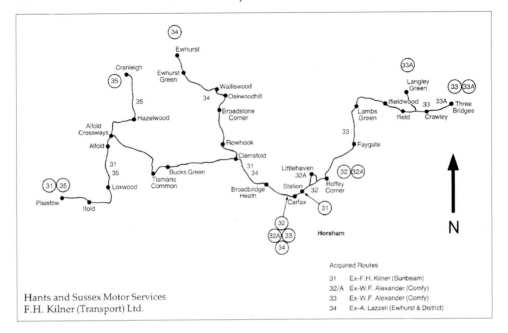

Hants and Sussex Motor Services
F.H. Kilner (Transport) Ltd.

Acquired Routes

31   Ex-F.H. Kilner (Sunbeam)
32/A Ex-W.F. Alexander (Comfy)
33   Ex-W.F. Alexander (Comfy)
34   Ex-A. Lazzell (Ewhurst & District)

The two FYD-registered buses were subsequently purchased by Williams, and 570 formally joined the Kilner fleet in June 1946.

The acquisition by Williams of the coach side of Fred Kilner's business from 21 March 1946, with the setting up of Sunbeam Coaches (Loxwood) Ltd, gave the new owner access to four more vehicles, followed in June by the delivery of two Bedford OB/Duple Vista coaches – FAA240 and 242. These were part of a batch of seven meant for use on a contract providing the transport for Clydeside shipyard workers from their camp at Chandlers Ford to Southampton Docks, where the liners *Queen Mary* and *Queen Elizabeth* were being refitted to resume their peacetime role. Instead, Williams collected together a motley collection of old buses more suitable, in his view, for carrying workmen, so he distributed the new OBs around his various companies.

Williams consolidated his position in the Horsham area with the purchase of Alexander's Comfy Coaches for F.H. Kilner (Transport) Ltd, from 3 October 1946, for a consideration of £9,600, involving seven vehicles, around a dozen staff, the use of their Roffey depot and the licences for bus services from Horsham to Roffey Corner and Three Bridges. The purchase of Arthur Lazzell's Ewhurst-Horsham bus service for a sum of £2,885 in November 1946 saw the completion of the basic Hants & Sussex route network in the area. The bus for this service was initially outstationed overnight in the old Surrey Hills bus garage in Ewhurst, as the timetable remained similar to that latterly run by Lazzell.

In August 1946, A&D made one of the first applications published after the resumption of normal licensing procedures, for a service 50 from Haslemere to Horsham, reviving their Summer 1944 proposal. There would be five return journeys on weekdays and four on Sundays, running at roughly three-hourly intervals. Basil Williams naturally lodged an objection and counter-proposed to extend his Plaistow service to Haslemere five times a day in winter and hourly in summer. At the hearing in May 1947, Williams said he was prepared to offer protection to A&D between Fisher Street and Haslemere and, if granted, the A&D application would cause wasteful competition with his existing service. A&D felt they were better able to effect overall co-ordination and would agree to the removal of pickup restrictions on some of the F.H. Kilner (Transport) Ltd journeys between Bucks Green and Horsham. The Commissioner decided in favour of A&D and an appeal by Williams against the decision was dismissed in November 1947. However, by entering Horsham, the service fell

In the first part of 1947, Basil Williams started allocating new Leyland Tiger PS1 and Bedford OB coaches to his Horsham area F. H. Kilner (Transport) Ltd operations. These replaced some of the motley collection of vehicles acquired with the Kilner and Alexander businesses. Here, Bedford OB FOR 817 is on the Ewhurst service taken over from Lazzell. (Author's collection)

partly within the Metropolitan Traffic Area and the Commissioner refused to grant a backing licence, suggesting that the two companies agreed to a co-ordinated service into town from Bucks Green. Eventually, A&D did start their service 50, from 19 January 1948, and exactly a month later some co-ordination did occur when F.H. Kilner (Transport) Ltd withdrew four journeys each way per day and the pickup restrictions were formally lifted, although in reality they had been ignored for some time.

At the end of 1946, Williams advised London Transport that he wished to put a double-decker onto his local service from Horsham to Roffey Corner, to which London Transport objected, as they had run single-deckers since October 1946 on their service 434 short-workings, due to a vehicle shortage. To restore the balance, they suggested that F.H. Kilner (Transport) Ltd curtail the hourly journeys via Littlehaven to terminate there, rather than Roffey Corner. This was done in April 1947 and a new Leyland PD1 double-decker, registered FCG 525 with attractive Northern Coachbuilders bodywork, was then the regular vehicle used on the Roffey service. However, on 25 February 1948 London Transport reinstated their double-decker, so the Kilner Littlehaven service was restored to Roffey Corner.

On 29 March 1947, a Hants & Sussex booking and enquiry office opened at 22 Richmond Terrace, Carfax, Horsham adjacent to that operated by Southdown. This was staffed by Celia Browne, Gordon Jellett and Frank Andrews and it was there that H.F. Harrison was based, being the local manager and also the traffic superintendent for the whole Hants & Sussex group, thus spending some of his time at the head office at South Leigh Road, Emsworth. Prior to this, office work was performed in a room at Harrison's house, and crews also had to go there to pay in the bus service takings. At Loxwood, Ron Salmon took over day-to-day management from Fred Kilner in 1946, but by 1947 the manager was Vic Candish, whose brother Ron performed a similar function at the Liss & District Omnibus Co. depot at Liss Forest in Hampshire.

The standard vehicle livery of Hants & Sussex was maroon, red and cream and, despite being owned by and licensed to F.H. Kilner (Transport) Ltd or Sunbeam Coaches (Loxwood) Ltd,

they carried the Hants & Sussex fleetname. New Hants & Sussex bus stop signs appeared along the routes and from 3 April 1947, to coincide with the issue of a timetable booklet covering all Hants & Sussex services, the Horsham services were thus numbered, Plaistow being 31; Roffey Corner 32; Littlehaven 32A; Three Bridges 33 and Ewhurst 34. Williams was extremely keen that an impression was conveyed to the public and to competitors that Hants & Sussex was far more substantial than it actually was and that a big company image was portrayed. The vehicles carried high fleet numbers, which bore no relation to the total fleet size, and were essentially decorative, with no system as such.

During the war, Basil Williams had speculatively placed orders with Bedford and Leyland for large numbers of new vehicles to be delivered if Britain gained a successful result to hostilities. Whereas small companies had lengthy waits to get a couple of new vehicles after the war ended, Williams's foresight seems to have paid off and, with business buoyant, could readily obtain hire-purchase facilities. In 1947 and 1948 the Hants & Sussex group took delivery of significant numbers of Bedford OB and Leyland Tiger PS1 coaches and Leyland PD1 double-deckers and single-deckers continued unabated into 1949 and 1950. F.H. Kilner (Transport) Ltd was allocated in 1947/48 nine OBs and six PS1s, as well as the PD1 mentioned earlier, while Sunbeam Coaches received three OBs. This modern fleet enabled virtually all the pre-war vehicles acquired from Kilner and Alexander to be replaced and gave Hants & Sussex a distinct advantage over other operators when competing for excursion, contract or private hire business, but this came at some cost, which brought difficulties later. Advertisements for coach business usually carried the wording 'entirely new post-war coaches only' or 'super luxury radio-fitted coaches', all of which conformed to the air of company grandeur that Williams wanted to portray.

Overall strategic and administrative control came from the Emsworth office, but day-to-day affairs were under the charge of the local depot managers. To enable operations to be monitored, most vehicles were fitted with swiss Zenith eight-day time recorder machines, a measure introduced by Williams during the war for works contract buses outstationed far from home. The graph produced by the recorder could prove if the bus had been running to the timetable, but the system got a mixed reaction from the staff. Most, however, were pleased with the devices, especially if they had been accused of early running by passengers who had

An interesting shot of seven Hants & Sussex Bedford OBs on private hire in North Street, Horsham at 7 a.m. on 22 August 1948. The vehicles and drivers from both Roffey and Loxwood depots are, *from left to right*: FAA 240 Barnes, FHO 790 Tidy, FAA 242 Sheppard, GAA 548 Robins, FOT 20 Rogers, OML 543 Gosling and FOT 19 Merritt. All staff were encouraged to promote private hire in their area. (Author's collection, courtesy T. Merritt)

Above: Occasionally, when Leyland PD1 FCG 525 was not available, a double-decker for the Roffey service was drafted in from other parts of the Hants & Sussex empire. Identical FCG 523 normally worked in Emsworth or Fareham. Is the policeman about to make pleasantries with the baby or caution it? (Supplied by M. Rooum)

Opposite: The regular Hants & Sussex vehicle on the Horsham to Roffey Corner 'Swingers' from 1947 to 1954 was this smart Leyland Titan PD1, with attractive bodywork by Northern Coachbuilders. It had fifty-six seats but on occasions carried nearly double that number at busy times. It is in North Street near Horsham Station. (W.J. Haynes)

The first of five Bedford OBs with Duple bus bodies arrived in January 1949. In Summer 1954, GOU 721 is on the new Langley Green section of route 33 Horsham–Three Bridges. (A. Cross)

Bedford OB GOU 887 is on service 33 from Horsham to Crawley and Three Bridges on 6 June 1949, three months after it was new. The high fleet number was only for effect and had no significance. (J.H. Aston)

Thought to be in Loxwood on the former Kilner service in July 1949 is Bedford OB bus HAA 563. The batch of five such buses delivered in 1949 formed the backbone of the Horsham area Hants & Sussex bus fleet until operations ended. (D.C. Fisk)

missed the bus. The machines provided a paper record and were sometimes given spot checks on the road by a roving inspector.

Stocks of bell-bunch-style tickets inherited from the operators of acquired services were initially used and Hants & Sussex sometimes used punch tickets of their own on short-distance services such as that to Roffey. However, for general use, T.I.M. ticket machines were introduced on the Horsham services from around 1947/48.

Coach scheduling work at Horsham and Loxwood could be frustrating for those responsible, especially at weekends. Local excursions would be cancelled or private hires refused if Williams had obtained a more high-profile job elsewhere, sometimes involving large numbers of coaches brought in from the various satellite depots. If a coach was destined for Southsea it would sometimes find itself with its weary Roffey or Loxwood driver working for either Triumph Coaches or Southsea Royal Blue Parlour Coaches, which Williams had obtained control of in 1947. Coach trips to Portsmouth were also a revenue-earning way of transferring a vehicle to the state-of-the-art Hants & Sussex workshops, which were opened at Cosham in 1948, although many repair jobs were still performed at Loxwood or Roffey in somewhat basic conditions. Williams apparently tried at one point to build a new garage in Queen Street, Horsham, but the planning application was refused.

On one occasion, long-serving Roffey driver Tom Merritt took a party down to Bournemouth and then had to report to Shamrock & Rambler Coaches to operate an afternoon tour on their behalf. Two vehicles from Liss Forest depot were also there and Merritt complained that they had come a shorter distance, but were scheduled to start their sub-contract work after him. Merritt reported late as he needed a break and when the management heard about it they threatened to sack him. Ted Frost, the depot foreman at Roffey, was ordered to suspend Merritt for three days and replied that he would when he could spare him, maybe in three months time! Both Merritt and Frost had worked together for many years since they were with Alexander.

While the matter of the proposed Haslemere service was still dragging on, Williams applied for another major service expansion in September 1947. He sought to increase the frequency of service 33 to every two hours, to extend service 32 from Horsham Carfax to Greenway via Bishopric and Rushams Road and to extend service 32A from Carfax to Broadbridge Heath, already covered by several other services. Whether there was sufficient traffic to warrant more journeys on the rural Crawley service, or to Broadbridge Heath, was questionable. As one would expect, London Transport, A&D and Southdown objected, with the latter counter-proposing to extend their town service 73 (Oakhill-Carfax) to Greenway via Hurst Road, North Parade and Rushams Road. Then, in October, Williams applied for a new service from Horsham to Brook, in Surrey, via Bucks Green, Alfold Crossways, Dunsfold, Chiddingfold and Witley Station. This carved a lonely rural cross-country course, intersecting with A&D services at various points. Quite what business of any substance Williams thought he would obtain from such a service is now hard to see. At the same time, he applied to increase the frequency of service 34 to hourly and to extend it from Ewhurst to Cranleigh, Alfold and Loxwood, with every third journey further extended to Roundstreet Common and Billingshurst, competing in fair measure with A&D. Connections were to be made at Alfold Crossways with the proposed Brook service.

The hearing for the first batch of applications before the Metropolitan Traffic Commissioner took three days. He decided in favour of Southdown in respect of a town service to Greenway, adjourned the Broadbridge Heath proposal, pending the hearing for the Brook and Billingshurst services and refused the application for service 33 in its original form. However, he said he might consider a more modest enhancement and this was eventually granted in May 1948 involving some additional journeys running between Roffey Corner and Ifield, including on Sundays. Passengers were obliged to change at Ifield onto London Transport service 426 for Crawley. In February 1948, the fate of the other applications was decided at a two-day hearing when they were refused on the grounds that the existing A&D services

Another Bedford OB coach is seen in Crawley in 1954. Note the board in the window for the Langley Green service, officially numbered 33A. HCG 601 was new in June 1949. (A. Lambert)

in those areas were quite adequate, although some lesser augmentation of service 34 could be considered. In August 1948 a revised timetable was granted, including the provision of a Thursday afternoon service and a rescheduling to allow the bus to work from Roffey depot, rather than being outstationed at Ewhurst.

In 1949 the fortunes of the Hants & Sussex group were at their peak. Petrol was still rationed and with private motoring restricted there was much demand for public transport. Basil Williams even treated himself to a new Rolls-Royce car, in which he was chauffeured on visits to depots. It had a radio and a machine so he could dictate correspondence while en route. Early in the year, five new Bedford OBs with thirty-seat Duple bus bodies were allocated to F.H. Kilner (Transport) Ltd to form the backbone of the single-deck fleet for the Horsham area services. These were followed by two with coach bodies, while Sunbeam Coaches received two earlier coach examples which were transferred from Emsworth. Some of the Bedfords delivered in 1947 were sold in 1949 after a very short life with Hants & Sussex and other coaches came and went. However, one Leyland PS1 (GOT 400) remained at Roffey from September 1948 onwards as the front-line private hire coach.

Following an increase in costs, the Horsham office was reluctantly closed in March 1950 and the registered office and administrative activities of F.H. Kilner (Transport) Ltd was transferred to the depot at Roffey Corner. To maintain a presence in the town centre, the Albion Music House in the Carfax was appointed as agent for excursion bookings, although much useful coach business was lost to competitors due to the relative inaccessibility of the depot.

The same month an application was made for a new bus service from Plaistow to Cranleigh via Loxwood, Alfold and Hazelwood on Wednesdays and Saturdays, with one journey each way, mainly for the benefit of shoppers. Despite an objection from A&D it was allowed, but did not start until 18 November 1950, numbered service 35. Such a route had been considered by Fred Kilner in the 1930s, but he was worried that it would abstract custom from his Horsham service. Concurrently, an application was progressed for tours and excursions from a point in Crawley and this was objected to by London Transport, Southdown, Sargents of East Grinstead and British Railways. The hearing finally occurred in January 1951 when the application was refused in favour of a competing one from Southdown.

A rear view of a Bedford OB at the Roffey Corner depot, which was previously used by Alexander. On Hants & Sussex coaches the fleet name appeared on the rear and not on the sides. (Author's collection)

Meanwhile, the wrangle between Hants & Sussex and A&D over the Plaistow route continued. In June 1950 Williams applied to reinstate those journeys on service 31 which had been withdrawn in 1948. This was granted and A&D were required to reduce their service 50 Haslemere-Horsham to just two return journeys on Wednesdays and Saturdays only. Naturally, A&D appealed against this major reduction but after further extensive argument it was dismissed and the new arrangements started on 4 June 1951.

In February 1951, Sunbeam Coaches applied for a programme of excursions from Dunsfold and this was granted in time for the summer season. Other villages were added so that by the following summer Hants & Sussex could offer trips from Loxwood, Alfold, Dunsfold, Cranleigh, Tismans Common, Ifold, Plaistow and Kirdford as well as those from Horsham and Roffey. From 1 August 1951 the Cranleigh service was rationalised and curtailed to start at Alfold Crossways (with connections from Plaistow and Loxwood by service 31) and was revised to provide two journeys each way on Fridays only.

Working for Hants & Sussex was not a restful occupation yet despite the pressures placed on them, some of the staff were keen to serve the public well. There was a feeling that some of the local supervisors appointed by Williams were not of the best calibre, which was perhaps aggravated by the distance from Emsworth. The men at Loxwood had a grievance over their working conditions. The local T&GWU representative met with Patrick O'Sullivan who had been Hants & Sussex assistant general manager since before 1945, and also chief engineer. The talks broke down and the staff at Loxwood went on strike on 25 August 1951 and at Roffey on 27 August in protest over pay rates, scheduling and the need for better toilet facilities at Loxwood, where comforts could be called primitive. Although affairs were conducted in a gentlemanly way, the company could ill-afford to lose revenue or goodwill through labour disputes and Fred Kilner himself convinced the staff to return to work. The latter had sold his house, Gaywood, and the Loxwood manager lived in a nearby bungalow called Hazelwood, an asset of Sunbeam Coaches (Loxwood) Ltd.

London Transport started to turn a financial screw to Hants & Sussex's disadvantage in June 1951, when they proposed to double the frequency to half hourly on their service 434 through journeys from Horsham to Edenbridge on Saturday afternoons, and would not offer Williams

Hants & Sussex HAA 564, another of the 1949 batch of Bedford OBs, lays over outside the Bulls Head at Ewhurst, prior to returning to Horsham on service 34. Was the car's learner driver calming his nerves in the pub? (Author's collection)

After the ending of operations on 21 December 1954, a number of Hants & Sussex vehicles from Horsham were driven to Southsea the following day, prior to disposal. Seen here are some Bedford OBs and Leyland PD1 FCG 525. The drivers, now redundant, were no doubt commiserating with each other over a pint in this pub en route. (Author's collection)

the chance of some compensation by letting him enhance his service 33. In June 1952, London Transport similarly increased the frequency on Mondays to Fridays and Saturday mornings, in conjunction with a new route variant numbered 473, which ran to Edenbridge via Rowfant, instead of Copthorne and Crawley Down. As London Transport did not require Road Service Licences by statute, Williams could do nothing except see his share of the revenue decrease on the financially important Roffey route.

The modest town of Crawley was starting to mushroom into one of the designated post-war 'New Towns'. In the early 1950s, the first of the new residential neighbourhoods were built as well as factories on the Manor Royal Industrial Estate. Basil Williams saw the potential for new business generated by essential trips and also leisure travel, perhaps helping to cross-subsidise his now increasingly ailing and unremunerative rural bus services. Both London Transport and Southdown, who were long-established in Crawley, were determined to stop him progressing any expansionist aspirations.

By 1952, the fortunes of the bus industry in general, and Hants & Sussex in particular, were on the decline. The Labour Government imposed huge increases in Fuel Tax from 1950 and by 1952 it had reached 200 per cent! Wages had been increasing since the war and bus operating costs were rising steeply. Fare levels, which had been fairly static since the 1930s, had to rise but as fares were controlled by the Licensing Authority, it took a long time for applications to increase them to go through. In the meantime, the operator had to absorb any deficit.

In total, some 130 new vehicles had been delivered to the Hants & Sussex group between 1947 and 1951 to cater for the healthy growth in traffic, which meant a very large hire purchase liability. Until 1951 receipts were such that it was possible to service the debt, but from then on, patronage declined, as private motoring increased and more people could afford to own televisions, thus reducing the demand for leisure travel to cinemas in the evening. Thus, the financial position became unbalanced. The introduction of hire purchase restrictions in 1952 called for a cash deposit of 33.3 per cent and repayment over eighteen months; thus when a small batch of new Bedford SB coaches was purchased by the Hants & Sussex parent company, a larger than expected deposit was needed. By August 1952, the debt to the bank had reached £55,000 and on 2 October the bank appointed a nominee director to the Boards of each of the Hants & Sussex companies, in order to monitor financial activities.

The nominee wanted to sell F.H. Kilner (Transport) Ltd and Sunbeam Coaches (Loxwood) Ltd to the British Electric Traction Co., which owned Southdown and A&D, but British Electric Traction Co. wanted to buy the whole group. Basil Williams fought at Board meetings to prevent this occurring, but he did approach London Transport to ascertain whether they would be interested in acquiring services 32, 32A and 33. London Transport rightly assumed that the routes were being offered as they were unprofitable and had no intention of paying for them, despite the past nuisance they had endured in the traffic courts. With the passing of the Transport Act of 1953, London Transport were once again obliged to obtain Road Service Licences for their routes outside the 'London Special Area' and when they submitted an application for a licence for services 434 and 473, Williams objected and suggested that the service 434 Roffey local journeys should be passed to Hants & Sussex, but to no avail.

London Transport also applied for a licence to cover their excursion programme from Crawley, which was granted; but not before Williams had submitted an application of his own for excursions from Crawley and Ifield. When it came to the hearing in January 1954, it was rejected without the objectors being heard, as Williams had no evidence of need. The Licensing Authority raised justifiable concerns over complaints from the public about poor timekeeping on the bus services, irregular operation and the state of the vehicles – caused by inadequate maintenance following reduced expenditure due to cash flow problems. He also posed the question as to whether F.H. Kilner (Transport) Ltd was a fit and proper undertaking to hold any licenses at all.

1953 had ended with a deficit of £4,600 on the company's bus services, which had costs of 13.75 old pence per mile against receipts of 10*d* on average. Williams stated that receipts of 15*d* per mile were necessary if the services were to be viable and made critical references to the lack of relief from fuel tax. Unlike today, there was no financial support available for bus services that were not commercially sustainable and garnered little sympathy or understanding from any authority or the general public.

In September 1953 Arthur Williamson applied for a licence to run excursions from Billingshurst. Sunbeam Coaches reacted by applying for a Billingshurst pickup point on their own licence. However, Williamson's application was refused, whereupon Sunbeam withdrew their counter-proposal.

On the Plaistow service there had only been one fare increase since the takeover of the Sunbeam Bus Service. In October 1953 F.H. Kilner (Transport) Ltd notified A&D that they wished to raise them, but the latter did not wish to do the same, saying that increases were counter-productive and suggesting that Hants & Sussex should look to economies such as a reduction in unremunerative mileage and the use of the one-man operation principle, where drivers collected fares instead of conductors.

Several of the 1949 Bedford OB buses had been converted to run on diesel, with Perkins engines, which were more economical but were too much for the lightweight Duple bodies that gradually shook to pieces with the vibrations from the engines. As there was no money to undertake remedial repairs, it became known locally that parts of the buses were held together with string and that when it rained, one put one's umbrella up inside the bus! However, in 1954 Williams tried to raise the finance to convert more vehicles to diesel to save fuel costs but this was not sanctioned because of the overdraft – a somewhat short-sighted move on the part of the bank. Somewhat surprisingly, two forty-four-seat underfloor-engined demonstration buses were used on services 32/32A in early 1954 – an AEC Reliance and a Guy Arab LUF. Needless to say, no orders were placed but permission was obtained to use one-man operated buses up to forty-five-seat capacity on service 33.

A hearing was held in March 1954 for the application to increase fares on service 31. A&D and Southdown objected as they did not wish to raise their fares over common sections of the route and in view of this the application was refused, despite acknowledgement that Hants & Sussex desperately needed additional revenue. Williams advised the Licensing Authority that many of his rural routes would have to be withdrawn, whereupon the latter sounded-out larger operators to see if they wanted to take them over. A&D replied that it had many non-viable services and did not want any more. Hants & Sussex's bank debt was increasing as income dropped, partly, no doubt, due to loss of customer goodwill when services ran unreliably.

Rival applications were made by London Transport and F.H. Kilner (Transport) Ltd to serve the new Langley Green residential area in Crawley. Sensing another battle on the horizon, the Licensing Authority suggested that they came to terms before the Hearing. After the usual horsetrading, it was agreed that London Transport would run a service 476 from Crawley to Langley Green via London Road. Hants & Sussex would operate a two-hourly frequency on service 33 and a new hourly service 33A on weekdays from Crawley to the edge of Langley Green (Rushetts Road), just off the Ifield Road on the route of service 33, utilising two vehicles overall. Three Bridges would also be served by services 33/33A at peak periods. Service 476 started on 19 May 1954 and service 33A on 25 May and at that time Langley Green was sparsely populated and the houses unfinished. Had Hants & Sussex survived, this might have been a stepping stone to bigger things in Crawley, although London Transport would have made it quite difficult.

As an economy measure it was proposed in May 1954 to curtail certain journeys on service 31 on Mondays, Tuesdays, Thursdays and Fridays so that they were withdrawn between Tismans Common or Loxwood and Plaistow. In general, it was proposed that the conductor on the outgoing bus from Horsham could transfer to the incoming one at Tismans Common, leaving the driver to collect the fares for the remainder of the journey and saving on wages for one conductor. The residents of Loxwood were not happy with this reduction and thirty-five people attended a protest meeting to put their case to Hants & Sussex's manager, C.F. Manley (appointed at Horsham from 1 July 1953 in succession to Gordon Privett, who had followed on from H.F. Harrison and R.A. Howard) and to Charles Dunbar, who was a friend of Williams and both a transport professional and enthusiast. Hambledon Rural District Council lodged an objection at the public hearing in July, but the application was granted, coming into operation from 1 September 1954.

Coincidentally, on 11 July a Hants & Sussex bus was in a collision with a car on the bend in the road in Loxwood near the Onslow Arms and the now demolished Tollgate Cottage. The car was forced into the garden of the cottage and it was recorded that the occupants continued their journey by taxi later, and not by bus!

A revised timetable was also introduced on service 34 from 1 September to effect further economies. Running time was reduced and turnarounds were tight, leading to a late and erratic operation. A resident of Ewhurst organised a petition of complaint and obtained 100 signatures from users there and in Walliswood and Oakwoodhill. A protest meeting was held on 11 October at Oakwoodhill village hall and four local people were to seek a meeting with the Hants & Sussex management, although the new timetable continued in operation,

As an aside, the new (temporary) order is seen at Ewhurst. London Transport Guy GS 81 is on service 852 which encompassed former Hants & Sussex service 34 from Horsham to Ewhurst from December 1954 until May 1955. (Author's collection)

probably losing more business and goodwill. The same day, by coincidence, F.H. Kilner (Transport) Ltd started a contracted express service for the staff of the Hawker Aircraft works at Dunsfold Aerodrome near Alfold. Granted by means of a short-period licence, the service started at Horsham Station and ran via Broadbridge Heath, Bucks Green and Alfold Crossways on weekdays. The return journey diverted via Loxwood and Tismans Common.

The downward slide in the fortunes of the Hants & Sussex continued and on 7 July 1954 the bank advised Basil and Irene Williams that the overdraft must be reduced and some progress was made. However, matters were brought to a head on 9 September, when Mr and Mrs Williams were forced to resign from most of their companies, therefore becoming majority shareholders but with no control. The bank had threatened to call in their loans and appointed its own directors to work with Patrick O'Sullivan of Hants & Sussex, who was made general manager and managing director. The registered office of F.H. Kilner (Transport) Ltd and Sunbeam Coaches (Loxwood) Ltd was transferred to the coach station in Cosham, and seeing the writing on the wall, some of the staff began to leave and management were not always in attendance at Roffey and Loxwood, hence some irregularities occurred. Some vehicles were running with windows boarded up, rather than money being spent on new glass, and paintwork had become shabby.

Basil Williams made some suggestions as to how to reduce the debt to the bank, but the latter was not impressed. Being unable to increase ordinary fares, F.H. Kilner (Transport) Ltd applied to abolish season ticket concessions, including those for scholars, whose transport demanded expensive peak-hour duplication. This was refused at a hearing during November by an unsympathetic Licensing Authority, and this was a pointer that the inevitable was about to occur.

From 6 December 1954, the bank appointed a receiver for the Horsham area companies, when it was realised that no buyer would be found. The receiver gave the reasons for the his appointment as the low fares that the company had been obliged to maintain, the difficulty in obtaining staff and the downturn in trade. At that time, Roffey and Loxwood depots accounted for sixteen vehicles and twenty-three staff, more of whom had sought alternative employment. The new directors suggested to Basil Williams that he might like to take over the bus services on his own account and he applied for licences in his own name. However, the three major local companies had applied for short-period licences to continue them, and these had already been granted.

The last day of operation under Hants & Sussex auspices was Tuesday 21 December 1954. The final journey on service 31 from Horsham to Plaistow, over Fred Kilner's original route, was at 9.53 p.m., performed by Bedford OB bus HAA 564 and driven by D. Budd, while Cynthia Budd and Reg Dawson were the conductors. Stuck in the bonnet was a Union Jack flag at half mast and in the window a placard displayed the phrase 'sentenced to death'. The next day, the premises were closed and the vehicles driven away to Southsea, pending sale. On the way, the convoy stopped at a public house, no doubt so that the drivers, now redundant, could cheer themselves up.

Service 31 was taken over by A&D and numbered 50A. Friday service 35 from Alfold to Cranleigh also passed to A&D, as 50B, and was extended to start again at Plaistow. London Transport introduced a service 852 which ran through from Ewhurst to Crawley via Horsham, combining erstwhile services 34 and 33 and was operated from Crawley Garage. The 32/32A to Roffey were absorbed into London Transport service 434, while Southdown gained licences for the Hawker works service and the excursions from Horsham. No perpetuation was made of service 33A, with Langley Green being adequately covered by London Transport service 476, while the licence for excursions from Loxwood was allowed to lapse.

When these companies submitted applications for substantive licences, Basil Williams's counter-proposals were also considered, although he was unable to lodge objections. Ironically for Williams, one of the first things that A&D had done in respect of the Plaistow service was to get approval to raise fares to a more remunerative level, now that the service was solely in their hands! At the hearings in April 1955 the licence awards to A&D, London Transport and Southdown were confirmed, except for the Ewhurst to Horsham service which was awarded to Brown Motor Services as already described. The large operators were not attracted to the services in the hope of gaining good profits, but more in order to keep small independent operators from exploiting the opportunity to expand.

The Licensing Authority criticised Basil Williams's past conduct as managing director of Hants & Sussex and refused his applications. On appeal, the Licensing Authority agreed that they should not have taken Williams's past conduct into account, but felt that A&D were better placed to absorb any losses and to sustain a service for the public. The inspector's view that the licence awards should not be cancelled and that there was absolutely no need to grant licences to Williams too was agreed with by the Minister of Transport.

On 19 April 1955, Sunbeam Coaches (Loxwood) Ltd was declared insolvent and voluntary winding up commenced. The sale of its vehicles realised £1,543 and the bank received £1,906 of the £3,414 amount owing. In January 1956, a statement of affairs relating to F.H. Kilner (Transport) Ltd showed a deficit of more than £20,000. Its vehicles fetched £2,200 and creditors received 15s 5d in the pound on an amount of £3,094, the company being formally dissolved in March 1958.

Since the 1950s, development in both Horsham and Crawley has been substantial, and had it survived, Hants & Sussex might have reaped some benefit. However, from 1951 onwards it became clear that a network of rural stage-carriage services was not sufficient to allow a reasonable profit – cross–subsidy was needed from town services and tours and excursions, from which Hants & Sussex was effectively kept at bay.

From 1955, Basil Williams continued to operate bus services around Midhurst in West Sussex and Emsworth in Hampshire, under the Southern Motorways name. At the time of bus deregulation in 1986, he secured a network of services around Eastleigh and Winchester, once again under the Hants & Sussex title. It was not until May 1996 that he finally ceased operating on his last services around Emsworth, Havant, Waterlooville and Portsmouth. Despite all the past problems and setbacks, he was one of the most prolific independent bus and coach entrepreneurs who continually tussled with the large combine operators and the Road Service Licensing establishment until the enactment of the Transport Act of 1985. He had started Hants & Sussex when just twenty-three years of age, and died on 27 June 1999 aged eighty-five, being remembered, fondly or otherwise, as one of the great characters of the industry.

TWELVE

NORTH DOWNS RURAL TRANSPORT

The short-lived North Downs concern was the first new operator of stage-carriage services in the Horsham area since the arrival of Hants & Sussex in 1945. Although operations started in 1969, the founder's involvement with running bus services went back to 1963, and events in the area surrounding the outer London dormitory town of Orpington, Kent.

John Wylde was a teacher who was the honorary manager of the Orpington Rural Transport Association, which had been set up by some local councillors acting in a private capacity, as a non-profit making organisation. From 22 June 1963 they ran a service from Orpington to Biggin Hill, using minibuses, after the withdrawal of a London Transport service which had lasted only four months. The service was gradually expanded and later extended from Biggin Hill to New Addington and also to Tatsfield for a short period.

In 1965 Rusper Parish Council and Horsham Rural District Council became aware of the success of the Orpington R.T.A. and asked them whether something could be done to provide some form of replacement service for London Transport route 852, which was about to be withdrawn. In the event, John Wylde hired one of the Association's minibuses and drove it on Saturdays, from 30 October to 27 November 1965, over the route of the 852 from Crawley to Horsham via Ifieldwood, Lambs Green, Faygate and Roffey. Marketed as North Sussex Rural Transport, the service was intended for shoppers, and while the response was encouraging, there was nobody living locally willing to act as organiser and promoter.

During 1968, Wylde tried to convince the Orpington Rural Transport Association to introduce a bus service from Orpington to Croydon, as London Transport did not seem to want to provide a direct one. The Association did not feel able to respond, so Wylde, in partnership with his wife Mary and Roy Edwards, set up North Downs Rural Transport and obtained consent from London Transport to run such a service. After some delay a Road Service Licence was obtained and the service commenced on 8 April 1969, running on Mondays to Saturdays. A new twelve-seat diesel-engined Ford Transit minibus with body converted to public service vehicle standard was used, registered APX 928G. It was white with *North Downs* painted in 10in-high red letters on the sides.

Concurrent with the planning for the Croydon service, Mabel Mitchell's decision to give up her bus services would have left the villages of Ockley, Rusper, Lambs Green and Colgate without links to Horsham. John Wylde discussed the situation with the clerk of Horsham Rural District Council and formulated a plan whereby the Mitchell services would gain regular two-hourly interval timetables operated by minibuses and would be extended to also serve Crawley. As time was short, temporary licences were sought from 8 April 1969, the same day as the Croydon service began, in order to continue the Mitchell services – Ockley to Horsham via Wamham village and Broadbridge Heath and a circular service from Horsham via Holbrook, Rusper, Lambs Green, Faygate, Colgate and Roffey back into town. Both ran Mondays to Saturdays, although there was no service outside of peak hours on Mondays.

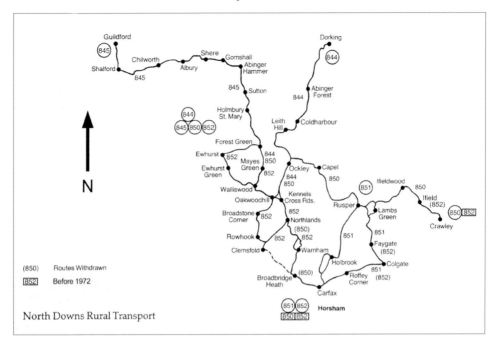

North Downs Rural Transport

Initially, one of Mrs Mitchell's coaches was hired but soon a twenty-nine-seat Bedford C5Z1 with Duple coachwork (TUX 416) was used intensively, with another Ford Transit (CBP 540G) as back-up.

The applications to introduce the planned enhancements were objected to by Southdown, on the grounds that children might be carried between the Carfax and Horsham Station for one halfpenny less than the Southdown fare! This appeared to be a delaying tactic, which once identified was soon resolved, and the North Downs services were restructured from 9 October 1969. The Rusper circular service was numbered 851, running basically two hourly, with several short-workings out to Holbrook Corner via Pondtail Road. The Ockley service was numbered 850 and extended to Capel, Rusper, Lambs Green, Ifieldwood and Crawley, again two hourly, providing connections at Rusper with service 851. One journey each way from Horsham to Crawley was a hybrid of the two services, running via Roffey, Colgate, Faygate, Lambs Green and Ifieldwood and was numbered 852, in line with its London Transport antecedent.

To try and make the minibuses look more like proper buses, Wylde arranged for Strachans to supply a slightly modified version of their standard high-roof personnel carrier body on a Ford Transit chassis, with sixteen seats and sliding door. Registered EPO 943H, it arrived two days before the start of the service improvements, in a white and red livery.

To supplement Vernon Brock on driving duties, Gordon Harris (previously with Brown Motor Services) and his wife Anne joined the staff. The vehicles were parked either on a piece of ground in Guildford Road, Broadbridge Heath or outside the Harris' house. Despite the increased service frequencies, the regular passengers could not be persuaded to avail themselves of the increased choice of travel time. For example, those in Ockley continued to travel to Horsham in fair quantity at 11 a.m. on Fridays, sometimes causing capacity problems on the minibus when it reached Warnham. At other times, usage from Ockley was nil or one person and quite a few journeys ran virtually empty.

In December 1969 another sixteen-seat Strachan-bodied Transit was purchased and licenced FPO 426H, which had a destination screen aperture fitted in the roof dome, and more comfortable seats. This allowed the withdrawal of the twenty-nine-seat coach. The Croydon

When North Downs took over Mitchell's bus services in 1969 a regular performer was TUX 416, a Duple-bodied Bedford C5Z1 coach, backed up by Ford Transit twelve-seat minibuses. (Bill Walker)

The second Ford Transit with sixteen-seat Strachan bodywork conversion arrived in December 1969. No.6 (FPO 426H) is in Horsham Carfax on a short-working of service 851 to Holbrook. (Author's collection)

The Country Bus Service
in 1970. Another view of
Ford Transit No.6, unusually
attracting custom for a
trip to Crawley, possibly at
Lambs Green. (A. Whitlam)

service (numbered 853 in September 1969) was doing well so the sixteen-seaters often had to be at Orpington, prompting the purchase of another twelve-seat Transit for Horsham, which was all that was available. FPO 427H was driven overnight from Manchester on 7 January 1970, as it was needed in Horsham for 7.15 a.m. on the day the children returned to school. It arrived with just an hour to spare!

During 1970, four more sixteen-seat Ford Transit/Strachan minibuses were purchased and, together with those already in stock, were based at both Orpington and Horsham. Maintenance was carried out by Gilbert Rice, the Ford main-dealer in Horsham. The new ones carried a red livery below the windows and white above, and were fitted with powered sliding-doors, operated by an electric motor which pulled them back and forth by means of wires. There was an increase in work at Orpington from 23 August 1970, when service 853 was increased to run every thirty minutes and a new service 855 was introduced from East Croydon to Forestdale, replacing a service provided by Wates, the developer of that estate. The vehicle requirement was then six at Orpington and two at Horsham. The year 1970 also saw the appearance of some new-style bus stop flags at strategic points on North Downs routes. They were to the new standard Ministry of Transport design, North Downs being the first operator in the United Kingdom to use them. With an amended style of a bus pictogram on them, the basic design is now more or less universal outside of London.

As recorded under Brown Motor Services, John Wylde purchased Tom Brady's business from 2 November 1970. A new company was set up – North Downs Rural Transport Ltd – to effect this and to hold the licences. Brady's Forest Green to Guildford service was numbered 845 and the Forest Green to Horsham service was numbered 852. By this time, the original journeys between Horsham and Crawley numbered 852 had been subsumed into the relevant part of services 850 and 851. Acquired with the Brady business were the Leyland Comet (OPB 536), the Bedford SB8 forty-one-seat coach (577 BYE), the Bedford VAS bus (3255 PJ) and the Albion Nimbus (335 KPL). These gained North Downs fleet names but retained brown and cream livery, this being adopted for certain vehicles on the Horsham area services. The former Brady vehicles also began to appear on services 850 and 851, intermixed with minibuses, which were not used on the Forest Green services. Barry King joined North Downs from London

Ford Transit twelve-seater No.7 (FPO 427H) lays over at the rear of Crawley Bus Station on service 850. Note the North Downs bus-stop flag with the pictogram then recently approved by the Ministry of Transport. (A. Whitlam)

An extremely rare view of former Brown Motor Services' Bedford SB8/Harrington coach 577 BYE being used on a North Downs bus service, seen at Rusper on service 851. The reason for this was that one of the Albions normally used at that time had developed defective brakes one afternoon in 1971. (A. Whitlam)

Former Brown Motor Services Bedford VAS 3255 PJ makes a somewhat rare appearance in Horsham on service 851. Normally North Downs used this bus on their service 845 to Guildford. (Vectis Transport Publications)

By the time it was photographed in the sylvan surroundings of Roffey Park Hospital in 1971, Brady's Albion Nimbus 335 KPL had the Brown Motor services fleet name on the front painted out and the bus given No.16 in the North Downs list. (A. Whitlam)

Representative of three Albion Nimbus vehicles once operated by Western Welsh and purchased by North Downs in March 1971, is No.17 (WKG 34), seen at Faygate on service 851 on 16 November of that year. (P. Wallis)

One of two former London Transport Guy GS vehicles hired from other operators by North Downs to cover for defective vehicles (the other was MXX 382 of Tillingbourne Valley) is MXX 343 of B.S. Williams Ltd (Southern Motorways) of Emsworth. It is parked at the entrance to the bus garage at Forest Green in November 1971. On the right is Tony McCann's garage – soon to become connected with bus operations. (P. Wallis)

A scene at Roffey Park hospital in November 1971 shows MOD 954, the first of three former Western National Bristol LS5Gs with ECW bodywork, which were acquired by North Downs and used during the last few months of operations in the Horsham area. They subsequently performed on service 853 from Orpington to Croydon. (P. Wallis)

North Downs turned the clock back in 1971 when they reintroduced the Bedford OB to Horsham. CFV 851 was in the Carfax shortly before North Downs ceased operations. (Bill Walker)

Country as manager, thus starting his long involvement in management and commercial matters relating to independent bus services in Surrey and Sussex.

In March 1971 three former Western Welsh Albion Nimbus dual-purpose thirty-seat vehicles were purchased. WKG 34 and 48 were repainted brown and cream, but WKG 37 remained red. They were obtained in view of the fact that the certificates of fitness were soon to expire on the former Brady Comet and Nimbus. Although North Downs now had premises at both Forest Green and Orpington for garaging vehicles and running repairs, they lacked the facilities needed to prepare vehicles for recertification, nor was the appropriate expertise available. Thus when their certificates ran out, the vehicles had to be discarded.

The licences for services 850 and 851 were transferred to the limited company from 14 April 1971, when revised timetables were introduced. Some journeys on service 850 within Warnham were diverted via Tilletts Lane, better-serving a residential area, rather than the route through the village via the church. Some journeys on service 852 were diverted between Forest Green and Walliswood via Mayes Green, to omit Ewhurst, while some buses ran on beyond Horsham, as far as Roffey Park, as part of service 851. Barry King realised that some economies were necessary in order to reduce costs and to equate the work performed with the number of drivers and vehicles actually available. As a result, service 850 had to be withdrawn from 3 July 1971 and a compensating diversion was made to service 852 so that some journeys ran between Rowhook and Broadbridge Heath via Northlands and Warnham, instead of the time-honoured route via Clemsfold and the main A281 road. From the same date, the service 851 short-workings from Horsham out to Holbrook Corner were revised so that although they went out as usual via Pondtail Road, they returned via North Heath Lane, a newly expanding area of housing.

On 3 June 1967 John Charlwood of Dorking, trading as Surrey and Sussex Coachways, started an optimistic and ambitious daily service running from Capel to Abinger Common (Parkhurst Corner) via Ockley, Coldharbour and Leith Hill. It was operated initially with a vintage Bedford OB coach. Patronage and revenue were predictably poor and from 5 August 1967 it was revised to run from Capel to Dorking via Ockley, Leith Hill and Coldharbour on Saturdays (and also Sundays until 4 November and then again from 14 April 1968). London Transport service 433 ran between Coldharbour and Dorking on Mondays to Fridays and when it was withdrawn, Charlwood expanded his service to run every day from 7 October 1968. However, this was short-lived and he reduced it to one round trip on Friday afternoons for shoppers from 1 November that year. The link between all this and North Downs Rural Transport was that the latter took over the service from 9 July 1971, numbered it 844 and altered it to run Friday mornings, starting from Forest Green via Walliswood and Oakwoodhill to Ockley, rather than from Capel. This was Ockley's only service at that time.

One of the Western Welsh Albions had to be withdrawn in August 1971, so a former London Transport Guy GS was hired from Tillingbourne Valley Services for a period. Trevor Brown, proprietor of that firm, and also a bus dealer, persuaded John Wylde that a good vehicle to operate would be the underfloor-engined Bristol LS-type, which the former Tilling subsidiaries of the National Bus Co. were then withdrawing, with about a year remaining on their certificate of fitness. Thus, MOD 954, with forty-one-seat ECW bus body arrived in September 1971, being North Downs' first full-size single-deck bus. When the company's fitter, Roy Burstow, inspected the engine, he went a funny colour and then said, 'Well, we'll have a go'. Three Ford Transits were sold in October 1971 and the following month a Bedford OB coach (CFV 851) was purchased, as well as two more Bristol LSs (OTT 51 and MOD 967), which had been converted to mobile classrooms by Western National in the run-up to the changeover to decimal currency. Before they could be operated, they had to be refitted with a full complement of seats.

Urgently needed revenue came from some additional school contracts but stretched the availability of the fleet to the limit, especially when service journeys on routes 845 and 852 had to be cancelled in order to prioritise resources for the school runs. A number of other operators' vehicles had to be hired at times. From 14 February 1972 revised timetables were introduced on services 851 and 852. On the latter, all journeys ran via Warnham with all running via the village centre except one off-peak journey each way via Tilletts Lane, and some were diverted between Oakwoodhill and Northlands via Kennels Cross Roads instead of Rowhook. Peak-hour journeys were extended from the Carfax to Horsham Station.

A new shoppers' service numbered 850, with one round trip on Tuesdays, was introduced between Forest Green and Crawley via Walliswood, Oakwoodhill, Ockley, Capel, Rusper, Lambs Green and Ifieldwood, which, like service 844, could be worked by a vehicle otherwise used on a school contract. Connections were available at Walliswood from/to Ewhurst and at Rusper to/from Horsham. Efforts were made to promote the services with a new timetable booklet, which also contained details of places of interest which could be reached by North Downs bus. A one-day rover ticket was introduced, valid on all North Downs and Tillingbourne Bus Co. services, for the princely sum of only thirty pence.

Requests to both West Sussex and Surrey County Councils for revenue support grants seem to have generated little interest. In those days, the response to such requests could be delayed pending consideration by appropriate committees, by which time it was too late for an operator to redeem its position. There was a continuing shortage of drivers and maintenance staff and some of the vehicles were put off the road by vehicle inspectors. Finance was not available to buy replacements and vehicles continued to be hired to maintain services which became increasingly erratic. The manager departed to work for Tillingbourne Bus Co. at Gomshall.

On 22 March 1972, John Wylde made applications to the Traffic Commissioner to introduce revised timetables on services 845 and 852, which allowed each service to be worked by a vehicle which was also used on a school contract. Service 852 was reduced to just one morning return journey to Horsham for shoppers, but with peak-hour journeys provided by the vehicle travelling to or from Horsham to maintain service 851. Tuesday service 850 to Crawley was withdrawn, although the number was retained for journeys at 8.00 a.m. from Forest Green to Ockley Station via Walliswood and Oakwoodhill, with a 5.00 p.m. return, which were school contract workings which would be made available to the general public. Although scheduled to be introduced from 4 April, Wylde advised Surrey County Council on 22 March that they were already effectively in operation, which was vital if any services were to continue in the absence of financial support.

By the beginning of April, the off-peak journey on service 852 had been withdrawn on Mondays and Thursdays. All operations ceased after 15 April 1972, when North Downs' vehicles were issued with prohibitions at Guildford testing station by vehicle inspectors and there was insufficient cash available to make them roadworthy. This to some extent mirrored what happened to the Hants & Sussex group in 1954, when rural, but socially valuable stage-carriage services could not be made sustainable without revenue support or cross-subsidy from other more lucrative work.

Rapid arrangements were made by West Sussex County Council for Tillingbourne Bus Co. to take over service 851 from 17 April, but services 844, 845 and 852 did not run at all for a week. However, Forest Green Garage had been owned since 1970 by Tony McCann, who had bought the business from Felday Engineering. By luck, rather than design, and venturing into a business unknown to him, he volunteered to serve the community as the new village bus operator. In lieu of payment for services previously rendered, he acquired North Downs' Bedford OB and an Albion Nimbus, and attended to them in his workshop so that at least the OB was fit for use again.

Wylde transferred the Bristol LS buses to Orpington and North Downs carried on running service 853. In June 1974, the vehicle parking site in Orpington had to be relinquished and the full-size buses were replaced with twelve-seat Ford Transit minibuses, as these could be parked outside drivers' homes overnight. John Wylde gained employment with Leicestershire County Council as transport co-ordinator, and moved on to Northumberland County Council in November 1975. The certificates of fitness for the minibuses were soon to expire and Wylde's relocation had a bearing on the decision to cease operations from 15 January 1976. Service 853 passed to Orpington & District Omnibuses.

As for John Wylde, he was later to be involved with two local taxi operators in starting bus services in Northumberland from October 1986 using, naturally, minibuses! They formed Taxibus Services (Berwick) Ltd, but that is definitely another story.

THIRTEEN

D.A. McCANN (BROWN MOTOR SERVICES)/TONY McCANN COACHES

With the financial collapse of North Downs Rural Transport, some villages in south Surrey suddenly found themselves without a bus service for the first time since the 1920s. There was local anxiety over the future of the links with Horsham and Guildford. Some were not keen to see a major operator take over, with the potential for rationalisation of the services. For those without access to a car, the prompt response of Donald Anthony (Tony) McCann must have been very welcome.

North Downs were unable to run any bus services during the week ending 22 April 1972 as their remaining buses were off the road. John Wylde had made arrangements for others to cover the school contracts. However, though McCann may have originally intended to sell the North Downs vehicles that he had acquired, concerns voiced locally about having no buses prompted him to meet with Wylde to establish a way forward. The result was that McCann would act as manager for North Downs and would continue the bus services by running on hire, as the Road Service Licences were still held by North Downs. As an interim measure, services 845 (Forest Green-Holmbury St Mary-Gomshall-Shere-Chilworth-Guildford, four journeys, Mondays to Saturdays) and 852 (Forest Green-Ewhurst- Walliswood-Oakwoodhill-Warnham-Horsham, one journey on Tuesdays, Wednesdays and Saturdays) were restarted on 24 April, while Friday shoppers' bus 844 from Forest Green to Dorking via Walliswood, Oakwoodhill, Ockley and Coldharbour was provided from 28 April. The former North Downs Bedford OB was used on services 844 and 852 and a Bedford SB coach hired from Tillingbourne Bus Co. was used on service 845.

Tony McCann received a number of telephone calls from grateful passengers, and while admitting that he was new to bus operating and had a lot to learn, he promised that the vehicles would be clean, reliable and maintained in good condition. Two drivers were recruited and the trading title of Brown Motor Services was revived.

McCann was not recognised as a contractor by Surrey County Council's education department, and they made arrangements for all the school contracts to be operated by Gastonia. This was unfortunate as the revenue from them could not be used by McCann to support the bus services. When applications were made to transfer the Road Service Licences from North Downs, objections were lodged by London Country and Tillingbourne Bus Co., who considered the services unnecessary, although this was mainly an attempt to reduce competition between Abinger Hammer and Guildford over roads covered by their services. Blue Saloon Coaches of Guildford also applied for a licence to cover service 845 but their application was withdrawn before the hearing in June.

McCann had good counsel and was able to produce letters of support from local organisations, parish councils, two rural district councils and members of the public. The outcome was successful and from 20 June 1972, Brown Motor Services increased service 845 to five journeys (two-hourly headway) and service 852 to a morning round trip on Tuesdays, Wednesdays and Saturdays, and an afternoon facility on Fridays and Saturdays.

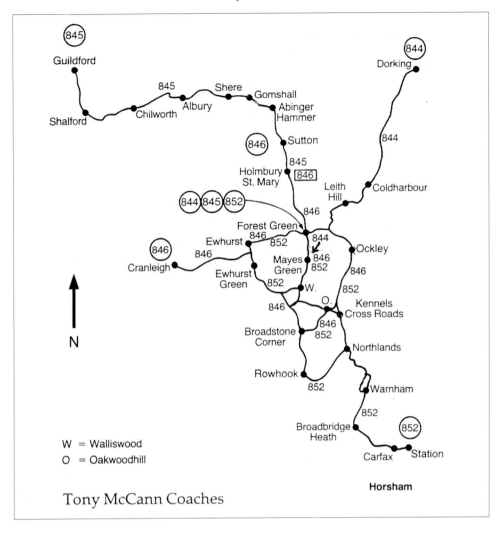

Tony McCann Coaches

In May 1972 a forty-one-seat Bedford SB8 with Duple Midland bus body was acquired, having been previously owned by Safeguard of Guildford and Banstead Coaches. This entered service later in the year on service 845 after a thorough overhaul. The next arrival was a forty-one-seat Bedford/Duple coach with butterfly-style radiator grille, affectionately known as *Daisy May* by virtue of its registration, 433 DMA, which became the mainstay of services 844 and 852. Both these vehicles were painted in the traditional brown and cream livery. Early in 1973, a Bedford/Plaxton forty-one-seat coach replaced the OB, but the new acquisition retained the grey and red livery it arrived with.

The public gradually regained confidence in the bus services which were now operating reliably again and loadings, especially to Horsham, were improving. In March 1973 proposals were put forward to increase the timetable on Saturdays on service 852 to four journeys each way. Half of these were to run via Mayes Green instead of Ewhurst and one each way would serve Ockley between Oakwoodhill and Northlands. Certain journeys would run through to and from Guildford on service 845. The increased service started on 19 May 1973 and soon after an application was made to operate a Wednesday afternoon service to Horsham via Ockley (which had previously run in December 1972 under dispensation for the Christmas-shopping period), as well as a service on Thursday mornings.

On this day in 1972, the independently operated normal-control vehicle reigned supreme in Horsham. Bedford OB CFV 851, by now owned by Tony McCann, was on the Forest Green service while Tillingbourne Bus Co.'s former London Transport Guy GS MXX 364 was on service 451. (Bill Walker)

While the Bedford OB ran the Horsham service, McCann hired Bedford SB3/Plaxton coach YUE 163 from Tillingbourne in Spring 1972 to maintain service 845 to Guildford. (J. Gaff)

From Summer 1972, the regular McCann vehicles on the Horsham and Guildford services respectively were 433 DMA (Bedford SB3/Duple coach) and 630 SPH (Bedford SB8/Duple Midland bus). Both were painted in brown and cream although in differing styles. (L. Smith)

In the meantime, Tillingbourne Bus Co. had applied for a service of two journeys on Tuesdays through to Horsham as an extension of their Guildford-Peaslake service via Ewhurst, Walliswood, Oakwoodhill, Ockley, Capel, Kingsfold and Warnham. At a Hearing in May, Tillingbourne Bus Co. were granted dispensation to operate on Thursdays and the service commenced on 21 June 1973, numbered 449. However, on 29 June, the Traffic Commissioner refused a substantive licence to both service 449 (which was consequently withdrawn on 12 July) and to McCann for a Thursday service, on the grounds of insufficient public need. McCann's application for Wednesday afternoon was granted, and it started in July, and was supplemented in December 1973 by a Tuesday afternoon service, also via Ockley.

In June 1973, McCann purchased UWX 277, a Leyland Tiger Cub with Duple Donnington forty-three-seat dual-purpose bodywork. This remained in the orange, grey and black livery of its previous owner, Pennine of Gargrave, North Yorkshire. Being somewhat unpopular with the drivers, UWX 277 stayed at Forest Green for nine months only. In August 1973, the business was constituted as Brown Motor Services Ltd, the directors of which were Tony McCann, Chris Hills and Allen Whitehart. The latter two had been assisting McCann full-time since earlier in the year; Chris Hills had run a coach business (Sussex Rural Rides) at Lindfield, near Haywards Heath and stayed about a year. Allen Whitehart had purchased Tom Brady's Leyland Comet for preservation when it was sold by North Downs.

From September 1973, Brown Motor Services started running school contracts for West Sussex County Council, to the Weald School at Billingshurst. These could be interworked with bus service 852. Fleet replacement in early 1974 was by means of two versatile forty-one-seat Bedford SB8 coaches with Duple Bella Vega bodywork. Rising operational costs meant that the bus services began to run with a financial deficit and in September 1974 an application for revenue support was made to Surrey County Council. The original garage buildings at Forest Green were replaced by a new workshop, office and car showroom, which provided better facilities for maintaining the buses and coaches. In April 1975, a forty-five-seat Bedford VAM14 coach was purchased – the largest up to that time to have worked from Forest Green. From the same date, certain vehicles were licensed to D.A. McCann trading as

Bedford SB3 257 EYB was in the McCann fleet about a year before being written off with frontal accident damage following an encounter with a lorry near Oakwoodhill. (Bill Walker)

Tony McCann Coaches, rather than to Brown Motor Services Ltd, and these were given a cream and red livery.

A return journey to Horsham Station on service 852 on Mondays to Fridays for workers and commuters commenced on 4 August 1975. It ran from Forest Green via Mayes Green, Walliswood, Oakwoodhill, Northlands, Warnham and Broadbridge Heath. This facility was made viable as the vehicle involved was travelling to and from Horsham in any case, to work a newly won school contract to the Forest Schools, from the Southwater area. Further vehicles acquired in 1975 and 1976 were run by Tony McCann Coaches, and from January 1977 all vehicles and services were licensed in the name of Tony McCann Coaches Ltd, the directors being Tony and Joy McCann and Allen Whitehart.

On service 845, the 5.30 p.m. departure from Guildford had run beyond Forest Green to Walliswood on request since 1974. This ceased from 3 June 1977 when a Friday evening return trip into Guildford was introduced for leisure travellers, such as those going to bingo, the cinema or theatre. It commenced from Ockley and ran via Oakwoodhill and Walliswood, before joining the normal route at Forest Green. It ran until December 1977 and then again from May until September 1978. There was another increase to service 852 from 28 November 1977 when a Friday morning facility to Horsham via Rowhook was introduced and a Monday and Thursday morning journey via Ockley. There were extra journeys on schooldays, to save otherwise dead mileage for vehicles operating on school contracts.

Three Ford R192/Plaxton Derwent forty-five-seat buses, previously in the Midland Red fleet, were purchased in 1978 and were smartly repainted red and cream, but were not as reliable as had been first hoped, being out of use by early 1980. Replacements in 1979 consisted of two Bedford YRQ buses purchased from Tillingbourne Bus Co., and a fifty-three-seat Bedford YRT coach from Hardings of Betchworth.

London Country service 412 ran from Sutton to Ranmore via Holmbury St Mary, Abinger Common, Westcott and Dorking. Surrey County Council found it financially advantageous to extend it on school days to cover Ockley and Forest Green, to replace separate contract services used by children attending schools in Dorking. For a marginal additional cost, off-peak

Leyland Tiger Cub UWX 277 with Duple Donnington dual-purpose body arrived at McCann's in June 1973. It remained in the orange, grey and black livery of its former owner, Pennine Motor Services of Gargrave, North Yorkshire. Nicknamed the *Orange Box*, it was not popular and stayed for a short time. (Author's collection)

journeys could also be projected from Holmbury St Mary to Cranleigh via Forest Green and Ewhurst, giving some new links. Tony McCann objected to this and proposed his own new (unsubsidised) service 846 from Ockley to Cranleigh giving shopping trips on Tuesdays and Thursdays via Oakwoodhill, Smokejack, Walliswood, Forest Green and Ewhurst, which could be fitted around school contract workings. After a traffic court hearing, London Country commenced their extended service 412 on 1 September 1979, while McCann Coaches service 846 followed three days later.

Service 412 in its new form was not as successful as envisaged, the off-peak service to Cranleigh being poorly used and withdrawn on 22 August 1981. McCann Coaches service 846, having been diverted between Smokejack and Walliswood to serve Snaky Lane from 8 January 1980, was back-extended on Thursdays from 3 December 1981 to start from Holmbury St Mary, travelling to Ockley via Forest Green pond. By July 1982 it had been further extended on Thursdays to start at Sutton.

In June 1980 Tony McCann took delivery of his first and only new vehicle – a Bedford YMT/ Plaxton Supreme Express fifty-three-seat coach, NMJ 279V, purchased with the aid of a government bus grant. On arrival at the Plaxton factory at Scarborough, he found that it was not ready for collection. Being known for having an extremely short temper when things displeased him, there were considerable fireworks when he discovered this and was obliged to return the next day, having told Plaxtons where they could stick their coach!

Tony had his own light aircraft, being an experienced pilot. However, he had a lucky escape when he suffered considerable injuries when he crash-landed near Goodwood Airfield in Sussex, after the Beechcraft Muskateer had developed difficulties.

One of a pair of versatile Bedford SB8/Duple Bella Vega coaches purchased by McCann in early 1974 was HCU 950. (N. Hamshere)

This forty-five-seat Bedford VAM14 coach with Duple Viceroy body was the largest vehicle to have been based in Forest Green in Spring 1975. Its appearance on bus services was quite rare. (N. Hamshere)

Allen Whitehart turns KEV 952J, a Ford R192/Willowbrook bus, in the car park at The Red Lion (now the Inn on the Green), Ockley, en route from Forest Green to Horsham. Originally a demonstration vehicle for Ford Motor Co., it was with Ebdons of Sidcup before being acquired by McCann. (Author's collection)

Three Ford R192 buses with Plaxton Derwent bodywork were acquired in 1978 after use by Midland Red. Such lightweight buses were purchased by National Bus Co. subsidiaries in the early 1970s and had short lives with their original owners. YHA 304J stands near the garage in Forest Green before setting off for Guildford. (Author's collection)

The only vehicle bought new by McCann, with the aid of government bus grant, was NMJ 279V a Bedford YMT with Plaxton Supreme Express bodywork. Here it waits in the former Onslow Street Bus Station in Guildford in about 1980. (P.R. Nuttall)

On the last day of service 844 to Dorking in October 1982, Bedford YRT KPC 208P is at The Plough at Coldharbour on the way back to Forest Green. It was one of three similar coaches bought by McCann from Hardings Coaches of Betchworth. (Author's collection)

30 October 1982 was the last day of stage-service operation by Tony McCann Coaches. Tom Muggeridge (*left*) and Bert Short started driving buses from Forest Green in 1950 and 1939 respectively. GGR 344N is a Bedford YRQ, acquired in October 1979 from Tillingbourne Bus Co. (Bill Walker)

During 1982, there were confidential negotiations between McCann and Tillingbourne Bus Co. concerning the latter's acquisition of the McCann Coaches bus services, and a contract from Peaslake to Tillingbourne Junior School at Chilworth. Tony had become disillusioned with running bus services and the somewhat lukewarm reception from local authorities when revenue support was requested. Thus it was that Tillingbourne Bus Co. took over the services after 30 October 1982, together with three vehicles – Bedford YRQ bus LPD 12K (which thereby returned to its original owner, although it saw no further use), Bedford YRT coach KAP 20L and Bedford YMT NMJ 279V. The revisions made by Tillingbourne Bus Co. to the services are covered under that company heading. No drivers transferred and McCann continued to operate school contracts and undertake private hire with four vehicles, but it was the first time in fifty-eight years that the bus services had not actually been based in Forest Green.

An undertaking was given by Tony McCann that he would not subsequently start any new services which were considered to be in competition with those of Tillingbourne Bus Co.. On the last day, service 852 was driven by Bert Short, who had been driving buses from Forest Green on and off since 1939, and Tommy Muggeridge who joined Brown Motor Services in 1950. Their vehicle, Bedford YRQ bus GGR 344N, and also LPD 12K on service 845, were decorated inside with balloons and streamers. A small group of enthusiasts gathered to mark the almost unnoticed passing of an era.

On 1 December 1984, the post office and store at Forest Green unexpectedly closed, causing considerable hardship for some residents. As in 1972, Tony McCann stepped forward to perform a community service and applied to take over the post office by transferring it to part of his car showroom premises. Planning permission was granted for the necessary building alterations and the post office approved his application so he could open for business from 1 April 1985. The last three coaches were sold in May 1986 when the school contracts ceased and in October that year Tony McCann closed his garage and post office store and left the village.

FOURTEEN

TILLINGBOURNE BUS CO. LTD

In recounting the activities of the Tillingbourne Bus Co. in Horsham and district, one needs to set some parameters. For many years, their bus services were contained within an area to the south-east of Guildford in Surrey, along the valley of the River Tillingbourne, which gave the operator its name. From 1972, it began to build a network in West Sussex and expanded its position in Surrey, culminating in a major increase in 1985, prior to extending its territory in the post-1986 deregulated environment. Between 1981 and 1983 it was even active in the Orpington and Croydon area of Greater London.

In 2001, when it unexpectedly and tragically collapsed, it also had services in north-east Hampshire and even a healthy tentacle into Wokingham and Reading in what was traditionally Berkshire. Its network covered an area bounded by Reading, Yateley, Fleet, Aldershot, Farnham, Godalming, Cranleigh, Petworth, Pulborough, Horsham, Redhill, Dorking, Woking, Staines and Camberley. There were even infrequent shoppers' services down to Chichester. The detailed history of Tillingbourne Bus Co. between inception and 1990 has already been published. Therefore we concentrate on the company's activities in Horsham and the surrounding area, but first, a little background.

In 1924, George Trice and J. Vic Smith of Chilworth started bus services from Guildford to Gomshall via Newlands Corner and Shere, and also from Guildford to Albury via Chilworth. These were soon extended to Peaslake and Farley Green respectively. The trading title of Tillingbourne Valley was adopted and soon Trice was sole proprietor. In December 1929, a local service up Warren Road in Guildford was taken over from Yellow Bus Service. An attempt by London Transport to take over the firm in 1933 was resisted, as were offers from Basil Williams and London Transport in 1950. The Peaslake service was operated in a co-ordinated way in partnership with East Surrey Traction Co. service 44, which eventually became London Transport service 448, some journeys of which ran beyond Peaslake to Ewhurst. London Transport found their share unremunerative, along with their Guildford local service 448A to Pewley Way. Agreement was reached with Tillingbourne Valley for the latter to assume London Transport's responsibilities on these services from 12 August 1964. A shortage of passengers and drivers prompted Derek Trice (George Trice's grandson) to withdraw the Peaslake-Ewhurst section and the Pewley Way service from 28 November 1965.

On 30 September 1970, Derek Trice sold the bus business to Trevor Brown in order to concentrate on his other interests, which were fuel conversions on domestic heating systems and the supply of heating oil. Brown brought in some elderly Bristol vehicles, which started to replace a fleet made up since 1963 consisting entirely of former London Transport Guy GS-type buses. The Warren Road service, which had been numbered 451, was withdrawn in October 1971 and the company entered a difficult period when unreliable vehicles caused services to run erratically and business to be lost. Tillingbourne Valley Services Ltd was heading in the same downward direction as North Downs at Forest Green. It was fortunate

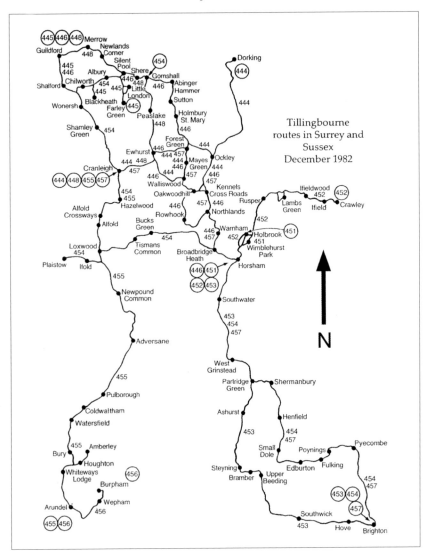

that Trevor Brown recruited Barry King in March 1972 to become manager and to start to put things right. The company started to evolve into the type of operation that is remembered during the 1980s and 1990s – strong, innovative, expansionist and fiercely independent, with a sound financial base and a well-presented modern fleet. The company's management made some smart moves and were to become a challenge for the traffic managers of National Bus Co., subsidiaries London Country, Alder Valley and Southdown.

Barry King took the opportunity created by the collapse of North Downs Rural Transport to move Tillingbourne into the Horsham area. Rapid arrangements were made with West Sussex County Council to guarantee some revenue support in order to maintain the Rusper circular service from 17 April 1972. It was renumbered 451 from 851 and also included was a Monday to Friday evening peak journey from Horsham to Warnham. The first vehicles to perform were ex-Western National Bristol SUL4As, together with a former London Transport Guy GS type, which were painted in Tillingbourne Valley's new livery of blue, grey and yellow. Soon, the bus used on service 451 was out-stationed overnight in the goods yard, off Nightingale Road near Horsham Station – the rest of the fleet was kept adjacent to Gomshall Station.

The first regular driver on service 451 was Charlie Bowler, who had previously worked for Tom Brady and John Wylde. In August 1972 the business was formally renamed Tillingbourne Bus Co. Ltd, deemed more appropriate for the expanded area of operation. To supplement further second-hand purchases, a government bus grant was used in June 1972 to buy a brand new bus (a Bedford YRQ/Willowbrook), and this was followed in January 1973 by a Leyland Leopard with dual-purpose Willowbrook Expressway body. This was used regularly in Horsham, as was a Bedford YRT/Duple Dominant coach purchased a year later and fitted with bus-type folding doors.

The need to transfer vehicles between Gomshall and Horsham resulted in a fair amount of dead mileage and an attempt was made in 1973 to link the two operating areas together by means of a service 449, which had a short life as described in the chapter on McCann's Brown Motor Services. Mainly for accounting reasons, a subsidiary company, Tillingbourne (Sussex) Ltd was set up in May 1974 to administer the Horsham service. The first vehicles licensed to it were Leyland Tiger Cub 9712 WX and Bristol SUL4A 269 KTA. Thereafter, certain vehicles were thus licensed, but these, and those of the main fleet, were always used indiscriminately on all the services.

Throughout 1973 and 1974, the company was under great pressure to find a new base for its fleet. Gomshall Station was sited in the green-belt and Guildford Borough Council served an enforcement notice preventing Tillingbourne from using the yard as a depot, as planning permission had not been obtained. As a result, Tillingbourne was given notice to quit by site owner, British Rail, and a plan to purchase the old Surrey Hills Bus Garage in Ewhurst for use as a workshop (which had been unused since 1971) met with much local opposition. After convoluted negotiations involving three councils and an appeal to the Secretary of State, it was agreed that Tillingbourne could park five vehicles at Gomshall as long as no maintenance was carried out. The company's proprietor, Trevor Brown, bought Ewhurst Garage in a personal capacity in October 1974, and leased it to the company, which was then granted temporary permission to use it as a garage and workshop. The company's occupation of it continued to be surrounded with much environmental controversy. From February 1975 the bus for service 451 was timetabled to run in service from Ewhurst via Forest Green, Ockley and Capel to join the route proper at Rusper, working in reverse at the end of the day.

Tillingbourne's next service in West Sussex started on 7 February 1975 – a Friday shoppers' bus numbered 452 from Wisborough Green to Cranleigh via Loxwood and Alfold – which could be worked in conjunction with a school contract to the Weald School at Billingshurst. In August that year it was diverted via Kirdford and Plaistow, making it a somewhat extended version of erstwhile Hants & Sussex service 35 of the early 1950s.

Development of the urban section of service 451 in Horsham commenced on 6 September 1976, when most journeys were diverted to serve the expanding North Heath Lane area, rather than travelling via Pondtail Road. Journeys at school times were extended to serve the Forest and Millais Schools, which enabled the county council to cancel a school contract route and brought useful revenue to Tillingbourne. By September 1978 the number of children using the service had risen to the point where a fifty-three-seat vehicle was inadequate. Thus a new Bedford YMT with sixty-one-seat Duple Dominant bus body (XPL 889T) was acquired, the capacity exceeding that of a standard 1950s double-decker by means of three-and-two seating in the back half of the bus.

From 29 January 1979 the service became primarily a circular route from Horsham to Holbrook Corner, outward via Pondtail Road, inward via North Heath Lane, with four journeys extended out to Rusper and Lambs Green. This resulted in an approximately hourly service on the town section and the whole operation was undertaken without revenue support. In order to replace the section of route through Roffey and Colgate, West Sussex County Council offered support to London Country to run a limited service 474 from Horsham to Crawley via Colgate and Pease Pottage, and then on to East Grinstead in parallel with service 434.

Regular performers on the Rusper circular service in 1972 after Tillingbourne took over from North Downs were various Bristol SUL4As including 355 EDV and 417 HDV, which originated with Western National. They are parked in the Horsham railway goods yard. (L. Smith)

Bedford YRT/Duple Dominant coach PWY 595M did a period of service on route 451 in the mid-1970s. It was the third new vehicle purchased by Tillingbourne after Trevor Brown acquired the business. (N. Hamshere)

This Bedford YRQ/Plaxton forty-five-seat coach (LPE 42P), seen in the Carfax, was licensed to Tillingbourne (Sussex) Ltd although it often performed on the Surrey services too. (RC Photos)

Leyland Leopard TRN 769 with Marshall bodywork emanated from the Ribble fleet of the National Bus Co. It is in Wisborough Green ready to work the Friday shoppers' service 452 to Cranleigh, *c.*1978. (J. Gaff)

With an unusual destination blind display layout, Bedford YRQ/Willowbrook GGR 344N puts in a turn on service 451. It joined Tony McCann Coaches in October 1979. (J. Gaff)

The frequency of service 451 on Mondays to Fridays was increased to every thirty minutes from 24 September 1979, thus a second vehicle was required, which was out-stationed at Horsham goods yard. An extra departure from Horsham to Holbrook was introduced at 6.45 p.m. and as the Tillingbourne driver could not perform this in the time allowed for his shift, and the expense of a relief driver could not be justified, arrangements were made for London Country to work it using a Leyland National on a layover from their service 414. Tillingbourne's country journeys to Rusper/Lambs Green were renumbered 452, and those in the morning were adjusted on Tuesdays and Fridays to provide a shoppers' bus to Crawley from those villages from 22 July 1980. As a result of reductions in Alder Valley's service 269 (successor to A&D service 50) between Plaistow and Horsham, Tillingbourne introduced a service 446 on Fridays from 5 September 1980 from Dunsfold to Horsham via Plaistow, Ifold, Loxwood, Tismans Common and Bucks Green.

West Sussex County Council and Southdown (and Surrey County Council with Alder Valley and London Country) had introduced extensive revisions to services from 31 August 1980 as a result of the nationwide Market Analysis Project, which in reality meant a reduction in bus mileage and therefore the subsidy requirement. Included was a new Southdown shoppers service 299 between Plaistow and Horsham on Tuesdays and Saturdays. This operated via Slinfold between Bucks Green and Broadbridge Heath, being another partial replacement for Alder Valley service 269.

Service 299 enjoyed revenue support, whereas Tillingbourne's service 446 did not. Southdown was beginning to become interested in Tillingbourne's activities, and when the latter were expanding their facilities in the North Heath area, Southdown had the temerity to suggest that they themselves should be providing any urban services within Horsham, as Tillingbourne had no experience of such operations. Also from 31 August 1980, London Country service 414 was withdrawn from the Horsham area and replaced by an extension of Green Line service 714, which worked through from London via Dorking. Thus the 6.45 p.m. departure on service 451 was withdrawn.

In Rusper after the country part of service 451 was renumbered 452 is MPE 248P, a Bedford YRQ/ Plaxton forty-five-seat bus, new in April 1976. (J. Gaff)

Tillingbourne took delivery of another high-capacity Bedford YMT/Duple Dominant bus (CCG 550V) in September 1980 and this with XPL 889T were the most frequent performers on service 451 for the next two years, usually driven by Mick Greenfield and Rodney Trout. It came as a great relief when at last the company was able to secure a lease on suitable premises at Littlemead in Cranleigh, which had previously been used by Waverley Borough Council, offering parking for the whole fleet, a workshop, offices and staff facilities. The station yard at Gomshall was vacated in December 1980, when vehicle parking commenced at Cranleigh, and the company moved in full to Littlemead from 16 March 1981. The site of Ewhurst Garage was subsequently disposed of for housing, and certain parts of the building, notably the doors, found there way into a replica Southdown Bus Garage at the Chalk Pits Museum at Amberley in West Sussex.

From 1 June 1981, the off-peak journeys on Rusper service 452 on Mondays, Wednesdays and Thursdays were withdrawn in favour of a new service 453 from Horsham to Steyning via Southwater and Partridge Green. A new Tuesday service 454 provided one round trip from Ewhurst to Brighton via Cranleigh, Horsham, Henfield, Small Dole and Fulking and it provided a replacement for withdrawn Southdown service 106 south of Henfield. In order to generate some publicity for the launch of the 454, Barry King made an arrangement with a small brewery at Edburton so that they could deliver real ale to one or two pubs on the line of route by transporting barrels in the boot of the coach! This novel additional service was not perpetuated for long.

Service 451 was diverted to serve Wimblehurst Park Estate in the North Heath Lane area of Horsham from 5 July 1982. The roads had been built with buses in mind and there was good support for a service, but this did not stop a few selfish residents from objecting on perceived road safety grounds and forcing a hearing before the Traffic Commissioner, at which Tillingbourne were successful. At the same time, adjustments were made to service 452, which was withdrawn on Saturdays, while service 454 was expanded to serve Plaistow and Loxwood and introduced on Fridays between Cranleigh and Horsham to replace service 446. Service

Together with similar bus XPL 889T, this sixty-one-seat Bedford YMT with Duple Dominant bus body was a stalwart performer on service 451 in the early 1980s. However, it is seen here on the short-lived Saturday Horsham local service 292 to Oakhill in early 1987. (J. Gaff)

Bedford YMT FOD 941Y with the then newly introduced Plaxton Bustler body is in Wimblehurst Park Estate in Horsham in February 1984. (E.C. Churchill/Southdown E.C.)

453 was altered to run on Tuesdays only and was interworked with the 454 as a round trip from Brighton to Horsham via Steyning.

The acquisition of Tony McCann's bus services from 1 November 1982 involved the restructuring of a number of Tillingbourne services in the area between Guildford and Horsham. McCann services 845 and 852 were combined into a service 446 which offered a number of new through-travel opportunities. A Thursday service 444 from Ockley to Cranleigh via Walliswood, Forest Green and Ewhurst replaced McCann service 846, while the latter's Friday 844 to Dorking was not replicated. However, it became apparent that a large section in the middle of service 446 was unremunerative and in June 1983 it was truncated to work only from Guildford to Forest Green, the southern section being numbered 450. The off-peak journeys through Walliswood, Oakwoodhill, Ockley and Rowhook were reduced to run on Tuesdays, Fridays and Saturdays only, while Forest Green lost its link with Horsham except on Saturdays.

For some time, the management of Tillingbourne Bus Co. had been making proposals to Surrey County Council for the transfer of bus services to the company from London Country and Alder Valley. By integration with their existing services, the company would incur lower operating costs than the National Bus Co. subsidiaries and consequently the demands on the council for revenue support subsidy would be reduced. In June 1983, a proposal was made to take over Alder Valley services on the Guildford-Cranleigh-Horsham corridor on a non-subsidised basis. The county council engaged consultants to analyse the independents' proposals and also the counter-measures put forward by the larger operators. Their report largely supported Tillingbourne's aspirations, although it emerged eventually that Alder Valley had no intention of vacating the Guildford-Cranleigh-Horsham corridor. After much discussion and hard negotiating, and with the support of the council, Tillingbourne greatly expanded its network in the Guildford-Dorking-Cranleigh triangle from 14 April 1985, but Alder Valley consolidated its position south-eastwards from Guildford. Tillingbourne introduced a two-digit service-numbering scheme, based on local numbers used many years ago by East Surrey and A&D. Services 450, 451, 452 and 454 serving Horsham had the 4 removed from their number.

In July 1984, while Surrey County Council's consultant was engaged on the Cranleigh Bus Study, the government published a white paper titled *Buses*, which mapped out intentions to deregulate the operation of bus services and to sell state-owned bus companies to the private sector, leading to the break-up of the National Bus Co. Bus services would no longer require a licence and under normal circumstances, no objections could be lodged and hearings would no longer be held. Instead, operators had to register their services with the Traffic Commissioner at least forty-two days in advance of their intention to start, amend or cancel a service. They could therefore control the commercial destiny of services which were to be run without local authority financial support.

The term 'stage-carriage service' was replaced with 'local bus service'. In Spring 1986, operators had to register the level of service they wished to run on a commercial basis from 26 October 1986, the date when the Transport Act 1985 became effective. The local authorities could then decide whether they wished to supplement them by securing 'socially necessary' services, mainly through a competitive tendering process.

As far as Horsham was concerned, Tillingbourne Bus Co. registered service 51 and parts of services 50 and 53. Surrey County Council arranged for retention of a peak-hour service for Walliswood and Oakwoodhill on service 50/53, along with a Tuesday link from Forest Green to Horsham. After the tendering process, Tillingbourne were awarded contracts from 27 October 1986 by West Sussex County Council to provide a twice-weekly shoppers' service on 52, a once-weekly facility from Alfold, Loxwood and Plaistow on service 54, and a Tuesday diversion of service 50 via Rowhook. They also gained the contract for erstwhile Southdown service 294 from Brooks Green, Barns Green and Itchingfield into Horsham, which was renumbered 55 and for a service 56 on Tuesdays, Thursdays and Saturdays from Horsham to

A second-hand Tillingbourne Bus Co. purchase to help with extra work at the time of bus deregulation in October 1986 was ABR 778S, a Leyland Leopard with Plaxton Derwent bodywork. It is at Warnham on a local working of service 50. (J. Gaff)

Crawley via Colgate and Pease Pottage, which replaced London Country service 474. As an investment, and in order to obtain undercover vehicle parking in Horsham, Tillingbourne purchased premises in September 1986 at Foundry Close, an industrial area just north of the town centre.

At the end of December 1986, the architect of Tillingbourne's growth, Barry King, left the company to become an independent consultant advising various bus companies. Chris Bowler, son of former service 451 driver Charlie, had been chief engineer and was now made managing director. Stephen Salmon continued as traffic manager until May 1988, and was then succeeded by John Gaff, who went on to maintain the growth of the company and its financial stability by astute management, later becoming a director.

Southdown had less work in Horsham after October 1986, an early victim of post-deregulation cutbacks being their bus garage in Denne Road which closed from 25 January 1987. Henceforth, their remaining services were worked in the main from Brighton or Worthing depots. London Country South West, as it was by then known, was to introduce a fleet of minibuses on to its local services to the Roffey/Littlehaven area, as well as replacing Southdown's town services, from 21 February. In the interim, short-term arrangements were put in place to continue operation and as part of this, West Sussex County Council awarded Tillingbourne a temporary contract to maintain some of service 292 from Horsham Carfax to the Oakhill area of the town on Saturdays. In June 1987, Tillingbourne found it expedient to introduce a service 60 on Wednesdays, when a vehicle was spare, linking Horsham with Guildford via Barns Green, Billingshurst, Plaistow, Dunsfold and Godalming, taking no less than one and a half hours! This survived until February 1989 when network expansion in West Sussex meant that the bus could be better employed.

When certain contracted services in the Horsham area were retendered by West Sussex County Council, Tillingbourne were unsuccessful in retaining service 55 to the Barns

Tillingbourne purchased two of the new Dennis Dorchester chassis in 1983 and had them bodied by Wadham Stringer. Originally intended for deployment in the Orpington/Croydon area, the sale of those operations meant they were used in Surrey and Sussex. FOD 942Y, driven by Rod Trout, is on service 56 to Colgate in January 1988. (J. Gaff)

This photograph shows LCY 299X, one of several short Bedford YMQs with unusual Lex Maxeta bodies which Tillingbourne acquired from The Beeline in March 1988. It is at Wisborough Green in May 1989 on one of the short-lived commercial services run in competition with council-contracted Sussex Bus service 295. (J. Gaff)

This powerful Leyland Tiger/Duple Dominant bus C195 WJT has arrived in Horsham on service 50 from Warnham in May 1991. It was sold in May 1999 to Islwyn Transport in South Wales. (J.G.S. Smith)

One of the new services introduced during the short 'war' with London & Country was the 57 from Horsham to Southwater. The latter place is the setting for H422 GPM, a Mercedes Benz 709D with Phoenix twenty-seven-seat bodywork. (J. Gaff)

Mercedes Benz 709D/Wadham Stringer L432 APC was new in May 1994, ready for assumption of the contract for the main Horsham to Billingshurst/Petworth/Pulborough services from Sussex Bus. It is in Forge Way, Billingshurst. (J.Gaff)

Green area and it passed to London Country South West from 20 February 1989. The latter renumbered it H6 in their Horsham local route series. From the same date, the contract for Sussex Bus service 295 from Horsham to Billingshurst and Petworth fell due for renewal, but the service had been registered on a commercial basis by Paul Gascoine who was in the process of establishing his Badger Buses business in the Crawley area. In view of this, the council did not award the contract and Badger Buses collapsed with financial problems within a few days of starting operations in January 1989.

Thus, Tillingbourne registered their own commercial services between Horsham and Billingshurst, but were shocked to learn that the council had gone ahead and awarded a contract to their preferred bidder, namely Sussex Bus, and that this would not be rescinded in the light of Tillingbourne's intentions. The latter decided to press ahead and thus were running in competition with the subsidised Sussex Bus service. Both operators ran beyond Billingshurst to Petworth at peak times, and there were also shoppers' journeys out to Wisborough Green on Mondays, Wednesdays and Fridays, and to Pulborough and Storrington on Tuesdays and Thursdays. Most Sussex Bus journeys omitted Slinfold (now covered by Alder Valley service 283) but Tillingbourne ran through that village. The latter's services were numbered variously 57, 58 or 59. With Sussex Bus showing no sign of retreating, Tillingbourne withdrew from 28 April 1989, before they lost even more money!

On a more positive note, Tillingbourne started another local service, numbered 61, to the North Heath area from 20 February, now that additional housing had started being built adjacent to the new section of the Horsham bypass.

Another round of changes to the Horsham services from 28 May 1991 saw the recapture by Tillingbourne of the contract for service 55, while service 56 became a Thursday shoppers link to Crawley from Brooks Green, Barns Green, Horsham, North Heath, Roffey, Colgate and Pease Pottage. Service 61 was expanded to cover Rushams Road, Greenway, Merryfield

Leyland Tiger F279 HOD was the first of four such vehicles with Plaxton Derwent II fifty-four-seat bodywork acquired by Tillingbourne from Thames Transit of Oxford in 1995/96. It shows destination blinds for Horsham school service 62 and was photographed near Tillingbourne's depot and paintshop in Foundry Close, Horsham. (J. Gaff)

Drive and Redford Avenue, in competition with services provided by London & Country in that area. However, in general, the services of Tillingbourne and London Country were complementary rather than competitive, but during Summer 1991, London & Country and their subsidiary Alder Valley West Surrey, registered a number of new or enhanced services which competed directly with Tillingbourne. Ironically, London & Country's commercial manager (West) at the time was none other than Barry King, who had joined the firm in 1989, thus returning after eighteen years! From 31 August 1991 their service H7 linked Slinfold and Broadbridge Heath to Horsham (largely replacing service 283 which resumed its traditional route via Clemsfold), and then ran on to the North Heath Lane area, terminating at Cook Road.

A new service 251 linking Horsham with North Heath, Wimblehurst Park and Holbrook Corner was virtually a clone of Tillingbourne service 51. Also, Alder Valley West Surrey enhanced the number of journeys on the Guildford-Cranleigh corridor where Tillingbourne of course had a presence. Predictably, the management of Tillingbourne swiftly retaliated and introduced some measures to attack London & Country from 9 September 1991. They put on additional buses between Guildford and Cranleigh, directly competing on the main route via Wonersh. There was little evidence that either operator generated any appreciable additional patronage with all the extra journeys.

In Horsham, Tillingbourne enhanced service 61 to run also on Saturdays, introduced a service 71 to North Heath and Cook Road to mimic L&C service H7 and made an attacking move into Southwater with service 57, competing with L&C service H5. It soon became clear that neither party would be able to sustain the new level of service in the long term and, after some negotiations, the status quo was largely resumed from 14 March 1992. The L&C group withdrew services H7 and 251 and Tillingbourne removed services 57 and 71. However, the latter did maintain a facility for the Cook Road area by diverting service 61 off North Heath

This is one of four Optare Metroriders purchased new in 1997. Here it is in Wisborough Green on service 95 from Petworth. When Tillingbourne Bus Co. ceased trading, R504 VOR was bought by White Star (Garnett) of Lockerbie in Scotland. (J. Gaff)

Lane. From 27 July 1992, the North Heath and Wimblehurst Park service 51 was increased in a peaceful manner from every half hour to every twenty minutes. The additional journeys were numbered 71 and also served the new housing in Bartholomew Way and Lemmington Way, which lay to the east of the traditional route along Rusper Road.

When West Sussex County Council next re-tendered the services from Horsham to Barns Green and Billingshurst, Tillingbourne were successful in retaining the former, and securing the latter from Sussex Bus. From 31 May 1994 a revised and enhanced pattern of service gave a basically hourly facility between Horsham and Billingshurst, Mondays to Saturdays. Journeys ran either via Christ's Hospital, Barns Green and Coolham, or via Broadbridge Heath, and Five Oaks, with certain journeys also serving Slinfold. Beyond Billingshurst, journeys ran to Petworth during peak hours and on Mondays, Wednesdays and Fridays off peak, and to Pulborough off peak on Tuesdays, Thursdays and Saturdays. Journeys to or via Billingshurst were variously numbered 55, 65, 75, 85 and 95, which was all somewhat complicated. From the same date, a Thursday shoppers' service 53 linked Horsham with Crawley via Rusper, Newdigate, Leigh and Charlwood, which lasted until December 1995. All journeys on the North Heath service were diverted to serve the Bartholomew Way area.

Tillingbourne was awarded a contract by West Sussex County Council from 6 January 1997 to provide a Friday shoppers' bus into Horsham from Plaistow, Loxwood and Alfold, which had been absent since March 1992 when service 54 had finally been withdrawn. From 31 January 1998, service 61 was diverted to serve the southern end of Merryfield Drive, also Trafalgar Road and Kempshott Road at The Common, with the Cook Road spur being transferred to service 71. About a year later, the 71 was renumbered 51C.

In 1998, the government introduced a Rural Bus Grant to local authorities, to fund new or enhanced services which ran for at least three miles in a rural area with a population density of less than 10,000. From 2 November 1998, West Sussex County Council used some of their

Tillingbourne also purchased several full-sized buses in 1997 including three Mercedes Benz 0405s with Optare Prisma bodywork. R201 YOR is on school service 63 in Merryfield Drive. All three passed to well-known Leeds independent operator Black Prince of Morley. (J. Gaff)

In June 1999 T447 JCR, one of three Mercedes Benz Vario 0814Ds with Plaxton Beaver twenty-eight-seat bodywork acquired in February the same year is dropping off passengers in Billingshurst on the way from Horsham to Pulborough. The driver is Brian Punter. (J. Gaff)

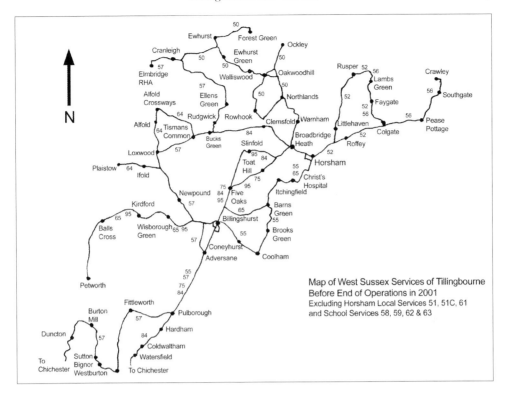

Map of West Sussex Services of Tillingbourne
Before End of Operations in 2001
Excluding Horsham Local Services 51, 51C, 61
and School Services 58, 59, 62 & 63

grant to improve Tillingbourne's Horsham to Petworth and Pulborough via Billingshurst corridor service. Frequency of service remained basically hourly to Billingshurst, but each of the onward legs was increased to operate every two hours, six days a week, something not seen for quite a few years.

Late in 1999, Managing Director Chris Bowler left the company and started his own Millennium Coaches business. Then, John Gaff left in summer 2000 due to, in hindsight, unfortunate circumstances not of his making. It is probably fair to say that from then on, Tillingbourne Bus Co. lost some of its leading edge and commercial acumen, as the departed management were adept at making good profits while keeping a number of inter-urban and rural services commercially viable by careful integration with supported bus services and school contracts, and by cost-effective scheduling, but at the same time offering the local authorities good value for money. Some unusual business purchasing decisions were then made: Trevor Brown passed control of the Tillingbourne Bus Group over to his son Nicholas, and a new management team maintained the routine business. Quite a few of the vehicles were re-registered with TIL 'cherished' marks.

In March 2001, the Tillingbourne Group had around sixty separately numbered bus services and operator licenses in the name of: Tillingbourne Bus Co. Ltd, Tillingbourne (Sussex) Ltd, Tillingbourne (Metropolitan) Ltd and Tillingbourne (Hampshire) Ltd. There were seventy-one buses and coaches in the fleet, operating from Cranleigh (Littlemead and also a parking area at Gaston Gate, behind George Weller's original premises, opened in January 1991), Horsham (Foundry Close), and from Hollybush Lane, on the outskirts of Aldershot, opened in December 1992. There were 140 staff, including 111 full- and part-time drivers. The portfolio of bus routes in West Sussex comprised the previously mentioned services 50, 51, 51C, 52, 55, 65, 75, 95, 56, 61 and 64. There were also four services around Horsham serving Forest, Millais and Tanbridge Schools (58, 59, 62, 63) and two Wednesday-only services to Chichester, service 57 from Cranleigh, Rudgwick, Loxwood, Pulborough, Fittleworth, Bignor, Sutton, Duncton,

Eartham and Crockerhill and the 84 from Horsham, Slinfold, Billingshurst, Pulborough, Coldwaltham and Bury.

It had become known that Tillingbourne was beginning to struggle to maintain its trunk services between Guildford, Cranleigh, Dorking and Redhill, which largely ran on a commercial basis, but with some financial support. Surrey County Council had issued to the market an invitation to tender to maintain these services on a contracted basis. However, before the closing date for bids had been reached, when Tillingbourne may or may not have been successful in winning the contract, a single day saw the collapse of the once well-ordered world of Tillingbourne and desolated its staff and regular, loyal customers, many of whom had been travelling with 'The Tilly' for years.

The group's bank became increasingly concerned at the cash-flow and the ability to trade. It had become apparent that financial problems had been allowed to occur and that significant losses had been mounting. It appointed Begbies Traynor, a corporate recovery and insolvency practice, to become receivers. On completing their investigations, they felt that the companies had to be put into receivership and that the situation was so grave that operations had to be suspended immediately. At lunchtime on Monday 19 March 2001, they made the shock announcement that all operations would be suspended that evening. Surrey County Council immediately offered tangible support which might allow something to be salvaged, or at least to allow an orderly termination of services, but to no avail. The word spread rapidly and was received by drivers and passengers while they were in the buses on various services.

Knowledge of the situation started to filter through to other bus operators and within minutes several had pledged their assistance to the local authorities in terms of maintaining essential services. By a concerted effort late into the evening, most of the main bus services and the majority of the school runs were in place for the following day. Several companies collected together drivers willing to work overtime, rest days or holidays and these were supplemented by some former Tillingbourne drivers who naturally made rapid enquiries as to alternative employment.

In West Sussex, Arriva assumed services 51, 51C and 61 on a commercial basis and carried on services 58 and 59 on contract. Other temporary contractual arrangements were agreed with Aventa (services 62 and 63) and Compass Travel (52, 55, 65, 75, 95, 57, 64 and 84). Even Brighton & Hove Bus Co. helped out on the Billingshurst services for the first few days. However, it was not until 27 April that service 50 could be resumed, with peak-hour journeys operated by Arriva, Tuesday and Friday shoppers' journeys by Carlone Buses and Saturdays by Compass Travel.

The receiver had several enquiries concerning the sale of parts of the Tillingbourne Bus Co. business, but none was to reach fruition. With the services all reallocated and operated adequately from premises elsewhere and with the staff gone, little could be done, with the vehicles being impounded in the depots. At an early stage, the receiver had suggested that the group's failure was largely attributable to the 'low rates of subsidy paid by local authorities'. This was quite unjustifiable as the company had submitted tenders for the work with the prices it required (and had accepted the award for a known period of time) or had negotiated prices which were mutually agreed. However, it was apparent that profit margins had been greatly reduced as costs had increased significantly in terms of fuel, wages, premises, maintenance and insurance, among other items. The fleet contained a proliferation of makes and models and this, it was said, would increase maintenance costs. Lack of management control and poor communications with supervisors on the ground were also cited.

The vehicles that were leased from finance companies were swiftly removed for resale through various bus dealers, while those owned outright, together with other assets of the business, were sold by tender after a viewing at Cranleigh on 26 and 27 April. The buses and coaches ended up spread over a wide area of the country, with a large batch being purchased by an operator in South Wales. And thus Tillingbourne was gone, but certainly not forgotten – an incredibly sad end to a respected operator in the Surrey Hills and the Weald of Sussex.

FIFTEEN

W.N.S. TRAVEL LTD (ARROW TRAVEL)

Until the early 1980s, the bus services of West Sussex were mainly in the hands of Southdown. However, some of the more rural parts of the Southdown network were thinned out following the implementation of changes as a result of the programme of 'Market Analysis Projects'. These involved re-designing (and reducing) services in order to equate better with actual usage patterns, to save money and to reduce the call on the public purse for a revenue support grant. Southdown's review of services radiating from Worthing and Littlehampton was implemented from 21 June 1981. One service to be affected was the 201 from Worthing to Midhurst via Storrington, Pulborough and Petworth, which was reduced west of Pulborough to only two journeys each way on Mondays to Saturdays. Journeys which had run between Storrington and Pulborough via Cootham (numbered 211) were withdrawn, as were services 278 Pulborough-Arundel and Ford and 279 Ashington-Storrington-Arundel-Angmering Green. The latter two services in the Arun Valley were the last remnants of Southdown's trunk routes 69 and 71 respectively, which had largely disappeared in the area in 1971.

Arrow Travel of Coldwaltham started in Spring 1979 as a partnership between Mick Stoodley and John Whatford. In February 1981 a company was formed – W.N.S. Travel Ltd – and Linda Kirk joined the business. On 16 March that year they started a service from Pulborough to Storrington via Coldwaltham, Bury, Houghton, Amberley and Rackham on Mondays, Wednesdays and Fridays. Arrow also ran taxis in the Pulborough area.

In June 1981 they commenced a schoolday service from Pulborough to Arundel and Ford (later extended to Barnham) and also began journeys on 27 July 1981 from Storrington to Midhurst, replacing Southdown service 211 and some of 201. In April 1982 there followed an extension from Storrington to Washington and a Saturday projection beyond Midhurst through to Petersfield. Two former London Transport vehicles joined the fleet – a Daimler Fleetline double-decker of the DMS class and a twenty-six-seat Bristol LHS6L. These were smartly painted in the yellow and white Arrow Travel livery.

In May 1982 two applications were made for new off-peak services. The first was a Tuesday round trip from Pulborough to Bognor Regis via Coldwaltham, Bury, Arundel, Barnham and Westergate which started on 8 June. However, this preamble concerning events not in the immediate vicinity of Horsham sets the scene for the introduction from 17 June of a Thursday service with two journeys each way from Arundel to Horsham via Bury, Coldwaltham, Pulborough, Billingshurst and Slinfold; part of which was over the route of Southdown services 295, 297 and 298. It restored the link from Arundel to Horsham, which disappeared in 1971 and was usually worked by the small Bristol bus. Arrow were then parking their vehicles at Codmore Hill Garage in Pulborough.

However, Arrow Travel's services received no subsidy and had to compete in some areas with established facilities provided for many years by Southdown. Promotion of the services was difficult over such a wide area and the travelling public was slow to recognise the new facilities.

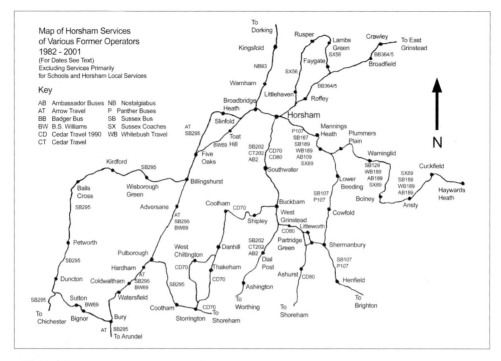

Map of Horsham Services
of Various Former Operators
1982 - 2001
(For Dates See Text)
Excluding Services Primarily
for Horsham Local Services

Key

AB Ambassador Buses   NB Nostalgiabus
AT Arrow Travel   P   Panther Buses
BB Badger Bus   SB Sussex Bus
BW B.S. Williams   SX Sussex Coaches
CD Cedar Travel 1990   WB Whitebush Travel
CT Cedar Travel

Arrow Travel used this little Bristol LHS6L with ECW twenty-six-seat bodywork, formerly of London Transport, on their short-lived Thursday service from Arundel in June 1982. Despite what it says on the destination blind, it is in Slinfold on the way to Horsham and demonstrating normal passenger loadings! (Author's collection)

During mid–Summer 1982, most services were reduced and then withdrawn, including that to Horsham which faded away in July, although nobody really noticed. Only the Barnham school service remained and Arrow then concentrated on school contracts and private hire.

Mick Stoodley left the business in 1982 and started his own coach operation, Ambassador Travel, in January 1983. W.N.S. Travel was later disbanded. In August 1983 Linda Kirk (now Linda Gander) became proprietor of Arrow Travel and operated until Summer 2003 from a number of locations. The Barnham service was not registered for public use at the time of deregulation in 1986. Mick Stoodley finished operating in 1994, having restarted bus services in April 1988 with a Monday to Saturday facility between Pulborough and Storrington under contract to West Sussex County Council. This was accompanied by a Storrington local service and later a Thursday service from Cootham to Storrington and a Friday service from Petworth to Worthing via Pulborough and Storrington. These routes were transferred to the ownership of John Whatford in September 1988, who subsequently ran services into Horsham as described later.

SIXTEEN

SUSSEX BUS LTD

By 1985, with the impending abolition of quantity licensing controls in the bus industry, Traffic Commissioners had to take a more laissez-faire attitude towards applications for new stage-carriage services. Under the Transport Act 1980 they were required to grant them unless it could be proved by objectors that they were against the public interest in some way. This was to benefit John Belson, who lived in Partridge Green, and being interested in public transport generally, had aspirations to do something to benefit the community by running a reliable, well-priced and locally orientated bus service, to supplement the efforts of Southdown, which were already diminishing. He was a pilot for British Caledonian Airways and owned a former Thames Valley Bristol L single-decker, as a preserved vehicle. He put together a business plan to operate one vehicle five days a week, which would be underpinned by a school run in the morning and afternoon, and he also negotiated a sponsorship deal with the Brighton-based *Evening Argus* newspaper. In view of his employment commitments, he recruited a full-time driver.

A Leyland Leopard registered (appropriately in view of the newspaper involvement) RAG 385M was purchased. This had been owned by Western Scottish, and had a forty-nine-seat Alexander Y-type coach body, so typical of major fleets north of the border. It was given a white and red livery and Sussex Bus fleet name. Parking was obtained at Bridge Garage, Henfield Road, Cowfold. The timetable leaflet and the bus displayed slogans advertising the *Evening Argus*, and the names of the places served were painted along the roof of the vehicle.

Operations commenced on 2 September 1985. The school service was numbered A3 and linked Cowfold and West Grinstead with Jolesfield Primary School in Partridge Green, and then continued via Ashurst to Steyning Upper School. A round trip on Monday to Friday mornings numbered A2 ran from Cowfold to Worthing via Partridge Green, Shermanbury, Henfield, Small Dole, Upper Beeding and North Lancing. On Wednesday and Saturday evenings a service A1 ran from Cowfold to Brighton, following service A2 to Henfield and then traversing Southdown's route via Woodmancote. By then, Southdown were no longer running in the evening. The inaugural trip to Worthing featured a champagne toast on arrival by the mayor of Worthing and the cutting of a special cake in the shape of the bus, while two *Evening Argus* promotions staff were on board.

Disappointing patronage resulted in the withdrawal of service A1 after 19 October 1985. However, following the acquisition of a second vehicle, operations expanded from 7 April 1986. A new service A1 with one round trip on Monday to Friday mornings linked Partridge Green with Brighton via Henfield, Small Dole, Upper Beeding, Shoreham and Hove, while service A2 was expanded to cover Steyning, Bramber, Upper Beeding and Shoreham. On arrival in the coastal towns, the buses from A1 and A2 were used on some journeys numbered A5 between Brighton and Worthing via. Portslade and Shoreham. At the same time, a service to Horsham on schooldays was started, numbered A4, from Cowfold via Shermanbury,

Opposite: JHA 232L, one of a pair of former Midland Red Leyland Leopards with Marshall dual-purpose bodywork acquired by Sussex Bus from Cedar Travel of Worthing. Seen in Billingshurst on 30 January 1989 working service 295 to Horsham. (A. Lambert)

Left: On the first day of Sussex Bus operations, Leyland Leopard RAG 385M stands at Worthing Pier after working the first journey on service A2 from Cowfold on 2 September 1985. (Author's collection)

In Henfield next to the Southdown Garage in February 1987 is the entire Sussex Bus fleet at that time. *Left to right:* 2501 LJ, an Alexander-bodied Daimler Fleetline, Leyland Leopard/ Alexander RAG 385M, UGP 478R a rare Sparshatt-bodied Leyland 550FG and ancillary vehicle Volkswagen KNF 128V. (Author's collection, courtesy J. Belson)

Working Sunday service 107 from Horsham to Brighton on 24 May 1987 is Sussex Bus Bristol LHS6L XPD 127N with thirty-five coach-style seats. This originated from the London Country fleet. (E.C. Churchill)

Partridge Green, West Grinstead, Copsale and Southwater. This could be used by students attending quite a few state and independent schools in the town.

From 27 October 1986 and the implementation of the Transport Act of 1985, Sussex Bus had the opportunity to expand in the way its owner wished. Service A1 was withdrawn, while A2 was reduced to run on Mondays and Wednesdays only, being complemented by a similar Southdown service 103, which ran on Mondays, Tuesdays and Thursdays. Two contracts were awarded by West Sussex County Council. These were for the off-peak journeys on the otherwise Southdown service 102 (Partridge Green-Henfield-Steyning-Washington-Ashington-Storrington on Tuesdays and Thursdays), and service A6 (Partridge Green-Henfield-Small Dole-Fulking-Poynings-Brighton on Fridays), which had previously been Southdown service 106. By that time, the Sussex Bus Ltd base had moved to The Garage, Partridge Green and, shortly afterwards, moved again to Station Road, Henfield, marking the beginning of a period of informal association with Chris Stepe's Travelfar Coaches business.

No changes were allowed to be made to services under the new deregulated regime for three months. Southdown took the first opportunity to close their Horsham depot and to reduce their services in the area. The contracts for some services were put out to tender by West Sussex County Council and Sussex Bus were successful in gaining four of them from 25 January 1987. Two were Sunday operations: 107 from Horsham to Brighton via Mannings Heath, Cowfold, Partridge Green and Henfield and 202 Horsham to Worthing via Southwater, Ashington, Washington and Findon. On Saturdays, service 189 provided a limited facility from Horsham to Haywards Heath via Mannings Heath, Plummers Plain, Warninglid, Bolney, Ansty and Cuckfield, which Brighton & Hove Bus Co. ran on Mondays to Fridays.

However, more substantially, Sussex Bus started service 295 on Mondays to Fridays, to replace Southdown services 295 and 298, from Billingshurst to Horsham via Five Oaks and Slinfold. There were six journeys each way, with a three-hour gap in the middle of the day, which Southdown filled with a residual service 298 round trip from Horsham to Billingshurst. The morning peak-hour journey started at Petworth via Kirdford and Wisborough Green, and returned there in the evening. John Belson left British Caledonian Airways to concentrate on running Sussex Bus on a full-time basis.

The increase in work resulted in a need to hire coaches from Travelfar and in February 1987 a Daimler Fleetline double-decker with Alexander body was acquired from Maidstone & District and was well-presented in Sussex Bus livery. This bus was converted to an open-top model in June 1988 after an unsuccessful attempt to drive it under the low railway bridge by Amberley Station! In July 1987, Horsham school service A4 was withdrawn, but from 17 November a contract was gained from Tesco to provide a number of free services to their store at Three Bridges in Crawley. These required two vehicles, and included a half-hourly shuttle from the town centre. Sussex Bus acquired two Ford R1114 coaches to boost the fleet in late 1987 and these were followed by two former Midland Red Leyland Leopards with dual-purpose Marshall bodywork, which were purchased from Cedar Travel in Worthing and became regulars on service 295. In 1988 the association with Travelfar largely ended and premises were obtained at the Rudford Industrial Estate on Ford Airfield. This helped shape the future direction of the business.

January 1989 saw the start of a shift of geographical emphasis in the Sussex Bus service portfolio, when they successfully bid for a package of contracted services around the Chichester area which had been run by Yellowline Tours. From then on, the majority of the company's operations were focussed on Chichester and quite a network of services, albeit a regularly changing one, was built up on both a commercial and contracted basis. Service 189 was given up in May 1988, followed by services 107, 202 and the original A2 service from 20 February 1989. This left just service 295 to extend as far as Horsham. New work was obtained when Cedar Travel ended operations in October 1989 and additional contracted services around Chichester, Worthing and Midhurst followed.

Service 295 was gradually developed. Two off-peak journeys on Mondays, Wednesdays and Fridays were extended to Petworth from 20 February 1989. On Tuesdays, Thursdays and Saturdays it was projected from Billingshurst to Pulborough and Storrington, but curtailed at Pulborough in February the following year. Following a successful bid to the Rural Transport Development Fund, it was enhanced from 10 September 1990 with a second bus which allowed through-journeys on Wednesdays and Fridays south of Petworth to and from Chichester via Duncton, Upwaltham and Halnaker, recalling the 'good old days' of the Horsham to Chichester regular Southdown service 63. On Wednesdays, the 295 also served East Dean and Singleton. From 28 May 1991 the Friday Chichester journeys were withdrawn, but 295's three-days-per-week Pulborough service was extended to Coldwaltham, Bury and Arundel. However, it was cut back to Watersfield from 26 October 1992 and then Pulborough again from 23 December 1993. The period of competition with commercial services operated by Tillingbourne Bus Co. is mentioned under the latter heading, and it was that company which finally took the contract away from Sussex Bus after 28 May 1994.

Between 1990 and 1992, Sussex Bus acquired four Leyland Leopards which had had their original bodies replaced with Willowbrook Warrior bus bodies. One was partly funded by Rural Development Council money, and they were a good-value option for presenting a reasonably modern image, becoming regulars on service 295 into Horsham. They had various internal features to make travel easier for the elderly and disabled. Fittings such as brightly coloured grab rails, clearly marked shallow entrance steps and palm-operated bell-push buttons were part of a national standard laid down by the Disabled Persons Transport Advisory Committee and vehicles with these fittings were specified by many local authorities in their contract specifications. This was a step on the road to the now prolific fully accessible low-floor bus and for a time, Sussex Bus added their own extra feature – a baby and toddler seat of the type one fits in a car – to make life easier for parents and carers travelling on their services.

Other vehicles used on service 295 included a Leyland Leopard/Duple Dominant bus, a similar bus but with AEC Reliance chassis and a former Southdown Bristol RE with Marshall body – all very smartly turned out in Sussex Bus red and white livery.

By 1990, a useful relationship had been established with Stagecoach, who had purchased Southdown from its management in August 1989. John and Sheila Belson were then living in Pagham and Sussex Bus vehicles were garaged at Southdown's depot in Chichester. Further service development saw a new minibus-operated frequent shuttle service around the centre of Chichester and out to the Tesco store at Fishbourne, followed by contract awards for two

At Chichester Bus Station,
Leyland Leopard/Duple
Dominant SSU 780W
is ready for a Wednesday
journey to Horsham
on service 295, through
attractive villages situated in
the South Downs. (Author's
collection)

In the latter phases of
Sussex Bus service 295
the usual vehicles were
Leyland Leopards, which
were once coaches and
had been rebodied with
Willowbrook Warrior bus
bodywork. There were four
of them and here is XSU
682 in the Carfax, which
had arrived in January 1991
and passed with the business
to Stagecoach in October
1996. (Author's collection)

services to Petersfield – the 54 from Chichester and the 61 from Midhurst. Vehicles were also
kept at Everyman's Garage at Maudlin, on the outskirts of Chichester.

While the business was doing reasonably well, John Belson realised that, without a
commercial service of its own, Sussex Bus was reliant on winning contracts from West Sussex
County Council, which brought uncertainty when they expired and fresh bids had to be
submitted. Rather than allow matters to deteriorate if important work was unfortunately
lost, it was decided that Sussex Bus should be sold. After negotiations with several parties
which did not reach fruition, the company was sold to Stagecoach in its local guise of Sussex
Coastline Buses Ltd. After operations on 18 October 1996, Stagecoach acquired the remaining
six services, mainly focussed on Chichester but also the Friday service 289 from Petworth
to Brighton via Billingshurst, Storrington, Steyning and Fulking which was a descendant of
Tillingbourne service 454. Eleven vehicles and thirteen drivers changed hands and Sussex Bus
continued for a considerable time as a separate operating unit within Sussex Coastline.

In its relatively short existence, Sussex Bus always took a professional approach, a friendly,
reliable service provided by well-maintained and turned-out vehicles, with a positive marketing
approach, good timetable literature and a sharp eye for an opportunity to satisfy customer
demand and to meet local needs. It was a quality example of an independent operator in the
post-deregulation period.

SEVENTEEN

C.J. CHATFIELD (CEDAR TRAVEL)

In May 1984, Chris Chatfield of Worthing set up as a minibus operator, trading as Cedar Transport and using two twelve-seat Volkswagen LT28s. In October that year he proposed to provide four bus services linking various West Sussex villages over a wide area – with Worthing – aimed at shopping trips and evening entertainment possibilities. He also planned a dial-a-ride demand-responsive service into Worthing, with door-to-door pickup around Goring, Ferring and Angmering. However, the scheme did not reach fruition, being just a little too early to allow such activities to have the total freedom to run in areas served by Southdown.

Chatfield increased his fleet to five minibuses and from October 1986 started running a local service within Worthing under contract to the county council, to replace a section of Southdown service 229, which was to be abandoned on a commercial basis. The following year, he expanded his activities with commercial services from Worthing to Findon and Durrington, in competition with Southdown, and gained some further contracts. In February 1988, having bought nine more vehicles, Cedar Travel (later restyled Cedarbus) introduced more local services in Worthing, mainly complementary to those of Southdown, and covering most areas of the town. In Summer 1988, two additional Iveco 49.10s and five MCW Metroriders were purchased new.

From 5 April 1988, one early morning journey on Mondays to Fridays on Cedar service C2 (Findon-West Worthing-Worthing) was extended to start at Horsham via Southwater, Ashington and Washington, under contract to the county council. This filled a gap in the timetable of Southdown service 202 and a connection was available at Findon for a direct trip into Worthing by Southdown service 201. Thus, Cedar Travel became the first new independent operator in Horsham after deregulation, but the contract was given up from 20 February 1989. Cedar then gained other contracted services in central West Sussex, although not to Horsham.

In July 1989, Southdown launched a competitive offensive against Cedarbus in Worthing. This came just after a Traffic Commissioner's hearing when Chatfield lost his operator's licence on grounds of poor vehicle maintenance, but had continued running, pending an appeal, although several drivers left and services began to run erratically. Having seen Cedarbus weakened, Southdown made their move and purchased part of the business on 24 September 1989, including seven services and eight vehicles. Southdown kept the Cedarbus trading name for a time and the vehicles retained their white and orange livery. Chatfield's licence was indeed revoked, as the appeal was lost, and the four remaining services and some vehicles passed to Sussex Bus after 28 October 1989. However, Chris Chatfield was to return, and his company's current important position in the Horsham area is described later.

EIGHTEEN

WHITEBUSH TRAVEL LTD

Whitebush Travel, based in Redhill, started with a sixteen-seat Ford Transit in June 1987. From 26 October 1987 they were awarded contracts by West Sussex County Council for three services previously provided by Southdown. These were the Haywards Heath to East Grinstead section of Southdown 770 on Mondays to Saturdays (renumbered 270), a Saturday service linking Wakehurst Place, Ardingly and Haywards Heath (renumbered 472 from 34) and Monday to Saturday evening journeys on service 773 from Gatwick Airport to Brighton via Crawley, Bolney and Hassocks. Two former Crosville coach-seated Leyland Nationals were acquired.

The contract for service 166 (Haywards Heath-Plumpton-Lewes) passed to Whitebush Travel from Lewes Coach Co. from 25 April 1988. From 31 May 1988, operations expanded dramatically with the award of contracts by both East and West Sussex County Councils for seven services radiating from the Haywards Heath area, including to Crawley and Lewes. Also involved was service 189 from Haywards Heath to Horsham via Cuckfield, Bolney and Warninglid, to replace former contracts with Brighton & Hove Bus Co. (Mondays-Fridays) and Sussex Bus (Saturdays). Whitebush Travel obtained premises at an industrial estate on the outskirts of Horsted Keynes and ran their new services with hired vehicles, which included two Leyland Nationals from Gatwick Engineering, two Ford Transits from Alder Valley South and five assorted Leyland Leopards from Hyndburn Transport, the municipally owned operator in Accrington. However, Whitebush Travel had clearly overcommitted itself and from the start, certain journeys were covered by Southdown or Lewes Coaches (by now owned by Brighton Borough Transport) at short notice.

To relieve the pressure on Whitebush Travel, West Sussex County Council terminated the contract for service 189 to Horsham on 11 June 1988, and it was taken over by Southdown, thus ending Whitebush Travel's very brief appearance in Horsham. Whitebush Travel's service reliability did not improve and many complaints were received by the councils. East Sussex transferred service 121 (Haywards Heath-Lewes) to Brighton & Hove Bus Co. from 11 July and on Monday 1 August 1988 Whitebush Travel vehicles did not appear on the road, the company having decided overnight to cease trading.

Emergency action by the councils saw the services restored the next day, with the assistance of Lewes Coaches, London Country South West and RDH Services. The Whitebush Travel hired vehicles were swiftly repossessed by their owners and the company disappeared. This hitherto-unknown small business was allowed to expand its bus service operations too quickly without, in hindsight, adequate foundation or resources, prompted, it must be said, by local authorities awarding their contracts to the lowest bidder without effective assurances that so many additional services could be sustained on a reliable footing.

Representative of the vehicles taken on loan by Whitebush Travel from Hyndburn's hire fleet was EHG 44S, a Leyland Leopard/East Lancs. It is outside the former Southdown Bus Station in Haywards Heath in June 1988 on service 166 from Lewes. (A. Lambert)

Also in Haywards Heath was TPD 195M, a Leyland National that Whitebush had hired from Gatwick Engineering. Whitebush only ran service 189 to Horsham for a few weeks in Summer 1988. (A. Lambert)

NINETEEN

B.S. WILLIAMS LTD (HANTS & SUSSEX)

The regime of local authority tendering for services of no interest to the commercial sector of the market saw the return in 1988 of a well-known name in the annals of independent bus operations in Horsham. This was none other than Basil Williams, who was last encountered in 1955 when trying unsuccessfully to salvage his local services following the collapse of the Hants & Sussex Motor Services Group.

At the implementation of deregulation in October 1986, his Southern Motorways operation was still running a network of rural services based on Midhurst and also local routes linking Emsworth with Thorney Island, Westbourne and Havant, as well as from Havant to Rowlands Castle via Leigh Park. Using his Glider & Blue Motor Services Ltd company, he had been awarded contracts by Hampshire County Council for local services around Eastleigh and Chandlers Ford and two services into Winchester. These were run under the Hants & Sussex name, before being sold to Solent Blueline on 1 October 1987. In the late 1980s, some commercial and contracted services were started in the Chichester area.

The Hants & Sussex/Southern Motorways fleet consisted of a number of former London Transport AEC Merlin and AEC Swift single-deck buses, and some Ford R1114 and Leyland Leopard coaches with Duple Dominant bodies, in a mainly cream and dark red or cream and brown livery.

By Spring 1988, all that remained of Southdown service 298 was a Thursday facility of one journey each way from Chichester to Crawley via Duncton, Bignor, Bury, Pulborough, Billingshurst, Slinfold, Horsham and Faygate. The contract for this passed to B.S. Williams Ltd from 23 June 1988, as service 69, recalling the old trunk Southdown service from Horsham to Pulborough and beyond. The sections of route between Chichester and Duncton and beyond Horsham to Crawley were not perpetuated, while it was diverted via Toat Hill instead of Slinfold. A coach was used on this somewhat ephemeral excursion into the Horsham area. It was withdrawn after 16 February 1989, being partly subsumed by an expanded Sussex Bus service 295 between Pulborough and Horsham three days a week.

After a thirty-three-year gap, Basil Williams gained a bus service to Horsham! JMJ 109V is a Ford R1114 in Southern Motorways cream and brown coach livery. Despite what it says on the front, it was arriving in Horsham from Duncton on short-lived service 69. (Author's collection)

TWENTY

R.D. GASCOINE (BADGER BUSES)

Richard Gascoine, from Partridge Green, was a former London Country South West bus driver who had ambitions of starting his own company to challenge his old employer in the Crawley area. In 1988 he stated that he would set up a forty-vehicle operation under the name Crawley Bus & Coach Co., but with a partner, Paul Gardner, eventually settled for a fourteen-vehicle operator's licence and an aim to employ twenty-four drivers on a network of bus services designed not to compete with London Country or Southdown. This allegedly involved an investment of £150,000.

Pending the start of operations, he obtained two former London Country North West Leyland Nationals and four new Ford Transits with sixteen-seat Mellor bodywork on lease. These were supplemented by no fewer than nine Leyland Leopard buses and coaches from the Hyndburn hire fleet. By November 1988 the name Badger Buses (North Sussex) Ltd appeared on notepaper, together with a strapline which suggested that Badger was a 'Member of the Rank Organisation', whatever that meant. An operating base was established at Crawley Football Ground at Town Mead, off Ifield Avenue. Some private hire work was undertaken and the first service was seemingly started on 21 December 1988, being numbered 300 and marketed as 'City Express', running basically hourly every day from Crawley to London's Victoria Coach Station via Gatwick Airport and West Croydon, needing, on paper, four vehicles. This ran intermittently, with several cancellations, breakdowns, and little or no publicity. It only lasted ten days, before fading away.

A number of bus services had been registered to start from 9 January 1989, being largely competitive with London Country, including some Crawley town services to be operated by the Ford Transits under the Badger Cub brand. There was also a daily service 370 from Crawley to Merstham via Gatwick Airport, Horley and Redhill and weekday services 364/365 from Horsham to East Grinstead (Stone Quarry Estate). These were to run hourly via Roffey, Faygate, Broadfield, Crawley, Copthorne, Crawley Down and Turners Hill, whence the 364 was to proceed via Kingscote and the 365 via Sharpthorne. However, the start date was delayed to Thursday 19 January and the whole business was a disaster from the outset. Apart from breakdowns there were insufficient drivers, reports of drivers not having been paid and little support from the travelling public. Those journeys that did run were somewhat erratic. Most of the services ran on 19 and 20 January, few on 21 January, two on the morning of the 22nd, then just occasional journeys on 23 to 25 January. This was somewhat at odds with Badger's press advertising which stated that 'The No.1 bus and coach company would put the public first'.

Six Leyland Leopard/East Lancs buses from Hyndburn, the two Leyland Nationals and the Ford Transits had been painted into Badger Bus dark blue and cream livery. The Nationals, Transits, two Leopards and three Bristol RE/ECW buses obtained from Poole Bay Services were active between 19 to 25 January 1989. Thus, Badger Buses collapsed, leaving fourteen drivers unpaid and debts quoted at £53,000 or £200,000 if you believed reports in the local press.

Shortly after Badger Bus operations collapsed, a Mellor-bodied Ford Transit is parked at their operating centre in Crawley. Four of these were used for a few days under the 'Badger Cub' brand on Crawley town services in competition with London Country. (Author's collection)

Having admitted he had run out of funds, and after surrendering his operator's licence, Richard Gascoine disappeared. Drivers were faced with a large number of unpaid bills from suppliers, and it transpired that the only assets actually owned rather than leased were some ticket machines.

Badger Bus had registered an hourly service 366 on a commercial basis from Horsham to Slinfold and Billingshurst, with some journeys projected to Petworth. This coincided with the retendering of the contract for service 295, which West Sussex County Council intended not to award. The collapse of Badger Bus required an about-turn, with Sussex Bus Ltd retaining the contract.

The Badger Bus episode brought out the worst side of deregulation. It is probably fair to say that it was a mixture of an overdose of enthusiastic amateurism, coupled with an almost Walter Mitty-like disregard for the financial realities and obligations in starting a passenger transport business. It would never have been easy to break into the Crawley bus market in a significant way, as others had found before and others would do in the future. The final irony was when BBC's London Plus news programme broadcast a report on Badger Buses's first day of operations more than a week after the company collapsed. A vision of a happy Richard Gascoine must have incensed those affected by the affair and confused a few bus passengers in Crawley.

As a postscript, it must be recorded that Richard Gascoine reappeared, but in Devon, in Autumn 1994 and started another business which traded as East Devon Buses, based on Crediton. A number of ever-changing, often short-lived and over-ambitious commercial services were run as well as several services under contract to Devon County Council. The operating territory covered much of East Devon, from Exmouth, Sidmouth and Seaton on the coast, up as far as Tiverton and Dulverton, with some services running over the border into Somerset. True to past form, Gascoine launched his venture as 'the newest bus company in Devon and backed by a multi-million pound organisation'. Gascoine's dreams of new services were sometimes manifest into printed timetables, which were put up at stops, but some services advertised like this never actually started.

In late June 1997, Devon County Council had to act on behalf of the travelling public and withdrew all of East Devon's contracts. A week later, the operator's licence was revoked by the Traffic Commissioner, but a new one was obtained in the name of East Devon Bus & Coach Co. Ltd, which ran a few services in a very erratic fashion until early October 1997, when it became bankrupt.

TWENTY-ONE

J. WHATFORD (AMBASSADOR BUSES)

John Whatford, of Coldwaltham near Pulborough, took over Leyland Leopard coach CUF 260L and the bus services in the Pulborough/Storrington area from Mick Stoodley in May 1988. Both men had of course been previously involved in the Arrow Travel business. The service registrations were formally transferred from 16 September 1988. Thus, for the next six years, John Whatford ran a generally one-vehicle business on a changing group of bus services in various parts of West Sussex. The Leyland Leopard was supplemented by TCD 487J, a former Southdown Bristol RESL6L/Marshall bus, in January 1989.

On 27 May 1989 all the bus services were withdrawn when the contract for the Storrington to Midhurst service passed to Cedarbus of Worthing. Instead, from 19 June that year, Whatford gained the contracts for service 189 from Haywards Heath to Horsham on Mondays to Saturdays and service 188 from Ardingly to Haywards Heath on Saturdays, which Southdown had maintained since the demise of Whitebush Travel. Whatford ran the Horsham service only until 26 May 1990, when the contract passed to Brighton Buses, and the Leyland Leopard was sold.

Services recommenced on 15 June 1990 with a Friday commercial service (numbered 1) of one journey each way from Petworth to Pulborough, Storrington and Worthing, which was expanded from 3 September 1990 with additional Monday to Saturday journeys from Pulborough to Worthing under contract to the county council. At the same time, the contract for the morning peak journey from Horsham to Worthing over Stagecoach service 2 was obtained.

The Bristol RE was replaced in May 1991 by a former Portsmouth City Transport AEC Swift with Marshall bodywork, which lasted until October 1991 when it was substituted with a Leyland National. From 29 August 1991 another contract was gained for a Thursday service 3 from Steyning to Storrington via Washington, Ashington and Thakeham, replacing Cedar Travel (1990) service 25. Services 1 and 2 were withdrawn after 23 May 1992 and, from 1 June, Whatford started a schoolday service from Pulborough to Collyers and Millais Schools in Horsham via Storrington, Thakeham, Ashington and Dial Post. It appears to have been unsuccessful as it was withdrawn at the end of term in July.

Whatford also ran a school contract to Steyning and, to find additional work for the bus as well as Thursday service 3, he began a contracted Wednesday service 4 from 28 October 1992 from Washington to Chichester via Storrington, Pulborough, Bignor, Duncton and Eartham. The Leyland National was replaced with a former Green Line vehicle – YPL 85T, an AEC Reliance with Duple Dominant coach body. In March 1994 the school contract finished and John Whatford finally decided to cease being an operator, with services 3 and 4 withdrawn at the end of May 1994 and being continued by others in various forms.

Ambassador Travel's former Southdown Leyland Leopard/Duple Dominant CUF 260L picks up passengers in the Carfax for service 189 to Haywards Heath on 10 July 1989. (D. Stewart)

Another former Southdown vehicle used by Ambassador on service 189 was TCD 487J, a Marshall-bodied Bristol RESL6L. However it is shown here in April 1991 parked near John Whatford's home in Coldwaltham. (A. Lambert)

TWENTY-TWO

M. JEAL (PANTHER BUSES)

In January 1990, Michael Jeal, of Ifield in Crawley, was granted an operator's licence and subsequently purchased two Leyland Nationals previously used by Yorkshire Traction. These were painted red and white and the name Panther Corporation Ltd was used: this was inaccurate as Panther was neither a corporation nor a limited liability company. The buses were used to launch a service from Crawley to London (Victoria) via Horley, Redhill, Coulsdon, Croydon, Streatham and Brixton, numbered variously 405A or 109A to mirror the traditional London & Country service 405 or London Buses 109, which the Panther route largely paralleled. Started on 1 March 1990 running Mondays to Saturdays, the Saturday journeys had ceased within two weeks and it then settled down, with some irregularity, offering three round trips. It disappeared after 11 October 1990 when the Nationals were sold.

West Sussex County Council awarded Panther a contract from 3 September 1990 for a single trip on service 107 from Brighton to Horsham via Pyecombe, Henfield, Partridge Green and Cowfold, which was not covered by Southdown. This departed Brighton at 5.15 p.m. on Mondays to Saturdays. However, Panther offered a number of additional journeys on a commercial basis, in competition with Southdown, and the bus was scheduled to run in service from Crawley in the morning, and back in the early evening. Southdown were not amused and just the contracted journey ran after a few days.

Panther replaced the original Nationals with three assorted elderly buses, none of which were to last long. A second contract was gained – to Holy Trinity School in Crawley – and to keep vehicles occupied during the day, Panther went into competition against London & Country's C7 service across Crawley, from Crabbet Park and Pound Hill in the east, to Gossops Green and Bewbush in the west. This marked the start of a series of competitive service developments and more Crawley town services were introduced.

By early 1991, an operating base was established at Oakhurst, Leechpool Lane in Roffey to replace premises in Crawley. Panther Engineering (as it styled itself for purposes of the depot) was immediately in conflict with those living in the surrounding residential area, who complained bitterly of noise, smells, verbal abuse and traffic problems. These aspects were strongly denied by the company, which maintained it was just trying to run a business to serve the travelling public, although an approach from North Horsham Parish Council received an antagonistic reply. However, a fire in March 1991 destroyed a bus and a lorry, and was suspected to be arson.

London & Country complained to the Traffic Commissioner of multiple instances of Panther not running to the correct timetable or route, perhaps in order to extract potential passengers from London & Country, and it was alleged that Panther buses had been seen with fare-paying passengers in parts of Crawley where they did not hold service registrations. As the 'bus war' escalated, Panther started local Horsham services over London & Country routes from 15 May 1991. Services 1 and 2 linked the Carfax with Littlehaven, Lambs Farm, Roffey

In Crawley, Panther's former Southdown Leyland National UFG 58S shows the 107 route number (Brighton-Horsham) on which Panther ran a contracted journey. It is still in the cream and red livery of its previous owner – Brighton & Hove Bus Co. (Author's collection)

Panther Buses took this Freight Rover Sherpa D402 ERE with PMT bodywork conversion on loan when they started competing against London & Country on Horsham town services. It was parked in the Carfax on 22 June 1991. (A. Lambert)

THX 230S was one of five former London Buses Leyland Nationals used by Panther on local services in Horsham and Crawley. It is on service S2 to Lambs Farm and Roffey during the period that Panther were obliged to run their vehicles on hire to Silver Fern of Crawley to circumvent a ban on running their own services imposed by the Traffic Commissioner. (Author's collection)

and South Holmes estate, giving a bus every half-hour, service 3 ran hourly to Depot Road, Comptons Lane and Oakhill, while service 4 ran hourly to Greenway, Merryfield Drive and The Common. Panther charged a flat-rate adult single fare of 40p, compared to London & Country's between Roffey and Horsham of 95p. The contract for the journey from Brighton on service 107 ended.

During 1991 Panther built up a fleet of second-hand Leyland Nationals, including four that had previously been owned by Brighton & Hove Bus Co., as well as several from London Buses. When the Horsham services started, a twenty-seat Freight Rover Sherpa was loaned to Panther for a couple of months. Shortly after the Horsham services started, a London & Country bus driver was assaulted in the town, while at Panther's depot a bus was deliberately put out of action. Police kept an open mind.

The Traffic Commissioner held a public enquiry in May 1991 to look at the complaints of irregular operation, when the former Panther Buses 'operations manager' admitted that he had instructed drivers to indulge in the same sort of tactics as London & Country were alleged to have used, apparently without the knowledge of Michael Jeal. The Commissioner was not impressed by this excuse and felt that the whole episode had been one of the most blatant cases in disregard of the regulations. He imposed a prohibition on Panther running any bus services for three months from 1 July 1991 and determined that a 20 per cent reduction in Panther's fuel duty rebate payment for the previous three months should be made.

Jeal lodged an appeal with the Transport Tribunal but was not successful in obtaining a 'stay' on the judgement in the interim. Therefore, Jeal made alternative arrangements. Four services in Crawley, and Horsham services 1 and 2, were registered by Silver Fern of Crawley, owned by J.W. Faulks. From 1 July 1991, Panther would be running their buses on hire to Faulks, under the Silverline name. No doubt disappointed that Jeal had been able to effectively circumvent the ban on running services, London & Country used their Randomquick subsidiary (Alder Valley West Surrey) to register two services starting on 2 September from Horsham to Roffey, numbered 1 and 2, which mirrored Silverline's routes but ran seven minutes in front of the Silverline journeys, by now officially numbered S1 and S2.

On 4 October 1991, Horsham District Council served a notice under the Environmental Protection Act to stop Panther's Leechpool Lane premises being used as a bus depot, with a three-month lead time. A few days later it was announced that the appeal against the Traffic Commissioner's decisions had failed. At the start of October, Jeal could resume running his bus services in his own name. The original Panther local bus registrations were cancelled on 15 October (Horsham services 3 and 4) or 28 October (Horsham services 1 and 2 and those in Crawley), while those of Faulks were cancelled from 3 November. During October, Saturday operations in Horsham had been erratic. From 4 November, new Panther registrations came into effect, with no Saturday operation, but Horsham services 3 and 4 were not included.

However, to resolve their problems, the Drawlane Group, which owned London & Country, purchased the Panther business from Jeal on 12 November 1991. The trading name used was Gem Fairtax, but service registrations and vehicle license discs were in the name of Tellings-Golden Miller Ltd. Fairtax was the name of an operator in Melton Mowbray in Leicestershire which had been purchased by another Drawlane subsidiary – Midland Fox – while Tellings-Golden Miller from Byfleet in Surrey was then also in the ownership of Drawlane. Eight of Panther's Leyland Nationals were taken over. The Horsham services were not perpetuated but four Crawley town services were maintained. However, a London & County spokesperson, quoted in the local press, denied all links with Gem Fairtax! The new owner continued to use the depot in Roffey until arrangements could be made to move in to London & Country's Crawley Garage. It followed quite naturally that Alder Valley West Surrey services 1 and 2 were withdrawn on 30 November 1991.

The Gem Fairtax brand was retained as a separate unit within the control of London & Country, no doubt as a means for dealing with any further competition. From 1 March 1992 a separate company – Gem Fairtax (1991) Ltd took over responsibility for licensing from Tellings-Golden Miller. From 5 June 1993, Gem Fairtax gained the contract for service 189 from Haywards Heath to Horsham on Saturdays, while from 6 November that year they started a contracted morning peak journey on Saturdays between Crawley and Horsham over London & Country's service 438. Gem Fairtax ended operations from 1 September 1995 when the contracted services were transferred to London & Country and the Crawley town services were amalgamated with the latter's own network.

TWENTY-THREE

R. WRIGHT (CEDAR TRAVEL 1990)

Richard Wright of Portslade, a former employee of Chris Chatfield's Cedar Travel, was to begin operating on his own account and although he obtained an operator's licence for three vehicles, some carried the discs of Sussex Bus Ltd. Perhaps in an attempt to gain recognition from Chatfield's old customers, he traded as Cedar Travel 1990. From 9 July 1990 he formally took over four services from Sussex Bus Ltd which had once been run by Chatfield. However, Wright had been using his vehicles on them prior to that date. These were the CL (Worthing local) on Mondays to Fridays, the 24 (Partridge Green-Henfield-Steyning-Worthing) on Mondays, Wednesdays and Fridays, 25 (Partridge Green-Henfield-Steyning- Washington-Ashington-Storrington) on Tuesdays and Thursdays and the 35 (Brighton Open Market to Tongdean and Westdene) on Mondays to Saturdays.

As well as gaining some minor contract awards subsequently, along the coast, 28 May 1991 saw service 24 extended to start at Cowfold, service 25 truncated to start at Steyning and new service 23 from Cowfold to Brighton on Tuesdays and Thursdays, again via Partridge Green, Henfield and Steyning. The contract for Brighton service 35 was given up after 4 May, while service 25 was withdrawn in August 1991. In March 1992 service 23 was withdrawn in favour of a Monday to Saturday facility on service 24, although on Saturdays it started at Henfield.

Horsham District Council was concerned that those without cars in several villages, once served well by Southdown, were unable to easily get into town. Without the involvement of West Sussex County Council, they funded the introduction of two services provided by Brighton & Hove Bus & Coach Co. from 7 April 1992, but the contract passed to Cedar Travel 1990 from 2 April 1993. Service 70 ran to Horsham from Shoreham via Steyning, Storrington, Coolham and Shipley on Wednesdays and Saturdays, with Thakeham also covered on Wednesdays and West Chiltington on Saturdays. Service 80 started at Shoreham on Tuesdays, or Small Dole on Fridays, and ran to Horsham via Steyning, Partridge Green and West Grinstead. From 13 October, service 70 was able to also stop at Upper Beeding and Bramber.

Wright owned a sixteen-seat Freight Rover Sherpa and acquired five Bedford coaches over a period of time. He also acquired the two Iveco 49.10s which Sussex Bus Ltd had taken over from Cedarbus, E306/7 FYJ, which were the vehicles normally used on the Horsham services.

Financial difficulties lead to Wright having to cease operating on 22 January 1994. The contract for the Horsham services 70 and 80 reverted to Brighton & Hove Bus & Coach Co., Worthing local service CL passed to Stagecoach and service 24 went back to Sussex Bus.

In July 1990 we see E307 FYJ, one of two former Cedar Travel (Chatfield) Ivecos operated by Richard Wright for his Cedar Travel 1990 venture. They were used on the two shoppers services to Horsham (70/80) under contract to Horsham District Council. (A. Lambert)

A Cedar Travel 1990 Bedford/Duple coach (FPJ 113V) appears to be operating service 23 from Cowfold to Brighton on 8 August 1991. (A. Lambert)

TWENTY-FOUR

ROYAL MAIL POSTBUS

Although a Royal Mail Postbus did not run into Horsham until 1994, the concept had been in existence for some considerable time, especially in very rural areas. The first experimental services in various parts of the country started in the mid-1960s, but it was the following decade that really saw their growth. The Postbus delivers and collects mail as its primary function and carries passengers when it does not clash with other bus services. Large numbers were introduced in Scotland, particularly the Highlands and Islands, where remote settlements with sparse populations meant they were a cost-effective solution for providing public transport where a conventional bus service could not be sustained. They were also introduced in smaller numbers in England and Wales – quite a few still run – although enthusiasm for them often depended on the attitude of the Post Office area managers. Postbuses have run under the auspices of varying controlling bodies: Post Office Corporation, Consignia and Royal Mail, the latter being the current operator. Two commenced service in Surrey in 1973, later being joined by two others.

Apart from Brown Motor Service's Friday route to Dorking, the village of Coldharbour was without public transport, an unfortunate situation especially as the only shop had closed in October 1972. The president of the local Women's Institute had heard about Postbuses at a conference and approached the Post Office Corporation to see whether they could provide one for Coldharbour. Eventually, there was a successful outcome with a service starting on 2 August 1973 under the control of the head postmaster at Redhill. The basic route was from Dorking to Coldharbour and Ockley. Certain journeys diverted to serve outlying farms and an early morning trip ran out as far as Oakwoodhill. On Friday mornings it was not supposed to pick up in Ockley and Coldharbour, to protect the conventional bus service. The Postbus replaced certain runs previously performed by ordinary mail vans, with drivers retrained to PSV standard. The timetable included lengthy periods of time between certain points on some journeys to allow for diversions to collect mail from pillar boxes and post offices and to deliver incoming mail to addresses in the area.

The first Ockley vehicles were eleven-seat Commer 2000LBs with Rootes body conversion in red and yellow livery. These were followed over the years by Freight Rover Sherpa 285s with Dormobile bodywork, a Leyland DAF 200 ten-seater and then a nine-seat LDV Pilot. The Ockley Postbus was unaffected by deregulation, and from 31 May 1994 the service was extended beyond Ockley in a circuit via Oakwoodhill, Walliswood and Forest Green, with some modest financial support from Surrey County Council.

The Horsham Postbus commenced on 31 May 1994, and was actually a car, being run with a red Peugeot 405 diesel estate with four passenger seats. It runs from Maplehurst via Nuthurst and Monks Gate, over the route of erstwhile Southdown service 80. There are two trips each way on Mondays to Fridays, but due to mail requirements there is one single trip on Saturdays at 10.00 a.m. from Maplehurst to Horsham. There is financial support from

West Sussex County Council. The vehicle is garaged at Horsham sorting office in Hurst Road, and the car was replaced with a new Peugeot 406 model in October 1998, which in turn was supplanted by a Peugeot Partner four-seater in February 2004 and a Vauxhall Combo in 2006.

The first vehicle on the Royal Mail Postbus from Maplehurst was actually a Peugeot 405 estate car! Seen in the Carfax before leaving on the late morning return journey, some time in the mid-1990s. (Author's collection)

In October 2006 the Postbus, by now a Vauxhall Combo registered EX06 YZN, waits in the Carfax to leave for Maplehurst. The service is officially designated 350 as shown on the vinyl on the bonnet. (Author's collection)

TWENTY-FIVE

HANDCROSS DISTRICT COMMUNITY BUS LTD

Since deregulation, several community bus schemes have been started in West Sussex to supplement one already running in the Harting area. These are Amberley & Slindon, from May 1988, Hurstpierpoint and Hassocks (January 1994), Midhurst (November 1994), Handcross (December 1994) and Selsey (September 1996). There was also a scheme at Arundel from 1999 until 2003. Unlike some community bus schemes, which operate on a flexible demand-responsive basis, these all have regular registered services with scheduled timetables and routes. Funded by West Sussex County Council (which supplies the minibuses) and other bodies, the drivers are local volunteers. The services generally complement existing conventional bus services but provide a number of unique links. Rather than full operators' licences, they run under community bus permits.

The Handcross District Community Bus waits to depart back home from Horsham. The Mercedes Benz 609D had a bodywork conversion by Pilcher Greene featuring a wheelchair tail-lift. Note the coach and horses logo. (Author's collection)

Service 451   Horsham—North Heath

Service 452   Horsham—Pondtail—Rusper—Ifield—Crawley

Service 453   Horsham—Steyning—Brighton

Service 454   Gomshall—Cranleigh—Horsham—Henfield—Brighton

Revised Timetables from Monday, 5th July 1982

For all bus and coach hire enquiries please contact:

> Tillingbourne Bus Co. Ltd.
> Little Mead
> Cranleigh
> Surrey GU6 8ND
> Telephone Cranleigh 6880

(This number will be changed to **CRANLEIGH 276880** when six figure numbers are introduced in Cranleigh later in the year).

Service 451 now via Coltsfoot Drive—Jackdaw Lane—Brook Street—Brook Road

The Handcross District Community Bus started on 5 December 1994 with four infrequent services to and from Handcross and surrounding villages, linking with Crawley, Haywards Heath and Horsham. The latter was served on Wednesdays with a route numbered 4 from Pease Pottage, Handcross, Staplefield, Slaugham, Warninglid, Plummers Plain and Lower Beeding. The previous bus service from Handcross to Horsham (Southdown 78) had been withdrawn in 1971. From 4 December 1995, it was diverted to serve Bolney and expanded to also run on Fridays. Horsham was also served on Mondays from 27 March 2000 by service 1 from Nymans Gardens, Balcombe, Handcross, Pease Pottage, Plummers Plain and Lower Beeding. The services commenced with M167 AGN, a Mercedes 609D with sixteen-seat bodywork by Pilcher Greene, featuring a wheelchair lift. This has now been replaced by a low-floor easy-access Optare Alero in a red livery.

Current operations comprise services 1 and 4 as described above with one journey each way and also a service 3 on Thursdays from Handcross and Pease Pottage to Broadfield and Crawley. The vehicle is also available for hire to the local community.

TWENTY-SIX

NOSTALGIABUS LTD

In the last fifteen years or so, a number of owners of vintage or heritage vehicles have obtained an operator's licence so that they can run them on a commercial basis for either private hire for special occasions or on scheduled bus services. One of these was Nostalgiabus Ltd, based in Mitcham in south London, which was to become one of the major players in this niche market.

In 1991 two bus enthusiasts got talking about using their privately owned vehicles so that they might pay for their upkeep. In November that year, the business was started by Roy Gould, a former train driver, who owned ex-London Transport twenty-six-seat Guy Special/ECW GS67, and by Jim MacNamara who owned RMC 1462 (an AEC Routemaster double-decker) and RF 136 (an AEC Regal IV single-decker), both of which had once been in London Transport's Green Line coach fleet.

From May 1995, the GS and the RF were used on rural summer Sunday leisure bus services 410 and 433, under contract to Surrey County Council, and such work was undertaken each year until 2000. The same local authority awarded Nostalgiabus a contract from September 1995 for bus service 808 on schooldays from Stoneleigh to Nonsuch High School at Cheam. Initially operated with RF 136, increased loadings meant that a fifty-three-seat AEC Reliance/Plaxton coach (RHC 51S) was used.

The Surrey County Council contract for the Sunday service between Horsham and Dorking via Broadbridge Heath, Warnham, Capel, Beare Green and Holmwood fell due for renewal from 29 June 1997. Traditionally run by London & Country and predecessors, and by then numbered 93, it passed to Nostalgiabus who normally used coach RHC 51 S, although on some occasions, a Routemaster double-decker with conductor appeared! Indeed, Nostalgiabus had built up a small collection of these famous buses, as well as some more modern double-deckers which were used on school services in south London that were contracted by London Buses. Between April and October from 1998, some journeys on service 93 were extended beyond Dorking to Leatherhead and Chessington World of Adventures, but the whole contract was terminated after 26 September 1999 as patronage was so poor that it no longer offered value for money for the council.

Nostalgiabus were successful in gaining more bus service contracts in Surrey over the following years, but more notably ran Routemasters on a substantial commercial service, in competition with London & Country service 406. Starting in December 1997, this was the 306 from Epsom to Kingston via Ewell, Tolworth and Surbiton on Mondays to Saturdays, but without subsidy became financially unsustainable and was withdrawn after 24 July 1998. However, another competitive service numbered 306 ran from Banstead via Epsom and Tadworth to Walton on the Hill from September 1999 until May 2002. Further bus service contract awards in Surrey saw six Optare Solo low-floor midibuses enter the fleet.

From 4 November 2002, Nostalgiabus Ltd (trading since May 2001 as Northdown Motor Services) returned to Horsham. They were awarded a contract by West Sussex County

At Horsham Station, Nostalgiabus AEC Reliance/Plaxton coach RHC 51S is operating the Sunday service 93 from Dorking under contract to Surrey County Council, around 1997 or 1998. (Author's collection)

Something of a rarity, but it happened from time to time, was the Nostalgiabus use of an AEC Routemaster on service 93, complete with conductor. Seen in December 1998, RMC 1462 was a former Green Line coach variant and had been preserved by Jim MacNamara, one of the firm's partners. (A. Murray)

Council for service 674 on schooldays from North Heath, Littlehaven and Roffey to Millais and Forest Schools, using a double-decker. This was part of a package of local school services which had been developed from those originally run by Tillingbourne Bus Co. and was taken over from Metrobus who had temporarily run it following the ending of operations by Aventa in April 2002.

Unfortunately, Nostalgiabus got into financial difficulties but was allowed to continue to trade from November 2000 by means of a 'company's voluntary arrangement'. Further money problems, coupled with uncertainty over premises, withdrawal of some contracts due to local authority cost savings, unreliability of the leased Optare Solos and a Traffic Commissioner's hearing over maintenance concerns, which saw a reduction in the number of vehicles authorised to be operated, all conspired to force the company out of business and it ceased trading after 19 December 2003.

TWENTY-SEVEN

C.J. CHATFIELD (COMPASS TRAVEL) & COMPASS TRAVEL (SUSSEX) LTD

Following the unfortunate break-up of Cedarbus in 1989, Chris Chatfield re-emerged in 1996 when he was granted an operator's licence, based once again in Worthing, running a selection of smaller-capacity buses. From small beginnings, he carefully expanded his new Compass Travel business so that he now has a portfolio of bus services covering much of West Sussex, and parts of Surrey as well, and as such is a major operator. Much of the growth in contracted bus service work has been due to Rural Bus Grant and Rural Bus Challenge funding, which West Sussex County Council has successfully obtained from the government. It was the collapse of Tillingbourne Bus Co. that saw Compass Travel active in a significant way in the Horsham area and the company has found a successful niche in the market to gain contracts not placed well enough to be attractive to major operators such as Stagecoach or Arriva.

From 8 May 1997 Chris obtained the contract from West Sussex County Council for service 71 on Thursdays from Steyning to Storrington via Washington, Ashington and Thakeham. From 1 April 1998, Compass Travel gained the contracts for the shoppers bus services from Shoreham to Horsham originally initiated by Horsham District Council and taken over from Brighton & Hove Bus & Coach Co. These were the 70 via Steyning, Storrington, Thakeham or West Chiltington, Coolham and Shipley (Wednesdays and Saturdays) and the 72 via Steyning, Partridge Green, West Grinstead, Maplehurst and Nuthurst (Tuesdays and Fridays).

From 1 November 1998, Arriva lost the contract to Compass Travel for the provision of service 63 on Sundays from Roffey to Cranleigh via Horsham, Slinfold, Bucks Green and Rudgwick (which continued until 25 March 2001 when it was regained by Arriva), while new services supported by West Sussex County Council through external funding were introduced on Mondays to Saturdays. These were the 73 from West Chiltington to Amberley Station via Thakeham, Storrington and Amberley village and the 100 – an hourly cross-country facility from Pulborough to Storrington, Steyning and Henfield. These offered a substantial increase in service in some rural areas over what had been provided for some years, and gave a number of new through-travel opportunities.

Bus service developments through 1999 and 2000 focussed on areas of West Sussex away from Horsham, although service 73 was restructured so that it was extended to run through to Horsham from Storrington via Coolham and Buckbarn from 7 June 1999. A number of Mercedes 811D or Mercedes Vario 0814 thirty-three-seaters entered the fleet, including the first of ten Mercedes 811Ds to be acquired from Nottingham City Transport between September 2000 and October 2001 These were partly to cater for new services in the Horsham area but also to replace some of Compass Travel's MCW Metroriders. In January 2001, the Compass Travel business was reconstituted as Compass Travel (Sussex) Ltd.

When Tillingbourne Bus Co. abruptly ceased trading, West Sussex County Council swiftly re-allocated some bus contracts to Compass Travel from 20 March 2001. These were services 55/65/75/95 from Horsham to Billingshurst, Petworth and Pulborough (Mondays to Saturdays), the 52 Horsham-Colgate-Lambs Green-Rusper circular (Tuesdays,

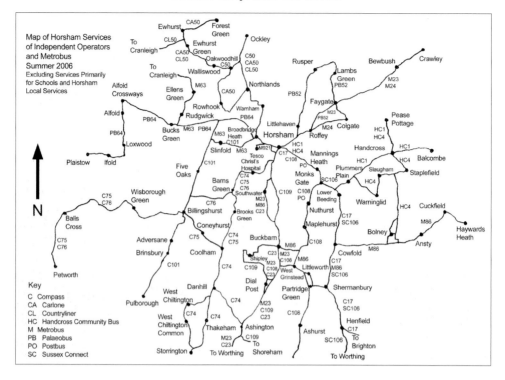

Fridays and Saturdays), the 57 Loxwood-Pulborough-Bignor-Duncton-Eartham-Chichester (Wednesdays), the 64 Plaistow-Loxwood-Alfold-Bucks Green-Horsham (Fridays) and the 84 Horsham-Slinfold-Billingshurst-Pulborough-Coldwaltham-Bury-Chichester (Wednesdays). Compass Travel were successful in recruiting several former Tillingbourne staff members and ran most of their Horsham operations from premises at Newhouse Farm, Upper Beeding. Vehicles were also based at Stane Street Nurseries, Codmore Hill, Pulborough.

Compass Travel was also successful in gaining a package of contracts for some mainly local Burgess Hill/Hassocks/Hurstpierpoint area bus services from 2 April 2001, previously run by Brighton & Hove Bus Co. These required the purchase of four new low-floor Dennis Dart SLF single-deckers with Alexander twenty-nine-seat bodywork. Compass Travel also acquired two Optare Metroriders in May 2001 from the erstwhile Tillingbourne Bus Co. fleet and two further similar buses which had been Optare Demonstration vehicles and, coincidentally, used by Tillingbourne earlier. Another former service of the latter company was reactivated under contract to Surrey County Council from 21 April 2001 – the 50 on Saturdays from Walliswood to Horsham via Oakwoodhill, Northlands, Warnham and Broadbridge Heath. This was diverted by popular request to also cover Ockley from 1 September 2001.

The short-term contracts for the former Tillingbourne services were replaced by substantive awards from 8 May 2001. Services 55, 65, 73, 75, 95 and also the original Thursday service 71 were replaced and expanded upon by means of four Rural Bus Grant-funded services, each running Mondays to Saturdays. The 73 and 74 combined to run hourly from Horsham to Christ's Hospital, Barns Green, Brooks Green, Coolham and Danhill, whence the 73 continued a two-hourly off-peak service to Thakeham, Storrington and Amberley Station and the 74 continued similarly to West Chiltington, Storrington and Ashington. The 75 and 76 combined to run hourly from Horsham to Needles Estate, Broadbridge Heath, Slinfold, Five Oaks and Billingshurst, whence 75 continued two-hourly to Adversane and Pulborough and 76 similarly to Wisborough Green, Kirdford, Balls Cross and Petworth. Between Horsham and Slinfold, the 75/76 supplemented hourly Arriva service 63.

MCW Metrorider F562 HPP joined the Compass fleet in October 1998 and is seen near Buckbarn on the A24 in February 1999 working service 70 from Shoreham and Steyning. (D. Stewart)

The church clock in Slinfold says 2.40 p.m. on a hot Sunday 1 August 1999, as Compass Travel's MCW Metrorider F133 YVP passes through the village on service 63 to Cranleigh, which on weekdays is operated by Arriva. (A. Murray)

On service 58, the shuttle to the RSPCA offices at Southwater is Compass Wadham Stringer-bodied Mercedes 811D M983 CYS, originally in the Nottingham City Transport fleet. Compass acquired ten Mercedes midibuses from that source. (Author's collection)

From the same date, services 70 and 72 were reorganised as service 108 (Shoreham-Steyning-Partridge Green-West Grinstead-Dial Post-Buckbarn-Maplehurst-Nuthurst-Horsham) on Wednesdays and service 109 (Shoreham-Steyning-Ashington-Dial Post-Shipley-Buckbarn-Horsham) on Saturdays, with one round trip on both.

Horsham service 52 was altered to run on Thursdays instead of Fridays from 5 November 2001, while service 64 was additionally introduced on Wednesdays and 84 on Fridays. From 4 September 2002 service 64 was diverted to run direct from Alfold Crossways to Bucks Green, omitting Tismans Common, while from 2 September 2002 services 57 and 84 were withdrawn when service 75 was extended from Pulborough to Coldwaltham, Bury and Chichester on Mondays to Fridays, thus reinstating the through bus link to the county town from Horsham. Compass Travel gained a contract from the RSPCA from 3 December 2001 to provide a service during peak hours and at lunchtime, Mondays to Fridays, from Horsham town centre to their new offices at Southwater. This was available to the general public as well as RSPCA employees and was numbered 58, but was withdrawn after 29 October 2004.

When Arriva closed their Crawley depot in April 2001 and withdrew their service network in that town (which was taken over by Metrobus), one of the few remaining services provided by Arriva (from Warnham depot) was the 23 from Horsham to Crawley via Roffey, Faygate and Bewbush. This was very much a shadow of the former intensity of service between the towns run by Arriva and their predecessors. This remnant of former days of glory (bearing in mind the titanic struggles between London Transport and Comfy Coaches and Hants & Sussex from the 1930s to the 1950s!) was finally withdrawn from 2 November 2002. However, Compass Travel decided to try a replacement Monday to Friday commercial service as West Sussex County Council surprisingly showed little interest due to budgetary constraints. Financial support was subsequently forthcoming from January 2003, while a Saturday service was restored from 30 August 2003. Two new Dennis Dart SLF/Plaxton low-floor single-deckers were obtained in April 2003 for operation on Horsham services 75 and 76 and further examples entered the fleet in subsequent years.

On 22 December 1981,
Compass Optare Metrorider
M440 AVG has just arrived
on Saturday service 109
from Shoreham complete
with Father Christmas and
seasonal decorations inside!
It was previously used by
Tillingbourne Bus Co. and
originated with Dereham
Coachways in Norfolk.
(J. Gaff Collection)

The manufacture of
Metroriders passed from
MCW to Optare. This
one had originally been a
demonstration/loan vehicle
and was acquired with
another in May 2001. T421
ADN works service 73 to
Storrington and Amberley
in November 2005.
(D. Stewart)

This former London
United Dennis Dart/
Plaxton Pointer J599
DUV is in Crawley in
July 2003 on service 23,
introduced in November
2002 when Arriva finally
withdrew from the
Horsham-Crawley route.
(D. Jones collection)

Typical of present-day Compass operations in Horsham is Dennis Dart SLF GX03 AZJ, new in April 2003. In November 2005 it is on service 76 to Petworth which is maintained with county council Rural Bus Grant funding. Behind it is the new Handcross Community Bus – an Optare Alero – which replaced the original Mercedes. (D. Stewart)

Further Rural Bus Challenge funding allowed Compass Travel to run some new and expanded services from 27 October 2003. Service 100 (Pulborough-Henfield) was extended to Burgess Hill, replacing previous service 37, but giving an enhanced hourly frequency. On Sundays, a two-hourly service was provided. This latter was interworked with a service 102 on Sundays providing a circular link from Storrington via Amberley, Bury, Coldwaltham and Pulborough back to Storrington. Finally, vehicles on service 100 worked through to a service 101 on Mondays to Saturdays between Pulborough and Billingshurst, supplementing service 75 over that section.

The contract for service 23 from Horsham to Crawley passed to Metrobus after 29 May 2004, while from 29 October that year, Rusper service 52 was withdrawn on Thursdays and Plaistow service 64 on Wednesdays. The section of service 75 between Pulborough and Chichester was renumbered 85 from 28 February 2005 and diverted to also serve Arundel, Westergate and Oving, replacing Stagecoach service 55 in that area. The May 2005 contract retendering programme in the Horsham area saw Compass Travel lose services 52 and 64 to Palaeobus, but they gained two Sunday services from Stagecoach. These were the 17 (Horsham-Cowfold-Henfield-Brighton) and the 23 (Horsham-Ashington-Findon-Worthing).

Thus, Compass Travel joined Arriva as major providers of bus services from Horsham. The Compass fleet then contained nearly fifty vehicles, smartly turned out in a white and maroon livery and by 2005 the bus network stretched from Chichester and Petworth in the west to Haywards Heath/Burgess Hill in the east, to Horsham and Horley to the north, and down to Worthing and Brighton on the coast.

However, from 28 May 2006 the operation of the services in the Haywards Heath/Burgess Hill area was assumed by Countryliner Sussex Ltd, together with a depot at Hickstead and eleven buses. The contract for services 100 and 102 on Sundays was lost to Stagecoach and changes were made to services into Horsham. The 73 was withdrawn and 74 diverted between Ashington and Storrington via Thakeham. The section of service 75 between Pulborough and Billingshurst was withdrawn in favour of service 101, which was extended from Billingshurst to Horsham via Five Oaks, Slinfold, Broadbridge Heath and Needles Estate. The management of services 100 and 101 also transferred to Countryliner Sussex, but only until 21 July 2006 when Compass Travel regained full control. The Petworth-Billingshurst-Horsham route was reorganised as services 75/76, all entering Horsham via Barns Green and Christ's Hospital, while journeys via Slinfold and Broadbridge Heath were replaced by the 101.

TWENTY-EIGHT

S.J. AYLING (SUSSEX COACHES)

Sam Ayling, of Sailor's Cross, Green Street, Shipley, was a bus driver who had previously worked for Tillingbourne Bus Co. He applied for an operator's licence in January 1998, which was granted in April, with vehicle parking at Rosier Farm Industrial Estate near Billingshurst. His first coaches were a Leyland Leopard and a Leyland Tiger, which were used on private hire and schools work.

A former Southdown (via Stagecoach Coastline) Leyland National 2 was acquired to coincide with the award of some local bus contracts by West Sussex County Council. These involved some funding through the Rural Bus Grant scheme. From 2 November 1998 some peak hour and school journeys were introduced over Tillingbourne route 52 from Faygate, Lambs Green and Rusper. Numbered 56, the journeys intended for general use continued via Littlehaven to Horsham town centre, while the schoolday journeys also covered Wimblehurst Park, Lambs Farm and Roffey on the way to Forest and Millais Schools. This was planned to provide some relief to Tillingbourne commercial service 51, which was deemed inadequate to cope with demand after the introduction of a quarter-fare scheme for students, but in reality it seemed to abstract patronage rather than enhance it overall.

An experimental Saturday service 57A was started on 7 November from Pulborough to Chichester via Fittleworth, Bignor, Sutton, Duncton, East Dean and Charlton and this was initially sub-contracted to Timetrak Passenger Transport Services of Shepperton, Middlesex, owned by John Appleford. Sam Ayling was also associated with that firm for a time. Sussex Coaches also gained the restored Saturday journeys on service 89 from Horsham via Warninglid, Bolney, Ansty and Cuckfield to Haywards Heath and on to Princess Royal Hospital and Franklands Village, that route gaining yet another operator!

From 1 February 1999 service 56 was reduced to just the school journeys, which were curtailed to start at Chennells Brook on the outskirts of Horsham and diverted to also serve Holbrook Corner and Bartholomew Way, as well as Beech Road and Falklands Drive in Roffey. Some positioning journeys for school contract vehicles were registered for public use as service 75 from Billingshurst to Horsham, travelling direct via Toat Hill towards Horsham but via Slinfold on the return. The afternoon journey was deregistered from 1 February 2000. A contract for a Monday to Saturday circular journey during the evening peak was awarded from 1 May 1999 over Arriva service 93 from Horsham town centre to Depot Road, Comptons Lane and the Oakhill area, which ran until 4 September that year. On 4 January 2000, service 56 was separated into two vehicle workings – the 56A covering the section from Chennells Brook to Littlehaven and the 56B covering Lambs Farm and Roffey. Service 57A was not successful and was withdrawn from 31 March 2001 when the contract for the Saturday service 89 passed to Arriva who already ran it on Mondays to Fridays.

Schoolday services 56A, 56B and 75 were withdrawn from 26 May 2001, being the last bus services to be operated to date by Sussex Coaches. However, a contract was obtained from

In April 2000, Sussex Coaches' ECW-bodied Bristol VRT XAP 638S is on the A272 between Ansty and Bolney, working service 89 from Haywards Heath. Originally a Southdown vehicle, it wears the livery of its intermediate owner – Brighton & Hove Bus Co. (A. Murray)

Sussex Coaches' Leyland Atlantean FBV 512W with ECW bodywork is positioning for Horsham school service 56 in June 1999. (A. Murray)

the RSPCA for a shuttle service to take their staff from Horsham town centre out to their new offices at Southwater and also to get them into town at lunchtime. This later passed to Compass Travel, who registered it as a public service numbered 58, as previously described.

The Sussex Coaches fleet has expanded since 1998, with a number of coaches including Leylands, DAFs, Volvos and a Scania. There have also been several double-deckers in use, including some Bristol VRs and a Leyland Atlantean. The fleet currently includes a fifty-one-seat Beaulas-bodied Iveco 391.E.12 bought new and a double-deck Plaxton-bodied DAF SB3000 coach. The Sussex Coaches livery is a very smart red with gold lettering. In 2003, the depot was moved to the Heveco Mushroom Growers' site at Thakeham.

TWENTY-NINE

METROBUS LTD

From small beginnings twenty-three years ago, Metrobus Ltd has seen rapid, careful and controlled expansion to become one of the most prolific bus companies in the south of England. Starting with six vehicles, it had seventy-three (including twenty coaches) in 1993 and now has around 350 buses, operating an extensive route network stretching from south London down to Brighton, including a number of high-profile and innovative services. Since September 1999 when it became part of one of the national transport groups, it has technically lost its independent status as defined in the parameters for this book. It was the astute approach by the founding directors to commercial opportunities and to the route tendering market that made Metrobus what it has become – a respected contractor to both London Buses and to several local authorities.

From the outset the quality ethic in terms of service performance and reliability, vehicle presentation and marketing, as well as the general air of professionalism surrounding its operations, were instilled by the directors in their staff, many of whom have served it for a long time. To properly record the activities of the company would demand a separate book, indeed one was published in 1994 covering the first ten years and a follow-up volume would be welcome. Metrobus has had three incarnations in the Horsham area and these need to be recorded along with a very brief sketch of its history.

Peter Larking and Gary Wood were the principal directors of Tillingbourne (Metropolitan) Ltd. This offshoot of the Cranleigh-based company was set up to run services in the Orpington/ Croydon area and spectacularly developed services between the two towns after both North Downs Rural Transport and Orpington & District Omnibuses had struggled to do so and then failed. Messrs Larking and Wood purchased the operations in their own right and from 24 September 1983 their new company, Metrobus Ltd, was launched. The depot at Green Street Green has been much enlarged into a facility which must be the envy of many operators.

Metrobus gained its first London bus contracts from 16 August 1986 – services 61 and 361 in the Orpington/Bromley area using thirteen former London Buses DMS-type Daimler Fleetline double-deckers. They went on to introduce their own commercial services as well as being awarded contracts for further routes in both Kent proper and the part of south-east London that the Post Office calls Kent. Throughout the 1990s several more London Buses contracts were secured for services focussing on Bromley, Woolwich, Lewisham, Eltham, Orpington and Croydon and it says much for the company's success that most were retained when they next fell due to be retendered. Metrobus are now one of the major contractors to London Buses (Transport for London).

The coaching side of the business was expanded with the purchase of Southland Coaches in October 1991, followed by Jason's Coaches in February 1993. However, it was decided to concentrate on bus work and the coach business was franchised in August 1998 to a new company – Southlands Travel Ltd based at Swanley. In July 1997 Metrobus took over

Former Eastbourne Dennis Dart with Wadham Stringer bodywork H908 DTP displaying the Metrobus East Surrey fleet name style used in the 1990s for non-London operations from Godstone depot. It is at Cowfold on service 86 in August 1999. (D. Stewart)

Leisurelink (Abacus Carriage Services Ltd) of Newhaven, owned by Cliff Jones. A depot was established at Lewes, trading as Metrobus (South Coast) and a portfolio of contracted services was run from it until July 2003 when the operation ceased.

More significant expansion had occurred on 2 June 1997 when Metrobus took over East Surrey Bus Services Ltd from Michael Walter, including a depot at South Godstone, twenty-three vehicles and twenty-three (mainly tendered) bus services in Kent, East Sussex, West Sussex and Surrey, featuring Sevenoaks, Tonbridge, Tunbridge Wells, Edenbridge, East Grinstead, Caterham and Redhill. However, Walter retained his associated firm – Cruisers – which moved to Redhill. The chosen local marketing name of Metrobus East Surrey was later dropped in favour of just the corporate Metrobus and further contract awards and commercial initiatives saw services expand to Haywards Heath, Uckfield, Crawley and other areas of east Surrey. In due course vehicles for certain London Buses contracts were relocated from Orpington to Godstone.

From 2 November 1998 Metrobus were awarded contracts from West Sussex County Council for two new Monday to Saturday services, funded by the Rural Bus Grant and restoring some long-vanished travel opportunities as well as some new ones. These were the 81 from Haywards Heath to East Grinstead via Ardingly, Turners Hill and Sharpthorne and the 86 from Haywards Heath to Horsham via Cuckfield, Ansty, Bolney, Cowfold, Partridge Green, West Grinstead, Dial Post and Southwater. Thus, the blue and yellow vehicles of Metrobus reached Horsham.

In 1999 Peter Larking and Gary Wood sold the company to the Go Ahead Group, which has substantial bus interests in various areas including London and Brighton as well as several important rail franchises, now including the Southern Railway, which serves West Sussex. This set the stage for yet further expansion of Metrobus, making it a major force in east Surrey and the Crawley area of West Sussex. Arriva took the decision to close its Crawley depot and to surrender the majority of its services (including the busy Crawley town network) from 31

In October 2002, representing Metrobus's second, but temporary, appearance in Horsham on schools services assumed after the ending of operations by Aventa that year, is B248 NVN, a Leyland Olympian/ECW previously owned by Arriva. (A. Murray)

March 2001. Complex negotiations between Arriva and Go Ahead culminated in the takeover by Metrobus of the Tinsley Lane premises in Crawley and some of the staff. As a small part of the whole deal the operation of service 86 into Horsham was transferred to Arriva and added to those run from the latter's Warnham depot.

Metrobus has become the dominant provider of bus services for Crawley, Gatwick Airport, Horley and East Grinstead. The breathless pace of expansion continued when on 21 April 2001 Arriva closed its Merstham depot, thus largely disappearing from the eastern flank of Surrey. The county council was obliged to invite tenders for Arriva's erstwhile network of trunk inter-urban services and also for the well-used services 430/435 running locally in the Redhill/Reigate area. Metrobus secured all of these, taking it as far north as Epsom and Sutton on a regular basis. The company ran its new services from both Godstone and Crawley, although Godstone has now been replaced by a new facility at Beddington near Croydon.

Metrobus made a reappearance in Horsham from 15 April 2002, when it stepped in on a short-term contractual basis to maintain local school services 651, 652, 661, 662, 674, 681 and 682 following the sudden demise of Aventa. The development of these services is recorded under the Aventa heading. This work was given up after 25 October that year when substantive contracts were awarded to other operators.

The company returned to Horsham when Stagecoach decided to withdraw its commercial service 2 on Mondays to Saturdays between Horsham and Worthing via Southwater, Ashington, Washington and Findon. Metrobus provided a replacement on a basic two-hourly frequency from 26 April 2004, after a vociferous campaign by bus users and local councillors to save this long-standing and important service. Some financial support was required from West Sussex County Council and the service was renumbered 23 in readiness for further developments from 1 June 2004.

The Worthing-Horsham service was then extended to Crawley to absorb Compass Travel's route 23. An additional two-hourly service 24 was introduced between Horsham and Crawley

Resplendent with the latest
Metrobus logo is P725 RYL, a
Dennis Dart SLF/Plaxton Pointer,
once in the London Central fleet.
On 25 November 2005 it is in
Horsham on service 23 en route
from Crawley to Worthing.
(D. Stewart)

The new apartments on the site of the site of the King & Barnes brewery form a backdrop
for this 2005 view of Metrobus T310 SMV, another variant of a low-floor Dennis Dart. It is
on the free shuttle service 921 between Horsham town centre and the Broadbridge Health
Tesco store. (D. Stewart)

but running via Colgate between Roffey and Faygate. This move gave Colgate its best level of
service for a considerable time and restored an hourly link between Horsham and Crawley. Also,
the contract for service 86 (Horsham-Cowfold-Haywards Heath) was regained from Arriva.

The contract for the network of free services to the Tesco store at Broadbridge Heath was
won at the expense of Crawley Luxury Coaches from 29 November 2004. These routes were
then registered for general public use. Metrobus operate the frequent link on Mondays to
Fridays from Horsham town centre themselves (service 921) but have sub-contracted those
from the outlying areas, which run one or two days a week, to Countryliner of Guildford.

From 28 May 2006 Metrobus gained the contract for two Sunday services at the expense
of Arriva, with one bus operating service 63 from Horsham to Cranleigh via Slinfold, Bucks
Green and Rudgwick and service 98 from Horsham to various parts of Roffey via Littlehaven
and Lambs Farm Road. Coming right up to date, Horsham received a direct bus link with
Gatwick Airport from 7 July 2007. Metrobus service 200 now operates hourly, seven days a
week, via North Heath, Roffey, Faygate, Bewbush, Ifield and Manor Royal Industrial Area.

THIRTY

AVENTA PASSENGER LOGISTICS LTD

In December 2000 an application for an operator's licence was made by Wingcrest Ltd, trading as Aventa, initially for three vehicles to be authorised. This was granted the following month but before operations started the licence was transferred into the name of Aventa Passenger Logistics Ltd in February 2001. The company's base was at the Gatwick Coach Centre, Old Brighton Road, Lowfield Heath – adjacent to Gatwick Airport. Originally set up as a coach hire brokerage business, the directors of Aventa were John Kateley and Peter Evans. Three Eos E180Z coaches were acquired for use on private hire and airport-related work.

When Tillingbourne Bus Co. abruptly ceased trading, West Sussex County Council awarded temporary contracts from 20 March 2001 to cover two of that company's Horsham school services (62/63). Aventa acquired three ECW-bodied Leyland Olympian double-deckers, together with a Leyland National Mk2 single-decker. At weekends these were used on railway replacement services when trains were not running due to engineering work on the line.

One of the double-deckers was also used from 28 April 2001 on a service X25 to Chessington World of Adventures and Thorpe Park from Crawley, Horley and Redhill. This was marketed as the 'Adrenalin Express' and operated at weekends, Bank Holiday Mondays and daily during the school holidays for the 2001 season.

Aventa secured the contracts for a package of seven school services around Horsham from 4 June 2001 when the county council expanded the original facilities, available on erstwhile Tillingbourne Bus Co. services 58, 59, 62 and 63 and also Sussex Coaches services 56A and 56B. New services 651, 652, 661, 662, 674, 681 and 682 ran variously to Forest, Millais and Tanbridge House Schools from residential areas such as North Heath, Bartholomew Way, Littlehaven, Lambs Farm, Roffey, Pondtail Road and Merryfield Drive. In addition, some school work was obtained in Surrey and some more coaches acquired.

Partly as a way of utilising buses during the day between school journeys and also because they thought they could offer a more reliable and good value service to the public, Aventa decided to compete with Arriva on local services around Horsham from 15 December 2001. Under the guidance of Aventa's operations manager Paul Churchman, registrations were made for services on Mondays to Saturdays to the major residential areas covered by Arriva.

Services 10 and 11 each ran hourly from Southwater into Horsham town centre, with service 10 then taking a loop via Depot Road, Comptons Lane and the Oakhill area east of Horsham and service 11 a western loop via Hurst Road, Redford Avenue, The Common, Greenway and Merryfield Drive, before both proceeded back into town and to Southwater. Service 14 operated every half hour to and from the town centre via Roffey, South Holmes Road, Beech Road, Lambs Farm, Littlehaven, Bartholomew Way, Holbrook Corner and North Heath, while the 15 (at a similar frequency) worked around the reverse of service 14, except that it covered Wimblehurst Park rather than Holbrook Corner. During the evening a hybrid hourly service 12 worked from Southwater to Roffey via the town centre and Lambs

On one of Aventa's Horsham town services in competition with Arriva is Leyland National 2 HHH 373V, in anonymous overall white livery, in December 2001. (D. Stewart)

Aventa used three ECW-bodied Leyland Olympians in Horsham on schools and town services, including A154 UDM, which originated with Crosville and, after Aventa, was used by Nostalgiabus. (Author's collection)

Three Plaxton Pointer-bodied Dennis Darts, once used by Armchair Transport of Brentford, turned up on lease to Aventa for Horsham town services. This view outside Horsham Station shows P28 MLE on service 15 which covered North Heath and Roffey on 16 March 2002. (A. Murray)

Farm. Each daytime service had gaps in the timetable while the buses covered the school journeys and the morning journey on service 674 was amalgamated with a service 15 trip, which was diverted via Millais and Forest Schools.

To supplement the fleet, Aventa leased three Dennis Dart/Plaxton Pointer thirty-seven-seat buses previously used by Armchair Transport of Brentford and these were given a livery of white with blue and grey swirls. Also taken on hire were some MCW Metrobus double-deckers.

It was fairly predictable that a war of words and fares broke out between Aventa and Arriva. Aventa opted for a 70p single fare, which compared well with Arriva's £1.10 from Roffey or Southwater to Horsham, but the latter responded with a return ticket for the cost of a single fare and reduced the price of their seven day Horsham traveller ticket. To launch their new services Aventa offered free travel for children and senior citizens.

However, competition with the mighty Arriva was no easier for Aventa than those who had previously taken on London & Country in Crawley and Horsham. Aventa fares policy became unsustainable and they ran into difficulties after a delay in being able to claim their fuel duty rebate, at a time when costs in the bus industry were rising faster than general inflation. It was also hard to secure customer loyalty when people will just get on the first bus that comes along. There were many instances of buses from the rival companies following each other with both being virtually empty. This showed that in Horsham at least there was still insufficient business to warrant competition.

Inevitably, Aventa took the decision at very short notice to abandon their services and resign from their school contracts from 12 April 2002. Twelve staff were made redundant and the buses were disposed of. The county council arranged for Metrobus to take up the contracts for the school services, but took no action in respect of the other routes which were already covered by Arriva in any case.

It was to be only three months later in July 2002, when Aventa ceased trading entirely. The depot near Gatwick is now used by Flights Hallmark Ltd; this company is described later.

THIRTY-ONE

CARLONE BUSES

It has already been recorded that when Gastonia Coaches Ltd suspended the operation of buses and coaches in 1984, part of the business was carried on by Martin Noakes. This comprised a sweet shop in High Street, Cranleigh and a taxi business run under the name Gastonia Chauffeur Cars, using cars and three Ford Transit minibuses previously owned by Gastonia Coaches. Although these activities were formally transferred to Noakes's new company Carlone Ltd on 18 December 1985, his re-emergence as a bus service provider saw the restricted operator's licence being in the name of M. Noakes, until April 1987 when an operator's licence in the name of Carlone Ltd was obtained to coincide with the takeover of three Ford Transit twelve-seaters and the business of Collier & Stone of Chilworth.

A restricted operator's licence allows the holder of a taxi licence to run scheduled local bus services with taxis. From 27 October 1986 Surrey County Council awarded Noakes contracts for three services which were operated with various cars and minibuses, including an eight-seat diesel Land Rover County Estate fitted with a roof-mounted luggage container and a telephone. Service 533 ran from Cranleigh to Dorking via Ewhurst, Forest Green and Ockley on Fridays and also into Dorking from Ranmore. From May 1981 this was curtailed to start at Ewhurst and was diverted to cover Walliswood and Mayes Green and still runs today. Service 588 provided a peak-hour link on Mondays to Fridays from Cranleigh, Ewhurst, Forest Green and Holmbury St Mary to Gomshall and Shere, where connections were available for Guildford. This was withdrawn in 1990 but the third service, 599 from Holmbury St Mary to Cranleigh and Guildford on Thursdays via Forest Green and Ewhurst, also still operates and additionally covers Walliswood, Smithwood Common and Wonersh. All of these were designed to replace facilities which had not been retained by Tillingbourne Bus Co. on a commercial basis at the time of deregulation.

In the ensuing fifteen years or so, Carlone went on to build up a portfolio of mainly contracted, infrequent, modest but socially valuable bus services in various parts of Surrey including into Godalming, Haslemere, Guildford and the surrounding areas. Several large coaches were owned in the period 1988-1993 for school contracts and this work has continued to be important, with a large number of minibus and taxi contracts for both mainstream pupils and for children with special educational needs. Some of the bus services are cost-effectively dovetailed around the school work.

Over the years many small vehicles – typically sixteen-, twenty- and twenty-five-seaters – have been owned, some of which are fitted with wheelchair tail lifts. Vehicles used on the bus services have included Ford Transits, LDV Sherpas and Convoys, Iveco 49.10s, as well as other assorted types. Six- or seven-seat people-carriers or taxis have also been used on some of the quieter journeys.

Carlone obtained premises at Wagstaff's in Catteshall Lane, Godalming and when Martin and Maddy Noakes bought Tom Brady's old house next to the garage in Forest Green in

Representative of the many and varied minibuses in the Carlone fleet is P177 EUJ, an LDV, just arrived in Horsham on service 50 from Forest Green and Walliswood. (Author's collection)

1988, some vehicles were kept there too. In the early 1990s they moved to live on a houseboat near Chertsey and the focus of the business partially shifted northwards with school contracts and bus services in north Surrey. Noakes then moved to another houseboat moored on the Basingstoke Canal at New Haw, before relocating to Wraysbury, near Staines. The principal depot is now at Warren Yard at Lyne, where there is a workshop facility, replacing that at Godalming.

As far as the Horsham area is concerned, Carlone Buses (the name Gastonia Chauffeur Cars was dropped in terms of bus service marketing) arrived on 27 March 2001. Surrey County Council awarded a contract to Carlone for a replacement for the Tuesday and Friday off-peak shoppers' journeys on withdrawn Tillingbourne Bus Co. service 50. This links Walliswood with Horsham via Oakwoodhill, Ockley and Northlands, and serving Forest Green, Ewhurst, Rowhook and Warnham additionally on Tuesdays only. Thus, as in several other cases, this little-known bus company is providing a rural lifeline service to a small number of mainly elderly people which offers good value to the taxpayer. Although Arriva runs the morning peak-hour journey on service 50, it is interesting to note that independent companies have maintained most of the service from the 1920s through to the present day.

THIRTY-TWO

SOUTHDOWN PSV LTD

Steve Swain, who lived in Horsham, ran a bus and coach dealer business known as Fleetmaster. Supplying both new and used vehicles to operators around the country and loaning vehicles to those in need, premises were occupied at Rosier Farm Industrial Estate near Billingshurst and subsequently at Silverwood Business Complex, Snow Hill, near Copthorne on the Surrey/West Sussex border between Crawley and East Grinstead. In September 2001 an operator's licence was granted for three vehicles in the name of Fleetmaster Bus & Coach Ltd. Rail service replacement work was carried out at weekends.

When Fleetmaster could no longer trade due to financial difficulties, Swain, in partnership with Peter Larking, set up Southdown PSV Ltd in April 2002. This should not be confused with the Southdown of old, or even the current legal entity of Stagecoach's local buses!

When Southdown PSV won the contracts for the majority of the Horsham school services from November 2002 they mainly used Leyland Lynx single-deckers, but also appearing was this former London MCW Metrobus EYE 321V, seen here in Lambs Farm Road in Littlehaven. (A. Murray)

Peter Larking had been a founder of Metrobus Ltd and left that company after concluding a sale on very favourable personal terms to the Go Ahead group. Using the Snow Hill site, Southdown PSV was formed to carry out bus and coach sales, to offer contracted engineering support and to run bus services locally, including rail replacements. A new operator's licence granted in July 2002 replaced that of Fleetmaster. In January 2003, Simon Stanford was made engineering director.

Bus service 646 on school days from Edenbridge to East Grinstead via Dormansland for Kent County Council started on 5 September 2002, as a prelude to the award of contracts for most of the Horsham area school services (651, 652, 662, 681, 682 and the late afternoon journey on 674) from 4 November. These replaced temporary contractual arrangements held by Metrobus. At the same time, the remainder of service 674 passed from Metrobus to Northdown Motor Services and service 661 to Coastline – what is now the other 'Southdown'!

HANTS & SUSSE**X**
MOTOR SERVICES, LTD.

LISS & DISTRICT OMNIBUS CO., Ltd.
Telephone: LISS 161

F. H. KILNER (Transport) LTD.
Telephone: HORSHAM 606

SUNBEAM COACHES (Loxwood) LTD.
Telephone: LOXWOOD 318

SOUTHSEA ROYAL BLUE PARLOUR COACHES LTD.

TRIUMPH COACHES LTD.
Telephone: PORTSMOUTH 31468, 32063, 32528

Head Office and Enquiries:

66, NORTH STREET, EMSWORTH, Hants.
Telephone: EMSWORTH 415

All communications should be addressed to Registered Office:

SOUTH LEIGH ROAD, EMSWORTH, Hants.
Telephone: EMSWORTH 415

B. S. WILLIAMS
Director and General Manager

As well as using vehicles drawn from the sales stock for short periods, Southdown PSV used various Leyland Lynx single-deckers on the school services, as well as a Leyland National Greenway (a former London General Red Arrow vehicle) and an MCW Metrobus Ltd double-decker. These carried a dark blue, turquoise and white livery.

In January 2005 Southdown PSV acquired two vehicles from Red Baron and took over the latter's contract for the remainder of service 674, while 28 February saw the acquisition of part of the Connexions Europe business, including a shuttle service from the Europa Hotel at Maidenbower near Crawley, to Gatwick Airport. However, Southdown PSV was unsuccessful in retaining the contracts for the Horsham school services when they fell due for retendering by West Sussex County Council and they passed to other operators from 6 June 2005. Southdown has since gone on to run several bus services in east Surrey for Surrey County Council from April 2006.

THIRTY-THREE

RED BARON TRANSPORT SERVICES LTD

In 2003 Tom Cunnington, a director and manager of Nostalgiabus Ltd, left the company and took up alternative employment. He also owned several of the vehicles used by Nostalgiabus and applied for an operator's licence, in the name of Red Baron Transport Services Ltd, from an address in London W4.

With the collapse of Nostalgiabus just before Christmas 2003, Cunnington approached West Sussex County Council to ascertain if they wished to reassign the contract for service 674 from North Heath, Littlehaven and Roffey to Forest and Millais Schools. Nostalgiabus had been out-stationing a double-decker in Horsham for this job, driven by a locally based employee.

From 5 January 2004 Red Baron took over the contract and the driver and used former Nostalgiabus Leyland Olympian A154 UDM. It was based at the transport depot in Langhurstwood Road, east of Warnham Station, along with an Optare Metrorider.

Unfortunately the regular driver, who administered the operation, was obliged to give up the job on medical advice. Therefore, Tom Cunnington decided to sell the vehicles to Southdown PSV and the latter took over the contract from the start of the school term in January 2005.

Former Crosville Leyland Olympian A154 UDM is shown here in the ownership of Red Baron on 19 November 2004. It is in North Heath Lane at the start of service 674 to Forest and Millais Schools. (A. Hamer)

THIRTY-FOUR

COUNTRYLINER COACH HIRE LTD

The round of contract retendering undertaken by West Sussex County Council for Spring 2005 saw three extra operators active in Horsham. One of these was Countryliner, based at Slyfield Industrial Estate in Guildford, which had started running the free services connecting various Sussex and Surrey villages with the Broadbridge Heath Tesco store from 29 November 2004.

Colin Brands acquired the Guildford-based Countryliner coaching operations of Arriva from 28 August 1998. The latter's predecessor, British Bus, had taken over the coach and bus operations of ABC Taxis (J. Lambley) Ltd, which traded as Blue Saloon, in April 1996 and had used the Horsham Buses Ltd licence for the vehicles acquired. Colin Brands had worked for the London & Country group since 1990 when they purchased his bus service in Crawley. In 1998 his initial fleet consisted of fifteen coaches and two buses.

In the following years, Brands's interest in Countryliner was progressively acquired by other directors including Bob Hodgetts and Roger Belcher, who had also held management posts with British Bus. Contracts for some of the former Tillingbourne Bus Co. services radiating from Woking were obtained from Surrey County Council commencing on 28 July 2001. When Arriva withdrew their service 479 from Guildford to Epsom via Leatherhead in February 2002, Countryliner took it over on a mainly commercial basis. Since then a substantial portfolio of contracted bus services in west Surrey has been built up, centred on Guildford and Woking, extending as far as Farnborough, Addlestone, Haslemere and Farnham. These are supplemented by school contracts, private hire, free services to Tesco at Brooklands near Weybridge and rail replacement work at weekends.

By 2005 the fleet strength was upward of forty vehicles, mainly in a white and lime green livery, operating from two sites at Slyfield under two licences – Countryliner Coach Hire Ltd and Countryliner Ltd. Of the buses, the low-floor Dennis Dart SLF predominates, while the coach fleet includes a number of the new Mercedes Touro models.

From 31 May 2005 Countryliner acquired the contract for Horsham local service 61 from Arriva who had run it since the demise of Tillingbourne Bus Co. in March 2001. This operates hourly between school times on Mondays to Saturdays on a circular route from the town centre via Ashleigh Road, Pondtail Road, Holbrook Corner, Cook Road and North Heath Lane. Arriva ran the 61 as part of the overall twenty-minute interval service to the North Heath area, but, on the loss of the contract, they added a third hourly journey on service 51 to compensate. From 6 June, Countryliner took over the contract for local school services 662 and 681 from Southdown PSV and, together with service 61, are operated with one vehicle, initially a high-capacity Dennis Lance single-decker. In addition, the vehicle for service 61 on Saturdays also operates one round trip on service 50 to Horsham from Cranleigh, Walliswood, Oakwoodhill, Ockley and Warnham on behalf of Compass Travel Bus.

From 13 January 2006 the bus operations of RDH Services of Ditchling Common, near Hassocks were acquired under the auspices of Countryliner Sussex Ltd. Services run

The most regular performer on service 61 from Horsham to the North Heath area since the contract was gained by Countryliner in May 2005 is J116 WSC, a forty-seven-seat Alexander-bodied Dennis Lance. The high capacity is needed for schools services 662 and 681 which the bus also operates. (D. Stewart)

On days when there are no school commitments, Countryliner uses one of their Dennis Dart SLF/Plaxton Pointer buses on service 61, as exemplified here by W364 ABD in Hurst Road, Horsham. (A. Murray)

in both East and West Sussex, radiating from Burgess Hill, Uckfield, Haywards Heath and Lewes, including local routes in the latter two towns. RDH Services, owned by Terry Hawthorne and Derek Hunnisett, retained their coaching activities. The purchase brought the total Countryliner fleet up to sixty vehicles. The operating base was later moved from Ditchling Common to Piltdown, near Uckfield.

This was followed from 28 May 2006 by the acquisition of the Burgess Hill/Haywards Heath area services and eleven buses from Compass Travel. The deal was to include the management of service 100 Burgess Hill to Pulborough and the linked hourly service 101 onwards to Billingshurst. The 101 was extended from Billingshurst to Horsham via Slinfold, Broadbridge Heath and Needles Estate, as a replacement for erstwhile Compass Travel services 75/76 over that section. However, in the event, Compass Travel regained

Sussex Bus faretables

SINGLE FARES

COWFOLD	COWFOLD					
West Grinstead	40	West Grinstead				
PARTRIDGE GREEN	40	30	PARTRIDGE GREEN			
Ashurst	50	60	30	Ashurst		
STEYNING	80	80	70	40	STEYNING	
HENFIELD	60	60	50	50	50	HENFIELD
Small Dole & UB	80	80	70	70	30	40 Small Dole & UB
WORTHING	150	150	140	140	100	100 100 WORTHING

RETURN FARES

COWFOLD	COWFOLD					
West Grinstead	70	West Grinstead				
PARTRIDGE GREEN	70	50	PARTRIDGE GREEN			
Ashurst	80	100	50	Ashurst		
STEYNING	140	140	120	70	STEYNING	
HENFIELD	100	100	80	80	80	HENFIELD
Small Dole & UB	140	140	120	120	50	70 Small Dole & UB
WORTHING	230	230	200	200	150	150 140 WORTHING

Reduced rates for children and OAPs

Sussex Bus

**Bridge Garage
Henfield Road
Cowfold
West Sussex
RH13 8DT
Telephone:
Cowfold 799**

Evening Argus

Right Up Your Street

full control of the 100/101 from 21 July 2006. An additional licence in the name of Countryliner Buses Ltd was subsequently applied for to cover operations from the former Compass Travel depot at Bolney Grange Industrial Estate at Hickstead, although a site at Burgess Hill is now used.

There was further expansion from 30 October 2006 when Countryliner opened an outstation at Heathfield in East Sussex following the award of contracts to run services 304/305 from Tunbridge Wells to Hastings via Hawkhurst and Battle (taken over from Arriva) and service 355 from Heathfield to Battle previously run by Autopoint. In 2007 Countryliner secured contracts for local services in Petersfield in Hampshire as well as for routes connecting Petersfield with Midhurst and Chichester.

THIRTY-FIVE

CENTRAL PARKING SYSTEM OF UK LTD (CENTRA) & FLIGHTS HALLMARK LTD (SUSSEX CONNECT)

Flights Hallmark is a diverse substantial bus and coach company with several operating bases, but is relatively little known in West Sussex. Until recently its operations formed the majority of the United Kingdom public transport activities of Central Parking System (CPS). The latter is a North American-based multinational corporation, which specialises in car-parking facilities and the decriminalised enforcement of on-street parking in many towns and cities.

In 1992 CPS started operating around Heathrow Airport on shuttle services between car parks and the passenger terminals and then on shuttles for British Airways aircrew and other staff. They also ran a fleet of transfer minibuses on behalf of Europcar car rental. Similar airport-related activities were then established at Luton, Bristol and Newcastle.

Trading as Centra Passenger Services, CPS appointed Paul Churchman in 2002, who had been involved with Aventa in Horsham. Two double-deckers were acquired in early 2003 for use on rail service replacement work. A luxury coaching business started in summer 2003 and a prestigious private hire customer base was established. The acquisition of Thamesbus Ltd on 28 October 2003 brought a number of contracted bus services in Surrey and premises at New Haw to supplement those already established at Heathrow and on the outskirts of Hounslow.

In January 2004 a base was opened at Lowfield Heath, next to Gatwick Airport (which had been used by Aventa), from where hotel to airport shuttle services were operated. Added to the CPS portfolio were the services of Local Link of Stansted, Essex in March 2004 and the twenty-two luxury and executive model coaches of Hallmark Coaches on 29 July that year. This brought more prestigious corporate private charter work and a depot at Coleshill near Birmingham. The old-established operator Mitcham Belle, owned by the Wilde family and in financial difficulties, was acquired from the receiver on 28 August 2004. This purchase brought premises at Mitcham and Croydon, seventy-one buses, some minibuses and coaches and contracts for six London Buses services in south London and some school contracts for the London Borough of Sutton.

Finally, from 11 October 2004, CPS acquired Flights Coaches of Birmingham from the Dunn Line group of Nottingham. A separate operator's licence – Dunn Line (Flights) Ltd – was perpetuated for the fleet of twenty-six coaches and thirteen buses and the acquisition gave CPS another 109 staff as well as twenty chauffeur-driven cars, bringing the combined CPS operation to 300 vehicles and 450 employees. A mainly red livery with some blue and yellow striping was adopted for Centra's south of England bus fleet.

So to Horsham, where it won the contracts for the operation of two double-deckers from its Gatwick base on school services 651 and 674, taking over from Southdown PSV from 6 June 2005. One of the buses also performs on service 106 which has one round trip on Mondays to Fridays from Mannings Heath, Cowfold, Partridge Green, Henfield and Steyning to Worthing. This was acquired from Stagecoach from 31 May 2005.

BROWN MOTOR SERVICES.

CAPEL, OCKLEY and HORSHAM,
Monday, Wednesday and Saturday.

	a.m.		p.m.	p.m.
Forest Green ...	8.45	Capel ...	7.20	9.25
Ockley ...	8.55	Ockley Station	7.25	9.30
Ockley Station ...	9.0	Ockley ...	7.30	9.35
Capel ...	9.5	Forest Green	7.40	9.45
			N.S.	S.O.

	a.m.	p.m.	p.m.	p.m.
Capel	9.20	1.20	4.20	7.20
Ockley Station ...	9.25	1.25	4.25	7.25
Ockley Village Hall ...	9.30	1.30	4.30	7.30
Kennels Cross Roads ...	9.37	1.37	4.37	7.37
Northlands Corner ...	9.41	1.41	4.41	7.41
Broadbridge Heath ...	9.53	1.53	4.53	7.53
Horsham Carfax ...	10.0	2.0	5.0	8.0
				S.O.

N.S.—Not Saturdays.   S.O.—Saturdays only.

	p.m.	p.m.	p.m.	p.m.
Horsham Carfax ...	12.30	3.30	6.30	8.45
Broadbridge Heath ...	12.37	3.37	6.37	8.52
Northlands Corner ...	12.51	3.51	6.51	9.4
Kennels Cross Roads ...	12.55	3.55	6.55	9.8
Ockley Village Hall ...	1.2	4.2	7.2	9.15
Ockley Station ...	1.7	4.7	7.7	9.20
Capel	1.12	4.12	7.12	9.25
				S.O.

S.O.—Saturdays only.

Fred Holmes, The Printer, 17, North Street, Horsham.

In Summer 2005 CPS decided to concentrate on its core activities and in readiness for a sale of the majority of operations a new operator's licence was obtained in the name of Flights Hallmark Ltd. In August 2005 all Flights Hallmark bus and coach activities (excepting the former Mitcham Belle operations and car park shuttles at Heathrow which remained owned by and licensed to Central Parking) passed to Rotala PLC. Flights Hallmark initially continued to use the Centra trading name but in October 2005 rebranded their southern England bus service operations as either Surrey Connect, Sussex Connect or Hotel Connect. This coincided with expansion of bus service work in Surrey which lasted until June 2007 when the New Haw depot was closed, but it remains to be seen if there is growth in the Horsham area.

THIRTY-SIX

C.N. ASLETT (PALAEOBUS)

The third new bus operator in Horsham in 2005 was Charlie Aslett's Palaeobus, based at the old cement works at Beeding, near Shoreham. Prior to starting operations in April 2003 when a three-vehicle operator's licence was granted, Aslett was transport manager for the erstwhile White Rose Travel based at Thorpe in Surrey. After driving for Compass Bus and a local coach company, he decided to earn some money with the two Leyland Nationals he had bought for preservation, by undertaking private hire, rail service replacement work and by working for other operators. Several more Leyland Nationals were purchased including examples that were once with Southdown, Alder Valley and London Country. The ones for service are mainly painted all-over dark green with a logo of an ammonite of the type excavated in Worthing in the 1930s.

One of the Nationals carried a black livery with green lettering and was used from April 2004 on services from Worthing town centre to surrounding areas on Friday and Saturday nights, to get people home after a night out at various pubs and clubs. Marketed as Niterider, each journey carried two security guards! It had to be withdrawn after a short time following opposition from the local taxi trade but restarted again and ran until January 2005. After that, Palaeobus was left with a couple of school contracts.

One Leyland National has found a use on a number of Horsham area bus services for which Palaeobus has gained the contract from West Sussex County Council. From 31 May 2005, two former Compass Bus services were operated – 52 Horsham circular via Roffey, Faygate, Lambs Green and Rusper on Tuesdays and Saturdays (no longer via Colgate due to Metrobus service 24) and 64 to Horsham from Plaistow, Loxwood, Alfold and Bucks Green on Fridays, to which a commercial Saturday service has been added. At school times Palaeobus run services 652 and 682 and the late afternoon journey on service 674, taking all three over from Southdown PSV. These serve Millais and Tanbridge House Schools.

So, why Palaeobus? The afore-mentioned fossilised ammonite had been titled 'Dinocerous Worthingencis'. Charlie Aslett studied palaeogeology at university and has lived in Worthing. Also *palaeo* is 'ancient' in Greek! For a fleet of Leyland Nationals, reawakening memories of the 1970s, it therefore seemed appropriate.

We end with a blast from the past! This is not the 1970s, but November 2005. Palaeobus uses a number of Leyland Nationals on its Horsham services including former Southdown BCD 802L. They carry a dark green livery – note the ammonite logo. (D. Stewart)

This Leyland National (YPL 388T) was once in the London Country fleet but passed through a number of hands before arriving at Palaeobus. In early autumn 2005 it is at Plaistow on Friday/Saturday service 64 to Horsham via Loxwood and Alfold, the last remnant of a route originally started by George Weller in 1929. (A. Murray)

APPENDIX I
OUTLINE OF MAJOR BUS GROUP COMPANIES SERVING HORSHAM

SOUTHDOWN MOTOR SERVICES LTD

Affiliated to British Electric Traction (BET) from formation. Between 1928-1942, BET interest vested in Tilling & British Automobile Traction Ltd. From November 1928, one third share held by Southern Railway, nationalised 1 January 1948 through the British Transport Commission. Remainder nationalised 14 March 1968 with sale of BET interest to Transport Holding Co., which was replaced by the National Bus Co. (NBC) on 1 January 1969. Sold to its management team on 21 October 1987 as part of the division and privatisation of the NBC. Sold to the Stagecoach Group 16 August 1989. Company renamed Sussex Coastline Buses Ltd 2 April 1992, trading as Stagecoach Coastline. Operator's licence reverted to name of Southdown Motor Services Ltd in July 2003 and trading name subsequently changed to Stagecoach in the South Downs.

ALDERSHOT & DISTRICT TRACTION CO. LTD

Affiliated to British Automobile Traction from formation. Followed path of Southdown 1928 to 1969. Merged with Thames Valley Traction Co. Ltd from 1 January 1972 to form the Thames Valley & Aldershot Omnibus Co. Ltd, trading as Alder Valley. Company split into two from 1 January 1986, with former A&D area being covered by Alder Valley South Ltd. Sold and privatised 1 November 1987 to Frontsource Ltd, owned by Robert Beattie. Sold to Q-Drive Ltd 19 November 1988, which was owned by Len Wright, David Stewart and Richard Soper. Renamed Alder Valley Ltd 1 January 1989. When Stewart wished to leave the business, Alder Valley activities based on Guildford, Woking and Cranleigh were sold to Drawlane Plc on 15 December 1990. Drawlane used a subsidiary company Randomquick Ltd, which traded as Alder Valley West Surrey and was managed by London & Country. Company and trading name became Guildford & West Surrey Buses Ltd 27 January 1992. Remainder of Alder Valley Ltd sold 26 October 1992 by Q-Drive to Stagecoach South Ltd, trading as Stagecoach Hants & Surrey.

LONDON TRANSPORT

East Surrey Traction Co. Ltd started by Arthur Hawkins of Reigate in 1911. Became affiliated to the London General Omnibus Co. Ltd (a member of the Underground group of companies). East Surrey effectively became General Omnibus's agent in the so-called Country Area to the south of London. Incorporated into London General Country Services Ltd 20 January 1932. Superseded by the London Passenger Transport Board (London Transport) 1 July 1933. London Transport's country bus and Green Line coach operations were required to be divested under the Transport Act of 1969, as London Transport was then controlled by the Greater London Council and could no longer operate wholly within the shire counties surrounding London. Country Bus and Green Line operations, vehicles, staff and premises transferred to the National Bus Co. on 1 January 1970.

LONDON COUNTRY

National Bus Co. operated their inherited responsibilities as London Country Bus Services Ltd. London Country split into four companies 8 September 1986, with that pertinent to Horsham being London Country Bus (South West) Ltd. Privatised 19 February 1988 by sale to Drawlane Transport Plc. Trading name London & Country started being used April 1989. Depot opened at Warnham Station 1 September 1990. A separate subsidiary company – Horsham Buses Ltd – used from 27 October 1990 to administer locally based operations from Warnham. Horsham base transferred to James Searle Industrial Estate, Parsonage Way, 2 November 1992. Drawlane renamed British Bus Plc December 1992. LCB(SW) Ltd renamed London & Country Ltd 14 February 1993. British Bus purchased by Cowie Plc 18 June 1996. Cowie subsequently became Arriva Plc. Horsham base transferred back to Warnham 1 December 1996. London & Country (and Guildford & West Surrey) operations around Horsham reconstituted 29 June 1998 under Arriva Guildford & West Surrey Ltd (Guildford and Cranleigh depots) or Arriva West Sussex Ltd (Crawley and Horsham depots). Their parent company is Arriva Southern Counties Ltd. The operations of Arriva West Sussex Ltd transferred to Arriva Guildford & West Surrey Ltd from 7 March 2007.

APPENDIX II

FLEET LISTS

General Note: In the interests of space only fleet lists for independent operators active in Horsham prior to 1980 are shown. Only those vehicles of North Downs Rural Transport while operating in Horsham are included. As an exception, Tillingbourne Bus Co., which operated in West Sussex from 1972, is not included. After 1980 several of the companies described had total fleets out of proportion to the scope of their activities in the Horsham area and only a relatively small number were seen in the town. The lists show all known vehicles, although available information is incomplete in some cases. In the 1920s and 1930s there may have been others for which details have not survived.

NOTES ON CODES USED TO DESCRIBE VEHICLE BODIES

The standard codes as recognised in most enthusiasts' publications have been used to describe
    body types and seating capacities.

Prefix:

B   Single-deck bus
C   Single-deck coach
Ch   Charabanc (open or with folding canvas roof) with bench seats
DP   Single-deck dual-purpose vehicle
H   Highbridge double-deck bus

Figures:

Seating capacity as stated

Suffix:

D   Dual entrance
F   Front or forward entrance
R   Rear entrance (with open platform on double-deckers)

J & M MITCHELL

Regn No.	Chassis	Body	Date In	Former Owner	Date Out
BP 5373	Ford Model T	Lorry/Bus 14	by 01/21	New	09/25
BP 7813	Ford Model T	Lorry/Bus 14	?/21	New	?
PX 333	GMC K16	B14	06/24	New	09/30
PX 383	GMC K16	B14	06/24	New	09/32
PX 2414	Guy BA	Rice B20	07/25	New	12/32
PX 6145	Dennis 30cwt	C19	04/27	New	11/35
UY 1110	Guy BA	C20	09/34	Woodyat, Malvern	?
BLC 692	Dennis Ace	Willmott B20F	10/34	New	11/38
HC 9153	ADC 416	Duple C24R	01/35	Southdown	01/36
APX 291	Dennis Ace	Willmott B20F	05/35	New	07/47
CLY 804	Bedford WTB	Duple C26	10/36	New	11/38
FW 1298	Dennis GL	20	06/37	?	?/46
FBP 189	Bedford WTB	Willmott C26	06/39	New	by 12/49
GPF 117	Dennis Pike	Dennis B20F	05/42	Hayter, Guildford	11/53
FPX 979	Bedford OWB	Duple B32F	04/44	New	08/55
GBP 555	Bedford OWB	Duple B32F	10/45	New	05/62
HBP 873	Bedford OB Duple	C27F	11/46	New	03/60
JPO 631	Maudslay Marathon III	Whitson C33F	03/48	New	06/60
JPX 15	Bedford OB	Whitson C29F	04/48	New	08/55
KBP 749	Bedford OB	Duple C29F	12/48	New	01/68
HUY 521	Maudslay Marathon III	Plaxton C33F	12/49	Smith, Fernhill Heath	01/67
LPX 729	Leyland Tiger PS1/1	King & Taylor C33F	09/50	New	01/67
JYA 880	Bedford OB	Duple C29F	02/54	Hedley, West Kingsdown	01/64
TBP 250	Leyland Comet 90	Duple C36F	06/55	New	04/69
LRU 5	Bedford SB	Gurney Nutting C35F	01/60	Shamrock & Rambler, Bournemouth	06/67
LEL 883	Bedford SB	Gurney Nutting C35F	02/60	Adams, Handley	12/66
VYR 337	Bedford SB8	Duple C37F	04/64	Fallowfield & Britten, London N16	09/71
WXP 718	Bedford SB8	Harrington C41F	01/66	Hall, Hounslow	06/73
223 JKL	Plaxton Bedford SB1	C41F	03/68	Don, Bishops Stortford	06/73

W.H. RAYNER & SON (HORSHAM BUS SERVICE)

Regn No.	Chassis	Body	Date In	Former Owner	Date Out
??? 92	Oldsmobile	Van / Bus 10	?/19	?	?
BP 5875	Ford Model T	Lorry / Bus 14	by 01/21	New	?
BP 8100	Ford Model T	? B14	by 09/23	New	?/30
KK 4403	W & G Du Cros	W & G Ch18	04/24	?	?
BO 9512	Vulcan VSD	? B18	?/24	?	?
DO 3633	Berliet 2 ton	? B18	?/26	?	?
PX 5776	Dennis 30cwt	Harrington B18F	03/27	New	01/35
PX 7090	Dennis 30cwt	Spicer B20	09/27	New	08/34
PX 9823	Dennis G	? C20	03/29	New	08/34
PO 1636	Dennis GL	Willmott C20D	02/30	New	08/34
PO 3840	AEC Reliance	? C32	04/31	New	08/34
YW 949?	Dennis G	? C20	?/32	?	08/34

W.F. ALEXANDER (COMFY COACHES)

Regn No.	Chassis	Body	Date In	Former Owner	Date Out
XV 7605	?	?	10/27	Minson, Roffey	?
PW 9949	Chevrolet LM	Waveney B14F	01/29	United	06/32
PO 1977	Chevrolet U	? C20F	04/30	New	02/35
WM 2350	Vulcan VWBL	? B30F	?	Masson, Hemsworth	09/35
RP 6092	GMC T20	?	?	Rhodes, Yelvertoft	?
PL 4385	Dodge	? B14F	?	Dodge Demonstrator	?
VB 3131	Dennis E	London Lorries	?	Bourne & Balmer, Croydon	?/39
PH 6304	Chevrolet	Reall B14F	?	Overington, Horsham	?
WM 3320	Star Flyer VB4	Spicer C20	?	Adnams, London	?
VB 8896	Layland Tiger TS2	?	?	Bourne & Balmer, Croydon	by 11/39
UR 9656	Gilford	?	?	United Travellers Club, Ponders End	by 07/38
KX 7469	AJS Pilot	Petty B20	12/34	London Transport	03/36
CN 3651	Renault	? 20	03/35	Worley, Low Fell	?
JK 1054	Dennis GL	Duple C20	?/35	Jackson, Eastbourne	by 03/39
DL 5191	Dennis E	Dennis B26F	09/35	Southern Vectis	by 06/42
BBP 339	Dennis Ace	? B20F	09/35	New	12/40
DL 5501	Dennis 30cwt	Margham B18	11/35	Southern Vectis	10/37
OY 3291	Dennis Arrow	London Lorries C32F	?	Bourne & Balmer, Croydon	?/39
OY 1060	Dennis Arrow	London Lorries C32F	?	Bourne & Balmer, Croydon	10/46
YW 5086	Dennis G	? B20F	12/36	King of the Road, Worthing	?/39
YD 1728	Dennis Dart	Strachan B20F	06/37	Gunn, South Petherton	02/39
PG 975	Thorneycroft A6	? C20D	?	Surrey Motors, Sutton	?
AG 6507	AEC Regal I	Mains B35	?	Western SMT	?
IJ 9644	Gilford 166OT	? B32	06/38	Sargent, East Grinstead	by 03/42

Regn No.	Chassis	Body	Date In	Former Owner	Date Out
JK 2916	Dennis GL	Duple C20	10/38	Jackson, Eastbourne	?/39
GK 8612	Gilford 168OT	Abbott C28D	11/38	Usher, London E3	09/42
RV 6259	Dennis Ace	? B20F	07/39	Parsons, Winterslow	12/40
RV 5736	Dennis Ace	? B20F	11/39	Lee, Winterbourne Gunner	10/46
CNC 559	Dennis Arrow Minor	Dennis C20F	?	Greyfleet Motors, Hulme	10/46
HJ 8610	Gilford 166OT	? ?	?	Rayleigh Motor Services	by 01/40
HV 1366	Gilford 168OT	? C26	?	Davis, London SW16	03/41
HV 1368	Gilford 168OT	? C26	?	Kirby, Bushey Heath	?
NJ 1371	Bedford WLB	Duple C20	?	Carter, Plummers Plain	10/46
AG 8612	Gilford 168OT	Wycombe C32R	?	War Department	10/46
VX 7851	Gilford 168SD	Duple C26F	11/40	Shotter, Brighstone	by 05/46
GN 8835	Gilford 168OT	? C32	12/40	Ardley, London N15	04/43
VV 11	Reo Pullman	Duple C26F	12/40	Dunkley, Southwater	08/41
AHK 852	Morris Viceroy	? C14	07/41	Thorne, Clacton	?
GX 1241	Gilford 168OT	Abbott C31R	02/44	Miller, Cirencester	10/46
GBP 292	Bedford OWB	Duple B32F	03/45	New	10/46
GK 8612	Gilford 168OT	Abbott C28D	07/46	Admiralty	09/46

A.T. BRADY (BROWN MOTOR SERVICES)

Regn No.	Chassis	Body	Date In	Former Owner	Date Out
?	Ford Model T	14	?/24	Lorry	?
?	Ford Model T	14	?/26	Capitol, London	?/27
?	Chevrolet	14	?/26	?, Chatham	?
PH 6304	Chevrolet	Reall 14	by 01/28	New	?
PK 3570	GMC	Duple B14F	by 10/28	New	by 07/36
PG 5063	Chevrolet LQ	London Lorries B14F	12/29	New	?/35
PL 4078	GMC T19C	Duple B20F	11/30	New	by 07/36
PJ 7633	Bedford WLB	Duple B20F	08/32	New	03/43
CPL 18	Bedford WLB	Duple B20F	?/35	New	?
EPC 47	Bedford WTB	Duple B20F	?/36	New	?
HPL 700	Bedford WTB	Duple C20F	?/39	New	09/52
JPK 817	Bedford OWB	Duple B32F	05/43	New	04/50
JPL 582	Bedford OWB	Duple B32F	04/44	New	11/56
MPE 59	Bedford OB	Duple B29F	06/48	New	04/62
NPC 430	Bedford OB	Mulliner B28F	06/49	New	06/59
OPB 536	Leyland Comet CPO1	Duple C32F	04/50	New	10/70
HOT 339	Bedford OB	Duple C27F	08/52	Grace, Alresford	03/68
GRU 104	Bedford OB	Duple C29F	05/55	Shamrock & Rambler, Bournemouth	10/61
JHP 895	Bedford OB	Duple C29F	10/56	Cobholm, Gt Yarmouth	04/62
335 KPL	Albion Nimbus NS3N	Willowbrook B31F	07/59	New	10/70
3255 PJ	Bedford VAS1	Marshall B29F	06/63	New	10/70
577 BYE	Bedford SB8	Harrington C41F	09/67	Farnham Coaches, Wrecclesham	10/70

S.S.T. Overington & Partners (Blue Bus Co.)

Regn No.	Chassis	Body	Date In	Former Owner	Date Out
PX 2017	Guy JA	14	01/25	New	09/32
PX 6030	Thornycroft A1L	C20	04/27	New	by 01/34
PX 7123	Reo Sprinter	B20	09/27	New	09/32
PX 8078	Thornycroft	20	04/28	New	07/33
PO 2396	Reo GE	C26	06/30	New	03/33
PH 6304	Chevrolet	Reall B14F	?	Brady, Forest Green	?
UF 1832	Dennis 2.5 ton	Duple C25	?	Southdown	?/35

A. Lazzell (Ewhurst & District Bus Service/Ewhurst Coaches)

Regn No.	Chassis	Body	Date In	Former Owner	Date Out
PK 2151	Dennis G	? ?	?/28	New	?
PL 9432	Chevrolet	Willmott C14	05/29	New	09/35
UA 6571	Dennis G	? 20	?	Hopley, Goole	?
CPL 91	Bedford WLB	Duple B20F	07/35	New	08/51
PL 7696	Bedford WLG	Duple B20F	02/39	Charman, Forest Green	06/50
ATB 233	Bedford WLB	East Lancs C20F	11/46	Sunbeam. Loxwood	08/49
BSC 878	Bedford WTB	Duple C26F	08/48	Moore, Jedburgh	03/60
ANT 226	Bedford WTB	Duple C26F	07/49	Williams, Wrockwardine Wood	01/56
ENK 150	Bedford WTB	Thurgood C26F	05/50	Smith, Buntingford	11/53
JUF 74	Bedford OB	Duple C29F	08/55	Unique, Brighton	04/61
VMV 702	Bedford OB	Duple C29F	02/56	Wimpey, London W6	02/64
VME 103	Bedford OB	Duple C29F	02/60	Beach, Staines	11/64
VVP 912	Bedford SB3	Duple C41F	03/61	Sandwell, Birmingham	08/71
NHO 190	Bedford SBG	Duple C36F	07/63	Dean, Maidenhead	05/67
ADL 486B	Bedford SB3	Duple C41F	02/65	Crinage, Ventnor	08/71
564 KCG	Bedford SB3	Duple C41F	04/67	Tourist, Hounslow	08/71

T.W. Carter (Carter Bros)

Regn No.	Chassis	Body	Date In	Former Owner	Date Out
?	Ford Model T	? 14	by ?/28	?	06/29
PO 413	Chevrolet LQ	? C20	06/29	New	01/31
PO 581	Chevrolet	?	07/29	New	?
PO 3551	Commer Invader 6TK	? C20	02/31	New	12/34

G. WELLER (GASTONIA MOTOR SERVICES)

Regn No.	Chassis	Body	Date In	Former Owner	Date Out
PF 6102	?	?	by 06/26	New	06/30
PF 8282	?	?	by 06/26	New	06/30
PK 1822	?	?	by 06/28	New	by 03/29
PH 9696	Reo Sprinter	? C20	08/28	New	?/36
XV 3508	Graham Dodge	? 20	11/28	?	07/38
PK 6935	?	?	by 03/29	New	06/30
PG ?	Chevrolet LQ	Willowbrook 14	03/29	New	?
PG ?	Chevrolet LQ	Willowbrook 14	03/29	New	?
PL 571	Morris 12cwt	Thurgood	06/30	New	?
PL 572	Morris 12cwt	Thurgood	06/30	New	?
PL 573	Morris 12cwt	Thurgood	06/30	New	?
PL 4707	Dodge	? B14F	?/30	New	07/32
PL 9047	Citroen 2 ton	?	?/31	New	?
XV 5729	Ford AA	?	?	?	?
DV 2984	Dodge	?	?	?	?/38
APD 387	Bean	? 20	03/33	New	?/38
BPH 79	Dodge	?	06/34	New	?/38

F.H. KILNER (SUNBEAM BUS SERVICE)

Regn No.	Chassis	Body	Date In	Former Owner	Date Out
PL 4707	Dodge	? B14F	04/33	Wise, Grafham	?
PO 7943	Bedford WLB	Duple C20F	07/33	New	03/46
VX 5364	Dennis GL	? B20	?	Eastern National	?
?	Morris Commercial	Strachan 8	?	?	?
KR 5405	Dennis G	? 20	?	Coppen, London N9	05/36
UF 3078	Tilling Stevens B10A2	Short B32R	05/36	Southdown	01/41
OU 8431	Ford F18C	?	05/36	Freelove, Bookham	?
CN 4097	GMC T30	? C24F	09/36	Olive, Billinghay	07/41
VW 9276	Chevrolet LQ	Eaton C14	?/37	Hempstead, Bucks Green	?
ATB 233	Bedford WLB	East Lancs C20F	?/38	Helliwell, Nelson	03/46
VX 9495	Gilford 1680T	? C32	?/39	Maidlow & Bell, London NW4	03/43
GK 3401	Gilford 1680T	Wycombe C32F	03/39	Grange, London E13	12/40
PL 8901	Dennis GL	Strachan B20F	05/39	Hayter, Guildford	?
VC 7790	Bean	? 20	08/39	?	?
AKE 725	Bedford WLB	Duple B20F	03/40	London Transport	02/45
AMH 881	Bedford WLB	Duple C20F	03/40	London Transport	02/45
APC 55	Bedford WLB	Duple C20F	03/40	London Transport	03/46
HMX 182	Opel 8W	? C27F	07/42	Foster, Twickenham	03/46
FPX 747	Bedford OWB	Duple B32F	05/43	New	02/45
PK 7511	Albion Valkyrie	Duple C31F	06/43	Eggleton, London SW19	by ?/45
DHR 432	Bedford OWB	Duple B32F	?/44	Wessex Aircraft Co., Middle Woodford	02/45

F.H. KILNER (TRANSPORT) LTD (HANTS & SUSSEX)

Regn No.	Chassis	Body	Date In	Former Owner	Date Out	Fleet No.
AKE 725	Bedford WLB	Duple B20F	02/45	Kilner, Loxwood	03/48	–
FPX 747	Bedford OWB	Duple B32F	02/45	Kilner, Loxwood	12/49	B48
DHR 432	Bedford OWB	Duple B32F	02/45	Kilner, Loxwood	05/48	B50
FYD 570	Bedford OWB	Duple B32F	06/46	Williams, Emsworth	02/49	B49
RV 5736	Dennis Ace	? B20F	10/46	Alexander, Horsham	04/48	–
CNC 559	Dennis Arrow Minor	Dennis C20F	10/46	Alexander, Horsham	04/48	–
OY 1060	Dennis Arrow	London Lorries C32F	10/46	Alexander, Horsham	04/48	–
GX 1241	Gilford 1680T	Abbott C31R	10/46	Alexander, Horsham	04/48	–
AG 8612	Gilford 1680T	Wycombe C32R	10/46	Alexander, Horsham	04/48	–
NJ 1371	Bedford WLB	Duple C20F	10/46	Alexander, Horsham	05/48	–
GBP 292	Bedford OWB	Duple B32F	10/46	Alexander, Horsham	12/49	–
HPO 431	Bedford OB	Duple C29F	12/46	New	04/49	108
FOR 169	Leyland Tiger PS1/1	Duple C35F	02/47	New	06/48	200
FOR 638	Leyland Tiger PS1/1	Duple C35F	03/47	New	12/48	201
FOR 567	Bedford OB	Duple C29F	03/47	New	05/49	109
FOR 817	Bedford OB	Duple C29F	03/47	New	09/49	111
OML 543	Bedford OB	Duple C29F	04/47	New	02/49	110
FOT 19	Bedford OB	Duple C29F	04/47	New	06/50	114
FOT 20	Bedford OB	Duple C29F	04/47	New	06/50	112
FOT 165	Leyland Tiger PS1/1	Duple C35F	04/47	New	12/48	202
FCG 525	Leyland Titan PD1,	Northern Coachbuilders H56R	04/47	New	12/54	LO54
GAA 548	Bedford OB	Duple C29F	10/47	New	06/50	115
GOR 869	Leyland Tiger PS1/1	Duple C33F	07/48	New	03/50	218
GOR 870	Leyland Tiger PS1/1	Duple C33F	07/48	New	03/50	219
GOR 880	Bedford OB	Duple C29F	07/48	New	03/50	138
GOT 286	Bedford OB	Duple C29F	08/48	New	08/50	139
GOT 400	Leyland Tiger PS1/1	Duple C33F	09/48	New	12/54	205
GOU 721	Bedford OB	Duple B30F	01/49	New	12/54	148
GOU 887	Bedford OB	Duple B30F	03/49	New	12/54	150
GOU 888	Bedford OB	Duple B30F	03/49	New	12/54	149
HAA 563	Bedford OB	Duple B30F	03/49	New	12/54	152
HAA 564	Bedford OB	DupleB30F	03/49	New	12/54	151
FOU 764	Leyland Tiger PS1/1	Duple C35F	03/49	Hants & Sussex, Emsworth	04/50	206
HCG 601	Bedford OB	Duple C29F	06/49	New	12/54	156
HHO 698	Bedford OB	Duple C29F	09/49	New	12/54	161

Long Term Loans

Regn No.	Chassis	Body	Date In	Former Owner	Date Out	Fleet No.
ARV 920	Bedford WTB	Mulliner C25F	10/45	from Liss & District	01/46	–
CWV 846	Bedford OWB	Duple B32F	01/46	from E Dennis, Trowbridge	03/46	–
FYD 569	Bedford OWB	Duple B32F	11/45	from Mid Somerset Motor Co., Shepton Mallet	03/46	–
FYD 570	Bedford OWB	Duple B32F	09/45	from Mid Somerset Motor Co., Shepton Mallet	11/45	–

SUNBEAM COACHES (LOXWOOD) LTD (HANTS & SUSSEX)

Regn No.	Chassis	Body	Date In	Former Owner	Date Out	Fleet No.
HMX 182	Opel 8W	? C27F	03/46	Kilner, Loxwood	07/46	–
ATB 233	Bedford WLB	East Lancs C20F	03/46	Kilner, Loxwood	11/46	–
PO 7943	Bedford WLB	Duple C20F	03/46	Kilner, Loxwood	06/47	–
APC 55	Bedford WLB	Duple C20F	03/46	Kilner, Loxwood	07/47	–
FAA 240	Bedford OB	Duple C29F	06/46	New	08/49	103
FAA 242	Bedford OB	Duple C29F	06/46	New	08/49	105
FHO 790	Bedford OB	Duple C29F	01/47	New	12/54	117
FOT 256	Bedford OB	Duple C29F	05/47	New	04/50	118
FOT 285	Bedford OB	Duple C29F	05/47	New	07/53	116
FOT 237	Bedford OB	Duple C29F	06/49	Williams, Emsworth	06/50	122
GHO 942	Bedford OB	Duple C29F	06/49	Williams, Emsworth	12/54	136
HOT 759	Bedford OB	Duple C29F	03/50	New	12/54	167
JAA 485	Bedford OB	Duple C29F	08/50	New	12/54	183

NORTH DOWNS RURAL TRANSPORT

Regn No.	Chassis	Body	Date In	Former Owner	Date Out	Fleet No.
APX 928G	Ford Transit	Deansgate 12	04/69	New	08/71	2
CBP 540G	Ford Transit	Deansgate 12	04/69	New	12/70	3
TUX 416	Bedford C5Z1	Duple C29F	04/69	Parfitt, Rhymney Bridge	01/70	4
EPO 943H	Ford Transit	Strachan B16F	10/69	New	10/71	5
FPO 426H	Ford Transit	Strachan B16F	12/69	New	10/71	6
FPO 427H	Ford Transit	Deansgate 12	01/70	New	10/71	7
HBP 478H	Ford Transit	Strachan B16F	04/70	New	09/72	8
JBP 699H	Ford Transit	Strachan B16F	07/70	New	06/72	9
KPO 310J	Ford Transit	Strachan B16F	09/70	New	01/74	10
KPO 311J	Ford Transit	Strachan B16F	10/70	New	06/73	11
OPB 536	Leyland Comet CPO1	Duple C32F	11/70	Brady, Forest Green	12/71	12
577 BYE	Bedford SB8	Harrington C41F	11/70	Brady, Forest Green	12/71	14
3255 PJ	Bedford VAS1	Marshall B29F	11/70	Brady, Forest Green	02/72	15

Regn No.	Chassis	Body	Date In	Former Owner	Date Out	Fleet No.
335 KPL	Albion Nimbus NS3N	Willowbrook B31F	11/70	Brady, Forest Green	08/71	16
WKG 34	Albion Nimbus NS3N	Weymann DP30F	03/71	Western Welsh	04/72	17
WKG 37	Albion Nimbus NS3N	Weymann DP30F	03/71	Western Welsh	08/71	18
WKG 48	Albion Nimbus NS3N	Weymann DP30F	03/71	Western Welsh	01/72	19
MOD 954	Bristol LS5G	ECW B41F	09/71	Tillingbourne, Guildford	09/72	20
OTT 51	Bristol LS5G	ECW B41F	11/71	Western National	05/73	21
MOD 967	Bristol LS5G	ECW B41F	11/71	Western National	02/74	22
CFV 851	Bedford OB	Duple C29F	11/71	Chivers, Elstead	04/72	–

BROWN MOTOR SERVICES/TONY McCANN COACHES

Regn No.	Chassis	Body	Date In	Former Owner	Date Out	Fleet No.
WKG 34	Albion Nimbus NS3N	Weymann DP30F	04/72	North Downs, Forest Green	08/72	–
CFV 851	Bedford OB	Duple C29F	04/72	North Downs, Forest Green	01/73	–
YUE 163	Bedford SB3	Plaxton C41F	04/72	Tillingbourne, Gomshall	08/72	–
630 SPH	Bedford SB8	Duple Midland B41F	05/72	Banstead Coaches	08/79	–
433 DMA	Bedford SB30oil	Duple C41F	08/72	North, Derby	02/76	–
257 EYB	Bedford SB30oil	Plaxton C41F	02/73	Seaview, Parkstone	03/74	–
UWX 277	Leyland Tiger Cub	Duple Midland DP43F	06/73	Pennine, Gargrave	03/74	–
HCU 950	Bedford SB8	Duple C41F	01/74	Clarke, Newthorpe	12/78	–
807 UDH	Bedford SB8	Duple C41F	03/74	Jones, Llanfaethlu	11/75	–
GVR 137E	Bedford VAM14	Duple C45F	04/75	Kingdom, Tiverton	by 03/81	2
KEV 952J	Ford R192	Willowbrook B48F	11/75	Ebdon, Sidcup	07/83	6
MAA 255F	Bedford VAM70	Plaxton C45F	11/75	Banstead Coaches	04/81	5
UUR 560E	Bedford VAM14	Strachan DP45F	09/76	Marchwood, Totton	09/78	–
HPM 263D	Ford R192	Duple Northern C45F	09/76	Marchwood, Totton	05/80	–
70 RME	Bedford SB3	Duple C41F	05/78	Watt, Horsham	12/78	–
YHA 304J	Ford R192	Plaxton B45F	06/78	Midland Red	by 06/80	7
YHA 313J	Ford R192	Plaxton B45F	06/78	Midland Red	by 06/80	8
YHA 294J	Ford R192	Plaxton B45F	09/78	Midland Red	by 06/80	1
LPD 12K	Bedford YRQ	Willowbrook B47F	05/79	Tillingbourne, Gomshall	10/82	4
KAP 20L	Bedford YRT	Plaxton C53F	08/79	Harding, Betchworth	10/82	3

GGR 344N	Bedford YRQ	Willowbrook B47F	10/79	Tillingbourne, Gomshall	04/84	9
NMJ 279V	Bedford YMT	Plaxton C53F	06/80	New	10/82	10
KPC 208P	Bedford YRT	Plaxton C53F	04/81	Harding, Betchworth	05/86	2
KPC 205P	Bedford YRT	Plaxton C53F	10/82	Harding, Betchworth	05/86	1
KAP 20L	Bedford YRT	Plaxton C53F	03/83	Tillingbourne, Cranleigh	06/86	3

BIBLIOGRAPHY

BOOKS

Akehurst, L., and Stewart, D., *London Country* (Capital Transport, 2001).

Blake, C., *One Man's Horsham* (Southdown Enthusiasts Club, 1995).

Boag, A., *Metrobus* (Capital Transport, 1994).

Burnett, G. and James, L., *Tillingbourne Bus Story* (Middleton Press, 1990).

Durrant, R., King, J. and Robbins, M., *East Surrey* (HJ Publications, 1974).

Holmes, P., *Aldershot's Buses* (Waterfront Publications, 1992).

James, L., *Independent Bus Operators into Horsham* (Rochester Press, 1983).

Lambert, A., *Hants and Sussex* (Alan Lambert, 1983).

Morris, C., *History of British Bus Services – South East England* (Transport Publishing Co., 1980).

Morris C., *Southdown Volumes 1 & 2* (Venture Publications, 1994).

Southdown Enthusiasts Club, Review of 1986/1987/1988/1989 (Southdown Enthusiasts Club, 1987-1990).

Wallis, P., *London Transport Connections 1945-1989* (Capital Transport, 2003).

Wylde, J., *Wylde's Adventures in Busland* (John Wylde, 1998).

MAGAZINES & JOURNALS (SELECTED ISSUES)

Buses and *Buses Extra*, Ian Allan Publishing.

News Sheets and Fleet Lists, PSV Circle.

Omnibus Magazine, Journal of the Omnibus Society.

South Eastern Branch Bulletin, Omnibus Society.

The London Bus, Journal of the London Omnibus Traction Society.

The London Bus Magazine, London Omnibus Traction Society.

Other titles of interest published by Tempus

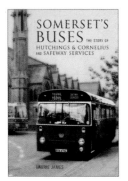

Somerset's Buses

LAURIE JAMES

The story of two of the most highly regarded independent bus companies in Somerset. Based in the village of South Petherton, the local reputation of Hutchings & Cornelius and Safeway Services is legendary. In the face of state-owned competition, they successfully offered cheap and reliable bus services to Taunton and Yeovil. Not simply a history of the companies and their vehicles, but a testament to people who work for the companies too.

978 07524 3171 0

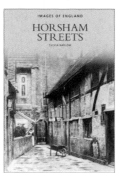

Saved from the Scrapyard

DOUGLAS G. MACDONALD

What happens to a bus when it reaches the end of its life? Most people would visualise a rusting frame residing in a scrapyard. However, many buses are rescued from this fate, and enjoy long and varied lives after their 'retirement'. Douglas G. MacDonald looks at the changing bus scene in Scotland since the 1950s and the fascinating range of tasks undertaken by the country's old buses thus exploring the afterlife of the rescued Scottish bus.

978 07524 3880 1

Horsham Streets

SYLVIA BARLOW

Horsham is a thriving and bustling market town with a sense of its own identity. From its early origins it has been known for its livestock and corn markets. Horsham Streets commemorates the town and shows how national events such as the Battle of Trafalgar have influenced its development. Many streets are covered, from the first to Belloc Close and Shelley Court after the famous poets who once lived around Horsham.

978 07524 4305 8

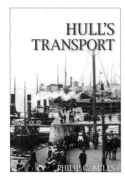

Hull's Transport

PHILIP MILES

This engaging book looks at the various forms of transport used in Hull from the 1880s to the present day. It includes a detailed look at Hull's bridges (including the world-reknowned Humber Bridge) as well as trams, ferries and trolleybuses. A fascinating read for anyone interested in both transport history and that of the area. Philip Miles lives in Hull and is a transport enthusiast.

978 07524 4206 8

If you are interested in purchasing other books published by Tempus, or in case you have difficulty finding any Tempus books in your local bookshop, you can also place orders directly through our website

www.tempus-publishing.com